NINA MAE McKINNEY

NINA MAE McKINNEY

AT THE DAWN OF BLACK HOLLYWOOD STARDOM

DABIAN T. WITHERSPOON

BearManor Media

2024

Nina Mae McKinney: At the Dawn of Black Hollywood Stardom

Published in the United States of America by:

BearManor Media

1317 Edgewater Dr. #110
Orlando, FL 32804

bearmanormedia.com

Printed in the United States.

Typesetting and layout by PKJ Passion Global

ISBN–979-8-88771-650-3

CONTENTS

Introduction

Nina Mae McKinney: At the Dawn of Black Hollywood Stardom is not just a biography. This book takes a different approach. It attempts to tell the story of Nina Mae McKinney's life and career while explaining the reasons for and the consequences of her experiences. That involves "filling gaps" and conducting careful analyses of people, places, and factors connected to or similar to McKinney and her life—logically, not randomly. I have tried to make this book accessible and relevant to academic and general audiences. This book is somewhat chronological but also thematic. Therefore, it briefly repeats ideas that overlap multiple themes, and its chapters can be read in any order.

Nina Mae McKinney (1912–1967) was a multi-talented actor, singer, and dancer.[1] She was also one of the first Black actors whom white and Black Hollywood movie audiences considered beautiful. McKinney's entertainment career began in Lew Leslie's Broadway musical *Blackbirds* in 1928, where director King Vidor discovered her. McKinney made her remarkable debut in King Vidor's Metro-Goldwyn-Mayer (MGM) film *Hallelujah* in 1929, becoming the first Black actor in a leading role in a Hollywood movie. She was the first Black leading lady in Hollywood, preceding Lena Horne's breakthrough, long-term contract with MGM in 1942, which made Horne the first openly and widely promoted Black actor in Hollywood. McKinney blazed a trail for Black actors to play characters who were not subservient to or degraded by white characters. Her becoming the first Black star in Hollywood was short-lived because institutionalized racism and sexism, which were even more pervasive in the 1920s and 1930s, prevented her from realizing her full potential. McKinney's story is also about dream-chasing, tragedy, the will to survive, the will to live and work on one's own terms, and redemption.

The career of Nina Mae McKinney and the appearance of her character Chick in *Hallelujah* mark the beginning of a significant rebellion against Hollywood's expectations for Black actors and Black characters in terms of agency and racial representation. McKinney's groundbreaking role as Chick established her as the archetype for Black female actors who would enjoy greater Hollywood success later, from Lena Horne and Dorothy Dandridge to Halle Berry. Although McKinney's performance as Chick did not immediately lead to similar opportunities for McKinney or other Black actors, it showed that Black actors could perform at the same level as their white peers and predicated Black superstardom in Hollywood. *Nina Mae McKinney: At the Dawn of Black Hollywood Stardom* investigates the career trajectory of Nina Mae McKinney, whose achievements in film and entertainment would have promised to leave a legacy on par with her white peers if not for the restrictions she faced because of her race.

The strict and innumerable forms of institutionalized racism as well as the socioeconomic and gender oppression facing McKinney throughout and beyond her career marginalized her. It contributed to a resulting negative personal image that mitigated her professional achievements and effectively erased her from our historical and artistic public imagination. Critics have either failed to give adequate attention to McKinney's career or downplayed her significance and her role as Chick. Some have even demonized McKinney at times. This book questions such critical views and establishes a connection between McKinney's talents and the sociohistorical factors she battled against. It provides a comparative analysis of McKinney and her contemporaries against the specific historical and narrative framework that informed the realities of Black and other nonwhite actors.

McKinney's Southern background and the mechanisms that were in place at the major film studios illustrate the challenges of an early twentieth-century society in which institutionalized racism was deeply rooted and upheld at all costs. Even in light of Hollywood's discrimination despite her well-received performance in *Hallelujah*, McKinney was not content to simply find work in race films, which were produced specifically for Black audiences in a segregated movie industry. In her attempt at agency, she chose strong, non-stereotypical, or at least balanced leading roles in race films. Similar to Josephine Baker, she also found more acceptance and appreciation for her talents when she traveled abroad. Despite McKinney's struggle to maintain her career after *Hallelujah*, her role as Chick remains timeless.

Although Nina Mae McKinney was posthumously inducted into the Black Filmmakers Hall of Fame in 1978, her name is rarely, if ever, mentioned when we ask today's actors, Black or otherwise, who influenced them most. Instead, they are more likely to refer to other actors such as Lena Horne and Dorothy Dandridge, who also broke the mold of mammy-like characters after they entered a door that McKinney cracked open, or Horne and Dandridge's successors. Since far too many entertainment industry professionals as well as moviegoers have not been exposed to McKinney's performances, including *Hallelujah*, the lack of instant name recognition is understandable. It is not that they should be faulted for failing to give more recognition to Nina Mae McKinney and her generation in the past. It is a matter of bringing McKinney to the forefront and ensuring that she receives proper recognition now and in the future.

I feel a special connection to Nina Mae McKinney and this book. I have found no direct family ties to McKinney that I can prove to solidify our kinship, but I was born and raised in her hometown of Lancaster, South Carolina. She even lived near my grandmother and great-grandmother's neighborhood on Gay Street in 1920.

I adapted this book from my Ph.D. dissertation. Earlier, in my M.A. in African American World Studies program, my coursework and research gave me a solid foundation in the study of Black people's contributions to the film and television industries. In narrowing this broad topic down for my Ph.D. dissertation later, I eventually chose the topic of Nina Mae McKinney because I did not want to be "married to" a topic that I hated just to complete my Ph.D. program, which was an approach or compromise that I had seen make some of the students I knew at various universities miserable. Someone even advised me that Eurocentric topics were safer, but I saw that as an unreasonable restriction. I thought Ph.D. programs were draining enough without adding that kind of torture to the mix. I wanted to do something different, and I did not worry about it being a gamble.

Researching Nina Mae McKinney's life and career gave me an opportunity to write something meaningful and lasting. It was for my hometown, my people, and an important historical figure whose story needed to be brought to light as fully as possible. After connecting McKinney to the movie *Hallelujah* and later standing before the Lancaster County Wall of Fame mural in downtown Lancaster that includes her likeness, I was convinced that I was on the right path. My work began organically, relying solely on the directions that my research took me. Soon, with a greater appreciation for Nina Mae McKinney's contributions and struggles, I sensed deeply where to go next. Clarifying her story and beginning the process of making her as well-known as other early film actors and her successors became my long-term goal.

Nina Mae McKinney: At the Dawn of Black Hollywood Stardom includes an introduction, seven chapters, and a conclusion. The chapters include "Southern Background," "Mechanisms at the Major American Film Studios," "Overseas Performances," "Choosing Race Films and Returning to the American Stage," "Personal Struggles and the Press," "The Groundbreaking Role as Chick in *Hallelujah*," and "The First Black Star in Hollywood." The conclusion is entitled "McKinney's Rightful Place in History." This book also includes the following appendices, which list Nina Mae McKinney's documented performances: "Firsts," "Credited Film Roles,"

"Uncredited Film Roles," "Stage, Theatre, and Club Appearances," and "British Radio and Television Performances."

The research that supports this book relies heavily on primary sources such as films, papers, and periodicals. These resources include, but are not limited to, archives and special collections such as the United States Bureau of the Census, the United States National Archives and Records Administration, the Warner Bros. Archives at the University of Southern California, the Margaret Herrick Library at the Academy of Motion Picture Arts & Sciences, the South Caroliniana Library at the University of South Carolina, the Lancaster County Library, *The Lancaster News*, and the Louise Pettus Archives & Special Collections at Winthrop University. This book uses in-text (parenthetical) citations that match the entries in the "Works Cited" section, a list of sources at the end of the book.

Nina Mae McKinney's legacy is greater than the treatment the topic has received thus far. A scarce body of work has acknowledged the apparent racial barrier that prevented McKinney from becoming a major Hollywood star, and it has recently recognized her as the first Black star in Hollywood. However, some critics have downplayed the long-term impact of the actor McKinney and the character Chick or unjustly reduced them to the status of Jezebel or vixen figures. *Nina Mae McKinney: At the Dawn of Black Hollywood Stardom* explores specific factors of the discrimination and other obstacles McKinney faced, and it digs deeply into Nina Mae McKinney's personal life and professional life, redefining her career and rightful legacy.

Chapter One

Southern Background

This chapter will discuss Nina Mae McKinney's Southern background. It will attempt to paint a clearer picture of her family history and early life than previously known. Then, it will illustrate the significance of her skin color and the power of racism during her lifetime.

Nina Mae McKinney was born Nannie Mayme McKenna in Lancaster, South Carolina. Her birthdate was June 12, 1912, according to the Woodlawn Cemetery ("Nina Mae McKinney, 12 Jun 1912 – 3 May 1967"). She confirmed that she was born in Lancaster, South Carolina, when she traveled internationally but consistently stated on her passenger lists that she was born on June 16, 1912. Examples include her voyages from Le Havre, France, to New York in March 1931 (Bourne 14); from Plymouth, aboard the ship *Lle de France*, to New York, arriving on December 25, 1934 ("Nina Monroe"); and from Sydney, Australia, aboard the ship Niagara, to Vancouver, British Columbia, Canada, arriving on March 12, 1938 ("Nina Mae Monroe"). Stephen Bourne, entertainment scholar and author of *Nina Mae McKinney: The Black Garbo*, correctly asserts that "a copy of her birth certificate has not been located and put into public domain" (Bourne 14). My efforts to obtain a copy from the Vital Records Office of the South Carolina Department of Health and Environmental Control (SC DHEC), both the Lancaster branch and the central branch in the state capitol Columbia, were unsuccessful. A representative in Lancaster said they were unable to locate it, but later, a representative in Columbia said that I would have to contact the South Carolina Department of Archives and History to locate anything older than 1915. According to the South Carolina

Department of Archives, South Carolina law did not require birth certificates until 1915. They clarified that it was not just that birth certificates were not required before 1915, but that they were not created at all before 1915. The law was passed in 1914, effective January 1, 1915 (Jones-King). Their website (2023) explains: "These records begin in 1915, because, while a few cities maintained their own records prior to this date, the state did not require registration of all births until the passage of a law mandating it in 1914" (Jones-King). The South Carolina Department of Health and Environmental Control's Vital Records Office holds them, and they "become public records 100 years following the birth" (Jones-King).

One of the purposes of a birth certificate is to establish paternity. It makes sense that no law required birth certificates before 1915 because early American laws—especially in the South—were sexist, protecting white men from their wives and any other mothers of their children. Married women had no recourse when their husbands abused them, cheated on them, or produced children outside of their marriage. Unmarried women had even fewer rights, including the judgmental way they were often treated after being abused or even raped. The plight of Black women was far worse. Certainly, the law did not respect the rights of Black people, in general.

McKenna seems to be the original spelling of Nina Mae's surname, or at least, it is the earliest found on official records such as the U.S. Federal Census. McKenna and McKinna, variations of the Scottish/Irish surname "McKinney," were used interchangeably between 1880 and 1920 (U.S. Federal Census, 1880, Napoleon McKenna; U.S. Federal Census, 1900; U.S. Federal Census, 1920, Nannie M. McKenna). The differences in spelling might also be accounted for by limited education or uncertainty about the spelling—the family's and/or the enumerators' uncertainty since enumerators (census takers) might have transcribed the family's oral responses.

Nina Mae McKinney's mother was Georgia Crawford McKinney (Pettus, "Nina McKinney"; Pettus, "Lancaster Brick Wall

Pays Tribute to Notable Citizens of That Area"; Pettus, "Nina Mae McKinney: Deserving of a Place in History"; Bourne 14). Georgia seemed to prefer being called "Georgie." Some sources refer to Nina Mae McKinney as a mulatto, but McKinney's parents were Black according to the U.S. Census (U.S. Federal Census, 1920, Nannie M. McKenna).

Although the publications on Nina Mae McKinney that predate this book cite her father as Hal McKinney, according to the 1920 United States Federal Census, her father was Napolian McKenna (U.S. Federal Census, 1920, Nannie M. McKenna). His name is spelled Napoleon in the 1880 United States Federal Census (U.S. Federal Census, 1880, Napoleon McKenna). Nina Mae's paternal grandfather, David McKinney (or Dave McKenna), is listed as the head of household in their Gills Creek home in Lancaster. Hal and Napoleon could not have been the same person since they are listed separately as members of David McKenna's household in the 1880 and 1900 U.S. Federal Census records. It could have been a simple mistake, but such an error would seem inexplicable. Both are listed as David's sons in 1880, but Napoleon is listed as his stepson "Napolian Thomson" in 1900 (U.S. Federal Census, 1880, Napoleon McKenna; U.S. Federal Census, 1900).

According to a McKinney relative who is a descendant of Nina Mae McKinney's grandfather but not of Nina Mae's, the Thompson and McKinney families relocated to Lancaster together and intermarried a few times. Exactly when and from where they relocated is uncertain, but it was common for enslaved people to be rotated from one plantation to another—in this case, covering York, Chester, Union, Newberry, and probably Lancaster. The movement of free Black people might have been similar, especially considering how common it was for newly freed people to go searching for relatives from whom they had been separated over time. Nevertheless, the McKinneys and Thompsons' resettling in Lancaster accounts for Napoleon's name being listed as "McKinney" in one census record and "Thompson" in another. The aforementioned relative added that although documentation is missing, the family believes that Nina Mae's great-grandmother on the McKinney side was white (European) and American Indian and that her great-aunt and great-uncle could pass for white.

Apparently, Hal's grandfather was also white. Hal's father was David McKinney, who was a mulatto according to census records. David's death certificate (September 30, 1918) states that his race was "non-white," his mother was Dinah McKinney, and his father was "not known" (South Carolina Death Records, 1821–1955). David's wife, Mary Ann (also recorded as "Mamy Ann") McKinney, was listed as a "mulatto" on the 1880 U.S. Federal Census. David was a "farm laborer," and Mary Ann was a "cook" (U.S. Federal Census, 1880, Napoleon McKenna).

The 1880 U.S. Census records Mary Ann's mother as Mary Faulkner. Yet it records Mary Ann's father as "unknown" (U.S. Federal Census, 1880, Napoleon McKenna; U.S. Federal Census, 1900). Therefore, it is possible that someone deliberately hid the identity of Mary Ann's father, Nina Mae's great-grandfather, from public record. Since Mary Ann and her husband David McKenna were listed on the 1880 Census as cooks (U.S. Federal Census, 1880, Napoleon McKenna), they might have worked for the Springs family or another wealthy family just as Nina Mae's great-aunt Carrie Sanders did later.

Nina Mae's maternal grandparents were John N. (aka Jack) Crawford and Nannie Crawford (1873–1911), after whom Nina Mae (Nannie Mayme) apparently was named (U.S. Federal Census, 1880, Nelson Crawford). It is more likely that Nannie Crawford's maiden name was unknown, but if she was already a Crawford and married a Crawford, they might have been from different sets of Crawfords. Having the same surname might indicate that the same slaveholders, white Crawfords, owned both families or that they came from different areas. Although many records of enslavement have been lost, some surviving inventory documents show that it was common for slaveholders to give their surnames to the people they enslaved. Since they typically treated human beings like livestock or farm tools, this was more about record-keeping than paternalism. Some slaveholders relocated after the outcome of the Civil War forced them to relinquish their slaves, and in some places, their surnames would become more commonly attributed to their former slaves' descendants than their own descendants.

According to the U.S. Federal Census, in 1880, Nannie's father (Nina Mae's great-grandfather), Nelson Crawford, age 80, was the head of household at their Gills Creek home in Lancaster, South Carolina. Nelson is listed as a "widower." The census also states that Nelson and his daughters—Caroline (Carrie, 19), Georgiana (16), and Nannie (6)—were mulattoes. Therefore, Nina Mae had at least one white ancestor on her mother's side of the family. The names of Nannie's mother, Nelson's parents, and their ancestors are unknown. Nelson was a "carpenter," Carrie was a "washerwoman," and Georgiana was a "house servant" (U.S. Federal Census, 1880, Nelson Crawford).

Information about Nina Mae's childhood is limited, and some of it is difficult to verify. Different versions of the story have named Hal McKinney as her father and treated Hal and Napoleon as the same person while other details about her family life vary. Nina Mae's mother, Georgie, moved to New York City seeking better opportunities when Nina Mae was a child (specific date unavailable), and Georgie's aunt, Carrie Sanders (born Carolyn Crawford in 1860 and married to Ed Sanders in 1884 according to the 1900 United States Census), raised Nina Mae in Lancaster until Nina Mae was about 13 years old. Then, Nina Mae joined her mother in New York, though details and dates are missing. Carrie Sanders was the maid of the wealthy white family of Col. Leroy Springs, who owned Springs Industries, the cotton mill company in Lancaster. Carrie lived in a small apartment in the Springs' backyard (Pettus, "Nina McKinney"; Pettus, "Lancaster Brick Wall Pays Tribute to Notable Citizens of That Area"; Pettus, "Nina Mae McKinney: Deserving of a Place in History"; Steen).

It is likely that Georgie left in search of better opportunities when Nina Mae was at least 8 years old because that age is stated on the 1920 U.S. Federal Census record that lists Nina Mae as a member of her grandmother Mary McKinney's household (U.S. Federal Census, 1920, Nannie M. McKenna). Mary McKinney died on March 18, 1920, not long after the census was recorded. That explains why Nina Mae went to live with Carrie Sanders the same year.

As a child in Lancaster, Nina Mae rode a bicycle, running errands for Lena Jones Springs, Leroy Springs' second wife. Lena gave her the bike to pick up her family's mail from the post office. At such an early age, Nina Mae was already demonstrating showmanship by performing stunts. Distant relatives have been unable to offer much information about McKinney's life in Lancaster, and records of her early life are missing. Some of her relatives never met her. Nina Mae's cousin, Mary Felder, did at least explain that part of the significance of Nina Mae's childhood errands and stunts was that Nina Mae was the only Black girl in Lancaster who owned a bike at that time. Ironically, Nina Mae would later use her skills as an expert bicyclist as an adult to save the life of a three-year-old child during the production of her film *Straight to Heaven* in 1939 (Bourne 14; Murphy 1; "Baby Playing on Trestle Saved by Nina").

Not foreseeing that her daughter would someday make it to Broadway and Hollywood, Georgie hoped that Nina Mae would become a schoolteacher (Matthews; "Didn't Raise My Daughter to Be an Actress"). In South Carolina, the racial climate their family lived in and the absence of Black stars in Hollywood limited Georgie's outlook, at first, as it surely did for numerous Black people who suffered racial oppression and suppression in the strictly segregated South. From an early age, Nina Mae told her mother that she would become a famous actor one day. Georgie understood how difficult it would be for a Black person to reach such a goal, but she never discouraged her daughter ("Didn't Raise My Daughter to Be an Actress"). Living in New York City, and attending Public School 126 in Lower Manhattan, Nina Mae was exposed to far more movies and entertainment venues than back home. Nina Mae felt even more encouraged to pursue her dream and taught herself how to dance. She stated, "Ever since I was a little kid, I used to get in front of the mirror and dance. I loved to dress up, too. But dancing sort of came naturally to me. I learned, of course, and started off my career in the chorus. Soon, though, I found I could wake up my own routines with better success than I could learn [from] anyone else" (Hanson 8, qtd. in Anae 125).

As a child, Nina Mae was multitalented, performing in school plays at the Lancaster Normal and Industrial Institute, the Colonel Leroy Springs-founded school for Black children (Pettus, "Nina McKinney"; Pettus, "Lancaster Brick Wall Pays Tribute to Notable Citizens of That Area"; Pettus, "Nina Mae McKinney: Deserving of a Place in History"; Steen). As a bright, young overachiever, Nina Mae not only knew her own lines but all of the other cast members' lines as well (Pettus, "Nina McKinney"; Pettus, "Lancaster Brick Wall Pays Tribute to Notable Citizens of That Area"; Pettus, "Nina Mae McKinney: Deserving of a Place in History"). This demonstrated a level of merit that foreshadowed her film career.

Another version of Nina Mae's family history repeats some of the information in the other version while partially contradicting the rest. In this version, Hal was an alcoholic who was abusive to Georgie. After Nina Mae was born, Georgie left Hal and often hid from him at the home of Col. Leroy Springs, for whom she worked as a maid. Hal made drug store deliveries to support the family until Georgie left him. Georgie moved to Savannah, Georgia, to work as a cook for Cynthia Withers around 1920, leaving Nina Mae with her grandmother Mary A. McKinney, who lived on Gay Street in

Lancaster's Gills Creek area. Georgie married James Edwin Maynor in Savannah and moved with him to Manhattan, New York. Shortly thereafter, Nina Mae joined them in New York, only for them to send her back to Lancaster to live with her uncle, Curtis, in Gills Creek. At the time, Hal was in prison for an unspecified crime, and he escaped the chain gang in 1923, never to be found. Nina Mae went to live with her grandmother, Mary A. McKinney, but when Mary died shortly thereafter, Nina Mae went to live with her great-aunt, Carrie Sanders, who worked as a cook and housekeeper in the home of Col. Leroy Springs (Bartira).

As stated earlier, Nina Mae's living with her grandmother on Gay Street is documented by the 1920 U.S. Federal Census, and Nina Mae's living with her great-aunt, Carrie, a domestic worker at the Springs' house is found in the Louise Pettus Archives & Special Collections at Winthrop University. Georgie's marriage to James Edwin Maynor is documented by the 1940 U.S. Federal Census and Maynor's burial records, which list Georgie as his spouse at the time of his death on March 8, 1949, in Queens, New York (U.S. Federal Census, 1920, Nannie M. McKenna; Pettus, "Lancaster Brick Wall Pays Tribute to Notable Citizens of That Area"; U.S. Federal Census, 1940, James Edwin Maynor; U.S., Find a Grave Index, 1600s–Current. James Edwin Mayor). However, the rest of the information in this version of the story lacks documentation.

In Leroy Springs' household, lived his son, Elliott White Springs, who was conceived by his first wife Grace Allison White. Grace was deceased at the time of the 1920 U.S. Federal Census (Elliot White Springs; U.S. Federal Census, 1920, Leroy Springs). Elliot, a World War I pilot and hero, was 23 and living in his father's household at the time of the 1920 census, which means Elliot was 15 or 16 when McKinney was born. This census does not indicate any other household members except Lena Jones Springs, Leroy's wife at the time, and two Black servants: Robert Brown and Reuben Brown (U.S. Federal Census, 1920, Leroy Springs). Leroy Springs' grandchildren were born around the time of Nina Mae's departure for New York. According to the 1930 U.S. Federal Census, Elliot White Springs' children—Leroy Springs and Anne K. Springs—were born around 1925 (U.S. Federal Census, 1930).

Since Nina Mae lived with Aunt Carrie within walking distance from the Springs house, it is quite possible that the Springs treated Nina Mae as if she was "the baby" of the household. In other words, in private, the Springs might have treated Nina Mae as if she was "one of their own," or like a relative, at least. This would be particularly noteworthy if that was the case because racist white people would have pressured them to "wear the mask" in public. There is at least a chance that Nina Mae was a blood relative of the Springs, considering the perpetual misinformation about who Nina Mae's biological father was and considering how her family was situated so close to the Springs home. It also opens the Springs' relationship with Georgie and Aunt Carrie to speculation. Although impossible to prove without a birth certificate, it is possible that Nina Mae's biological father was neither Hal nor Napoleon and that her father might have been one of the males in the wealthy Springs family, a white man closely associated with the Springs, or some other influential white man in town. The same can be speculated about Georgie's father. If that was the case with either of their fathers, the circumstances could have been voluntary—as in a secret, forbidden relationship between a white male and a Black female—or entirely involuntary—as in the predatory behavior of some white males toward Black females who had no recourse due to the power relationship and the indifferent legal system.

Some of the Black people who have the Springs surname trace their lineage to the white Springs family who owned property such as plantations, homes, and Springs Mills industries in York and Lancaster counties. According to genealogical threads on Ancestry.com, Col. Leroy Springs (1861-1931) had a brother, William, whose son, William Springs Jr., was a mulatto. William Springs

Jr. (1855-1939) married Betty Porter Springs. William Jr. had a son, Albert Springs (1894-1964), who was "the spitting image of Leroy Springs." Records establishing that Leroy and William Sr. were brothers have been unavailable, but William Jr. was buried in Fort Mill (York County) as the story goes ("Col. Leroy Springs—Re: I Have an Old Bible"; "Col. Leroy Springs—Re: The True Story of the Springs Mills Industries/African American Descendants"; "William Springs, 1855–18 Sept 1939"; Walter Albert Springs, 2 Mar 1894–24 May 1964; Col. Leroy Springs, 12 Nov 1861–7 Apr 1931). Mixed offspring may have been produced during the period of American slavery through voluntary or involuntary "unions." For example, the aforementioned William Springs who had a mulatto son, William Jr., hid in a cave until the Civil War ended, and William Jr. went to bring him home. From the end of the war until his death shortly thereafter, he lived with William Jr ("Col. Leroy Springs—Re: I Have an Old Bible"; "Col. Leroy Springs—Re: The True Story of the Springs Mills Industries/African American Descendants"). The circumstances and details of the birth of William Jr. are missing, but his behavior and his father's behavior in this story seem to indicate that William Sr. treated his son like family.

After emancipation, many free Black people worked for white employers such as Springs Mill industries. Hence, white men had frequent access to Black women, some allegedly resulting in the births of biracial children. The very existence of Black Springs, descended from William Sr. or otherwise, strengthens the probability of a connection between Nina Mae and the Springs family. If some of the white Springs men or other white men had taken advantage of their social status and power, as employers, with Black women who were powerless during those time periods, it would have been a closely guarded secret each time a child was produced. If one of the Springs men or a white man associated with them fathered Georgie or Nina Mae, it certainly would have been no different. The

Springs family would have felt compelled to protect its reputation, possibly with help from local officials. Georgie's family would have tried to protect her and later would have tried to protect Nina Mae. Thus, the timing of Nina Mae's departure at age 13 for New York might have coincided with her puberty. In slave narratives, Black women such as Harriet Jacobs aka Linda Brent describe how their master's behavior varied from or evolved from inappropriate sexual innuendo and "foul words" (Jacobs 29) to outright sexual advances and assaults, which typically coincided with the young girls' onset of puberty. The experience of free Black females with some white men would have been similar.

Due to the racial climate, especially in the South, it would not have mattered to a predominantly white society if any "relationships" between the Springs and Nina Mae (and her relatives) were non-consensual or consensual (based on romantic or familial love). Racist whites would have demanded secrecy from the family and those close to it, and they would have expected disapproval from outsiders. Harmful experiences in Nina Mae's lineage or experiences of her own might have been the reason for her unwillingness to return home after her career in show business had ended in the United States and abroad.

While the abuse of Black females at the hands of white men in America dates back to the slave period, the issue of voluntary unions between Blacks and whites must be addressed briefly. They were generally frowned upon in American society, especially in the South, and they were usually hidden if they existed. At any rate, there was no escaping the power dynamic involved. Prominent white males often dominated white females, including their wives, and sexist laws usually protected them from these women. Adding the factor of race placed Black females in an even more precarious position. That is undeniable, whether those women and young girls were taken by white men by force or they participated in supposedly consensual relationships with white men in which they typically were coerced by the possibility of attaining more comfortable lives for themselves and their children.

Nina Mae McKinney grew up in Lancaster, South Carolina, during a time of strictly enforced segregation. That included schools and public places. In the South, a Black person had to step off the sidewalk for a white person and avoid eye contact. Black males had to accept being called "nigger" or "boy," not "Mister," and Black females were rarely, if ever, called "Miss." Both were subjected to racist white people's disrespect for their right to even exist, and they often suffered violent verbal and physical attacks, whether they resisted such mistreatment or not. Unfortunately, it was common for white men, especially those who had money and status, to get away with abusing Black women and teenage girls between the American slave period and the mid-1900s. This was not limited to slave owners and overseers (and their associates). After slavery ended, some white employers and other white citizens behaved similarly. White people, in general, could enter Black communities and harass Black people with no legal consequences. White men came into Black neighborhoods, carried off Black women, girls, and sometimes boys, and returned them when they "were done with them." Sadly, this is the root of some family secrets. Older Black women taught younger Black females to be careful, and they watched over them as much as possible. Unfortunately, there was no legal protection, and usually, there was no justice when incidents occurred. Local law enforcement consciously overlooked white men's sexual abuse and other physical violence toward Black people.

According to racist whites, Blacks were less than human, and the abolition of slavery was both a mistake and a bitter memory. Those whites resented even the slightest progress made by Blacks, and they feared miscegenation or race mixing. Hence, racist whites perpetrated heinous and murderous tragedies such as the genocide that occurred in places such as Rosewood, Florida, and Tulsa, Oklahoma. Random disappearances and lynchings of Black people also occurred during this time period, especially in the South. When white men produced mixed-race children, some secretly looked after these children but took no direct part in their lives (e.g., Senator Strom Thurmond, to be discussed in Chapter Five) while others kept it a closely guarded secret and disowned them.

My search for more of Nina Mae McKinney's possible family ties has not been fruitful. For example, an interesting blurb appeared in *The Gaffney Ledger* when *Hallelujah* played at the Strand Theatre in 1930 in Gaffney, South Carolina. It stated that Nina Mae McKinney is "a cousin of Annabel Hill, who is the adopted daughter of Jane Hill, now in the employ of the L.G. Potter family" ("It May Be of Interest"), but I was unable to verify this information.

According to Louise Pettus and Ron Chepesiuk (Louise Pettus Archives & Special Collections at Winthrop University), Elliot Springs owned a scrapbook that contained a December 28 newspaper clipping about McKinney's benefit performance for Black senior citizens to be held at the Columbia Township Auditorium in Columbia, South Carolina. Since the year is missing, Pettus and Chepesiuk estimate the date around 1940 (Pettus, "Nina McKinney"; Pettus, "Lancaster Brick Wall Pays Tribute to Notable Citizens of That Area"; Pettus, "Nina Mae McKinney: Deserving of a Place in History"). The story lacks details, but Springs may have felt a sense of pride in seeing little Nannie Mayme (Nina Mae) all grown up and supposedly doing well for herself (Pettus, "Nina Mae McKinney—Deserving of a Place in History"). McKinney's brief return home may have also been emotional or symbolic for people who knew her as a child. Springs' possession of the clipping might also be an indication that a well-to-do white man in the South held a sentimental attachment to a Black extension of his family—family "by blood" or "by choice"—even if he felt pressure to avoid acknowledging it publicly.

Today, the Springs Close Foundation is a philanthropic organization based in Fort Mill, South Carolina. It funds various community projects in Lancaster, York, and Chester counties. My attempts to reach descendants of Col. Leroy Springs through the foundation to obtain any information they might have about Nina Mae McKinney or their families' relationship with her were unsuccessful.

My attempts to obtain information from several people who identified themselves as relatives of Nina Mae McKinney or members of the McKinney, Sanders, or related families, have not yielded much either. A McKinney from Lancaster who claims Nina Mae as a relative knew of Nina Mae's fame but knew nothing about her personal life, and a member of the Black Springs family told me they had no information about Nina Mae and were not related to her as far as they knew.

The issue could be a simple lack of information. Another possibility is the unwillingness to share information, especially something that could be a family secret, or the fear of being identified as the person who spoke up. Alternatively, it could be apathy or failure to value the topic. If secrecy is the reason, that would be most unfortunate for everyone involved. If Nina Mae and Georgie were conceived in love but not to the fathers that stories about their family have attributed them to, there is nothing for them or their family to be ashamed of. If they were not conceived in love, their situations still need to be acknowledged for the sake of receiving closure and beginning the healing process. When we refuse to come to terms with the past or even talk about something as traumatic as a family secret, we can never receive healing or be made whole; therefore, part of our humanity and our identities remains hidden or lost.

On the other hand, it is possible that there is no secret involving Nina Mae's immediate ancestry and no connection to the Springs family other than their employer-employee relationship, despite the red flags and inconsistencies. For example, as stated earlier, Nina Mae McKinney was the only Black child in Lancaster who owned a bike, which she received from Lena Jones Springs, and Col. Leroy Springs founded a school for Black children: the Lancaster Normal and Industrial Institute. Perhaps Springs and his family believed that Black people should eventually gain equality in America, not just have "separate but equal" schools and accommodations. The Springs and some other whites in Lancaster might have treated Nina Mae like family.

Nevertheless, it is important to note that when people are a family, by blood or by choice, inappropriate behavior occurs sometimes. Too often, children are harmed by family members or friends of the family, only for family members to cover it up, as if protecting the secret is more important than protecting the children. That encompasses short-term and long-term physical, mental, and emotional protection and support. At any rate, failing to address the possibilities where uncertainties may exist would be an injustice to Nina Mae McKinney, who was wrongfully denied a chance to tell her story before she left this world.

During McKinney's adulthood, the racial climate of the South had not changed much. While the Black press existed in some cities in the United States during her lifetime, the dominant white-owned media still did not consider the lives of Black people newsworthy in the South. Stories about Black people were scarce, and they tended to be stereotypical or harmful. *The Lancaster News* has long since shed the Old South's racial norms, but during McKinney's childhood and early adulthood, any mention of Black people was quite limited. For illustration, consider several brief articles *The Lancaster News* ran in 1929. One story in the August 9, 1929, issue states that four unnamed Black men were arrested for allegedly attacking a white man ("Blacks Attack Man"). The September 10, 1929, issue ran a story about the impending execution of four Black men, possibly the aforementioned men, in Columbia, South Carolina ("Four Awaiting Death in Chair"). A story in the September 24, 1929, issue reinforces the Black stereotypes of dysfunction and the love of knives—the "I'll cut ya" stereotype ("Negro Pastor Knifed After Church Meet"). The white press, in general, was more concerned with promoting whites' fear of Black people to justify segregation and providing comforting news for racist whites who wanted to believe that whites could still keep Blacks "in their place" and prevent the scourge of Black anarchy to white order and harmony.

Two of the remaining three stories do not fit the same stereotypical mold, but that is only because they are brief announcements found in the "News About Town and County" section of the September 3, 1929, issue. After all, some Blacks did buy newspapers. The first of these stories is a blurb that announces school openings for Black children and white children. It names teachers such as Mary Donnom Witherspoon, who later wrote for *The Lancaster News*, and W.L. Rucker ("City Schools Open Thursday"). The other story states that someone found the dead body of Blake Davis, a Black man about age 50, near Cane Creek on Charlotte Highway and that he apparently died of heart failure ("Negro Man Found Dead"). The last story, which appears on October 29, 1929, is hypocritical. Here, *The Lancaster News* printed a story about racial discrimination abroad. At first glance, the story may seem laudable, as it explains that whites did not allow entertainer Paul Robeson and his wife to enter a London grill, even though another group of whites had invited them ("Color Question Stirs England"). However, the paper had discriminated locally and had consistently failed to report incidents of racial discrimination in a legally segregated American society, especially in the South. On the other hand, perhaps the paper intended for the Robeson story to shift the focus on racial injustice to distant places or to underscore white liberalism, which racist whites perceived to be a growing problem.

Hallelujah premiered on August 29, 1929 ("Hallelujah"), but there was no mention of it in *The Lancaster News* between August and October of 1929. While ignoring Nina Mae McKinney and other Black entertainers, *The Lancaster News* ran two examples of stories that shined the spotlight on white entertainers within the same time frame. The September 6, 1929, issue, as a typical reflection of American society, upheld the white woman as the standard of beauty and femininity. Including a photo of entertainer Patsy O'Day, the paper described Florenz Ziegfeld's new showgirls as "harbingers of the return to the chorus of feminine curves" ("Chorus Girl, Latest Model: No Boyish Figure Here"). In the September 27, 1929, issue, a story explained that Blanche Sweet filed for divorce from her husband, director Marshall A. 'Mickey' Neilan ("Screen Actress Files Suit for Her Husband"). This was front-page news, but there was still no acknowledgment of Nina Mae McKinney or *Hallelujah*.

The November 5, 1929, issue of *The Lancaster News* proclaimed the public's excitement over talking movies, running an advertisement, labeled "'The Talkies' Are Here!" The paper also ran a brief story, entitled "Sound Pictures Please Crowd: Sparkling Musical Show Makes a Big Hit at the Imperial Theater," in reference to the success of Fox's *Movietone Follies* ("'The Talkies' Are Here!"; "Sound Pictures Please Crowd"). All of this is relevant to McKinney since her film debut bypassed the silent era and began with talkies. However, McKinney's hometown paper still had yet to acknowledge her breakout role in King Vidor's *Hallelujah*. In the same issue, *The Lancaster News* merely mentions her name, reprinting a brief story by an unnamed feature writer of the North American Newspaper Alliance about a Clara Bow interview in which Bow objected to people referring to Nina Mae McKinney as "the Black Clara Bow." Bow absurdly retorted that she did not have a "double chin" like McKinney ("Objects to Negress Named After Her" 2; "Clara Bow Resents Compliment to Nina"). Even if it was not racially motivated, Bow's comment was an insult and a gross exaggeration, especially considering that Black and white audiences considered McKinney beautiful. Since the birth of sound movies made some silent film actors insecure and considering the racial climate, it is logical that Bow might have been uncomfortable with or intimidated by a Black actress who, arguably, was equally talented, if not more talented, and more of a "natural" in talkies. The comment by Bow, who had struggled to adapt to sound pictures, illustrated that she and Hollywood, in general, were well aware of McKinney's presence but were reluctant to talk about McKinney as an actor. Some whites viewed McKinney's breakout role as a mistake, feeling that no Black woman should be on equal footing with their beloved white starlets. Unfortunately, this newspaper blurb certainly was not a celebration or an acknowledgment of McKinney's talent.

Even though McKinney was one of only a few "celebrities" who hailed from Lancaster, she would not make the front page of *The Lancaster News* until February 3, 1950, when the paper ran a story, entitled "Lancastrian in Top Rated Movie" and again in a similar story published on February 10, 1950 (Witherspoon). These were blurbs, not full stories, that the paper ran when McKinney played the minor role of Rozelia, the maid and the antagonist's girlfriend, in Elia Kazan's *Pinky*. The paper ignored McKinney's trailblazing leading role in 1929 but finally gave her some acknowledgment when she only appeared in a few scenes and delivered a few lines in another major motion picture 20 years later.

Pinky first screened in New York City on September 29, 1949, but when it was officially released on November 11, 1949, Southern theaters were reluctant to show it or even acknowledge its existence because of its content. White leading actress Jeanne Crain's titular character, Pinky, was a Black woman who had been passing for white to escape discrimination. Certainly, some whites would conclude that it would not be too controversial since *Pinky* ends in the typical heartbreak of a tragic mulatto. It was Hollywood's standard, covert anti-miscegenation message under the guise of a story about family values or pride in one's identity. Four other movie theaters in Lancaster County regularly advertised their showings in *The Lancaster News*. However, Midway Theater was the only one that advertised *Pinky*. The ads ran on January 13, 1950, and January 20, 1950 ("Watch for Pinky"), and Midway Theater screened the film for three days—ending on February 10, 1950 ("Last Day Friday for Pinky").

Early attempts to draw renewed attention to the career of Nina Mae McKinney occurred in the 1970s and 1980s when African American newspaper columnist and local historian Marjorie Clinton McMurray made periodic attempts to spark interest in McKinney. McMurray was a Lancaster native who published the following articles: "Black Lancaster" in *Tap Journal* in 1977, "Nina Mae McKinney Receives Award Posthumously" in *The Lancaster News* in 1978, and "Nina Mae McKinney Was Lancaster's Only Cinema Star" in *The Lancaster News* in 1986. Eventually, McMurray's efforts garnered enough attention for McKinney to have McKinney's portrait painted on the Lancaster County Wall of Fame mural across from the courthouse in downtown Lancaster in 1985. Nina Mae McKinney appears alongside other important historical figures, such as President Andrew Jackson, "father of modern gynecology" Dr. J. Marion Sims (although later revealed that he conducted inhumane experiments on enslaved women), author/businessman/World War I hero Colonel Elliot White Springs (interestingly), and astronaut Charles Duke. According to Ralph Waldrop, the mural's artist, McKinney's portrait represented "two minorities: Blacks and women" (Pettus, "Lancaster Brick Wall Pays Tribute to Notable Citizens of That Area"; Pettus, "Nina Mae McKinney—Deserving of a Place in History").

Attempts to publicly acknowledge Nina Mae McKinney outside of her hometown include *Nina Mae*, a free biographical play written by Vince Venturini and directed by Sameerah Muhammad "of the Potpourri Theatre of Jackson" in 1988 in Jackson, Mississippi. The play grew out of a Black history art exhibit idea. The production of this public performance at the Johnie Champion Center was funded by "the City of Jackson and the Hinds County Board of Supervisors through the Arts Alliance of Jackson/Hinds County" ("It's a Premiere"; King, "Local Resident's Play Features Pioneer Star").

Today, if asked who Nina Mae McKinney was, many people in her hometown still either do not know who she was or may only vaguely state that she was an actress who was born in Lancaster. Besides film historians, people outside of Lancaster typically know even less. *Nina Mae McKinney: At the Dawn of Black Hollywood Stardom* seeks to begin the process of undoing the public erasure of McKinney's important professional achievements and of ensuring that McKinney and her legacy become as well-known as her Hollywood successors, in America and abroad.

Chapter Two

Mechanisms at the Major American Film Studios

The career of Nina Mae McKinney and the appearance of the character Chick in *Hallelujah* (1929) mark the beginning of a significant rebellion against Hollywood's expectations for Black actors and Black characters in terms of agency and racial representation. Therefore, it is important to understand how the mechanisms or institutional practices at the major film studios illustrated the challenges of an early twentieth-century society in which institutionalized racism was deeply rooted and upheld at all costs. The majority of executives at Hollywood studios were European Jews, immigrants whose decisions were based on their own assimilation and newfound status as the model minority. Hence, they upheld the status quo of gender and racial inequality during the early years of Hollywood. This chapter also explores MGM's careful consideration of race during the production of *Hallelujah*; the struggle of elite white female actors—such as Miriam Hopkins, Barbara Stanwyck, and Carole Lombard—to demonstrate agency in their careers in the 1930s; and a comparison of non-white actors such as Anna May Wong, Lupe Vélez, and Nina Mae McKinney, who were never allowed to break the glass ceiling.

To explain the socioeconomic necessity for immigrants to assimilate, one must understand the backgrounds of the major studio executives in Hollywood. Most of the executives at the major studios—MGM, Universal, Paramount, Warner Bros., RKO Radio Pictures, Columbia Pictures, and Twentieth Century Fox—were non-Anglo European minorities who assimilated into the dominant white culture of the United States. Most of Hollywood's executives were Jewish immigrants from Europe and the children of Jewish immigrants from Europe. Since Nina Mae McKinney's breakout role was in *Hallelujah*, an MGM release, this section will focus on MGM.

Metro-Goldwyn-Mayer (MGM), though initially called Metro Goldwyn, was formed in 1924 after Marcus Loew, owner of the Loew's Theatres chain, purchased Metro Pictures Corporation, Goldwyn Pictures, and Louis B. Mayer Pictures ("Mary Pickford: Timeline"). Loew was a non-practicing Jew who was born in Queens, New York, and he was the son of a poor Viennese waiter ("Marcus Loew Biography"). Louis B. Mayer, CEO of MGM, had emigrated first from Russia to Canada, where he grew up. Then, he emigrated to the United States. Producer David O. Selznick was Mayer's son-in-law and the son of silent film producer Lewis J. Selznick, who had lost his fortune. David was born in Pittsburgh, Pennsylvania, but his father was born in Kyiv of the Russian Empire, which now is Ukraine ("David O. Selznick Biography"; "Lewis J. Selznick Biography").[2] Samuel Goldwyn, the namesake Goldwyn, emigrated from Poland ("Samuel Goldwyn Biography"). Young prodigy and super producer Irving Thalberg was born in Brooklyn, New York, but his parents were Jews from Germany ("Irving Thalberg Biography").

Universal Pictures' founder Carl Laemmle was born in Laupheim, Baden-Württemberg, Germany ("Carl Laemmle Biography"). At Paramount Pictures, Adolph Zukor, who had partnered with Marcus Loew in the nickel arcade business prior to their film production ventures, was born in Ricse, Austria-Hungary—which is now Hungary ("Adolph Zukor Biography"). Benjamin Warner, great-grandfather of the Warner Brothers—Albert, Sam, Harry, and Jack—relocated his family to America from his ancestral home of more than 300 years in Poland (Sperling 17). David Sarnoff of RKO Radio Pictures was born into a Jewish family in Uzlyany, Minsk Governorate of the Russian Empire, which is currently known as Vuzlany, Minsk Oblast, Belarus ("David Sarnoff"). Harry Cohn,

President of Columbia Pictures was the son of a Poland-born Jewish tailor ("Harry Cohn"). Twentieth Century Fox Film Corporation merged Darryl F. Zanuck and Joseph Schenk's Twentieth Century Pictures with William Fox's Fox Film Corporation. Zanuck, a former Warner Bros. producer, was the only non-Jewish major executive in Hollywood. He was a Protestant born in Wahoo, Nebraska ("Darryl Zanuck Biography"). Schenk, former president of United Artists, immigrated from Russia, and William Fox immigrated from Hungary ("William Fox Biography").

Race holds no physiological significance, as the dominant group adapts the notion of race over time to best suit its need to oppress and suppress other groups. Nevertheless, it is important to specify that the skin color of these European Jews was "white" since "Jew" is a term that denotes religion and ethnicity, not race, and since their skin color kept them out of American society's bottom caste, to which Black people were restricted.[3] European Jews assimilated in terms of appearance, culture, and names in order to reduce social barriers and enable themselves to compete in a capitalist market more effectively. Considering white privilege and applying the theories of "whiteness as property" and "master scripting" to the film industry, clearly, it was important socially and economically to become white.[4] The growth of industry could not ignore gender, class, ethnicity, and race (Leiman 6). Capitalists' position on racism varied according to whether the market structure was competitive or oligopolistic. Of course, Hollywood was an oligopoly. Other factors included "technical labor input requirements, cyclical and secular factors, the weighing of short-run economic factors against longer-run political factors, and the extent of a perceived threat from the working class" (Leiman 7). During the formative years of Hollywood, ethnic whites believed it was in their best interest to uphold the dominant society's discrimination against women and Black people. According to Michael Rogin, they had escaped the severe anti-Semitism of Central Europe where they were treated as the outsiders who "united the disparate nationalities and classes" (63). In the United States, however, Jewish immigrants understood that the color of their skin ensured that they would never replace Black people as the primary targets of "racial nationalism" (Rogin 63). European Jews benefited from Black people being restricted to the bottom caste. Although stated in a much later era, in his 1965 speech "Educate Our People in the Science of Politics," Malcolm X presents a compelling definition of whiteness in America that can also be applied to the early twentieth century: "When you get the white man over here in America and he says he's white, he means something else. You can listen to the sound of his voice—when he says he's white, he means he's a boss. That's right. That's what 'white' means in this language. You know the expression, 'free, white, and twenty-one.' He made that up. He's letting you know all of them mean the same. 'White' means free, boss" (Malcolm X 92).

Although some Jewish immigrants from Europe indeed related to the plight of African Americans and opposed racism more openly than any other white ethnic group, others such as Hollywood studio heads were careful to avoid upsetting the status quo of the society they were trying to fit into and profit in economically. At least publicly, they upheld its social ideology, even at the expense of other people. Hence, they appropriated the culture of African Americans, in music and film, while denying African Americans equal opportunity. Regarding the overlapping of race and gender, these "Jews were middlemen not only in their economic and cultural positions but also in their racial and sexual identification: They were positioned between white and black and between men and women" (Rogin 68). Hence, the studio heads also upheld paternalistic and sexist American norms.

Blackface minstrelsy, the earliest form of popular entertainment in the United States, was how Jewish immigrants became full-fledged Americans. Socioeconomic class status changed the meaning of whiteness over time, gradually absorbing ethnic European immigrants. Jewish European immigrants followed the model that Irish immigrants had already established by the 1850s. During the 1840s, when blackface became "American national culture," 1.7 million people immigrated to the United States, and they became a significant sector of the working class by the 1850s (Rogin 56). Most of them came from Ireland. Having comprised the "first mass post-revolutionary immigration in the United States," Irish immigrants participated in the denigration of Blacks—people whom they outranked in a white-dominated society based on skin color—in order to gradually reduce the anti-Irish sentiment and "political polarization" they faced upon their own arrival (Rogan 56). They soon became chief purveyors of blackface. Irish Americans were afraid to openly support Irish independence since the cause also supported the abolition of American slavery. It would have presented them as un-American, more loyal to their home country than to the United States. It would have also led to white Americans' retaliation with an even greater anti-Irish backlash that would have associated the Irish as savages along with Africans since the British "conquest, dispossession, and stigmatization of the Irish" occurred simultaneously with their displacement of American Indians and their enslavement of Africans (Rogin 56).

By the early 1900s, most blackface performers were Jewish, and this means of income flourished as European Jews abandoned their "Old World identities" for new Americanized ones (Rogin 57). As Jeffrey Melnick argues in "Ancestors and Relatives," Irish Americans, and later, Jewish Americans became "culturally pluralist within the melting pot" (qtd. in Rogin 57). Jewish Americans accomplished this as vaudevillians, songwriters, and movie moguls who "revitalized popular culture with white versions of African American folk productions" and helped transform it into a "mass culture" (Rogin 58, 60-6). On the other hand, contrary to the fantasy that white Jews were plotting to take over the world, the early assimilating Jews understood their precarious position in American society and were much more apprehensive about their own marginality than they were forward-thinking or concerned about their power (Rogin 68-69), which only came in time, through financial success.

The birth of Hollywood, even with ethnic minorities at the helm, was not a threat to the racial order in the United States. According to the Black-white binary and differential racialization theories, relations between whites and Blacks will always serve as the barometer for whites' relations with other racial minorities (Delgado 68-71). The film industry began as an inexpensive means of entertainment for working-class white people. After the birth of the studio system, it continued to benefit the majority in terms of profit and to benefit the economy.

Although King Vidor had already established himself as a liberal during the silent film era, his work was never a major threat to the dominant ideology. For example, *The Big Parade* (MGM, 1925) was not as radical as it now appears to be superficially. It simply was bold for its time. Vidor presented the film during a period in which films were normally used as propaganda for issues such as colonization, anti-miscegenation, and pro-war/patriotic sentiment. Yet, *The Big Parade* dared to question the Great War, World War I, and the nation's sudden sense of patriotism. In the story, his protagonist merely follows the bandwagon, literally and figuratively, even leaving his car parked in the middle of the street to go enlist as soon as he finds a street parade exciting and sees that a few of his friends are already leaving. While *The Big Parade* also questions the notions of valor in battle, the killing of other human beings, and the effect of war on the personal life of the individual, it might have been more radical if it had been released during the war, not seven years afterward. However, it does foreshadow King Vidor's willingness to conduct an experiment like *Hallelujah*.

Race films, even with their more positive and more balanced counternarratives, were not a threat to the social order in the United States, either. While the race film industry—which Blacks,

European Jews, and others financed—coexisted with Hollywood, race films lacked the major studios' production budget and level of distribution. Thus, the presentation quality of race films tended to appear crude and unprofessional compared to Hollywood productions. Since race films presented opportunities for Black actors such as Nina Mae McKinney who were underused or misused by Hollywood and for Black actors who never had the chance to appear in Hollywood films, local Black audiences treasured these films, even the most cheaply and poorly produced ones (*Midnight Ramble*). Nevertheless, this version of "stardom" was not on the same scale as national and international Hollywood stardom.

Hallelujah was not a race film. It was a Hollywood film, and MGM perceived *Hallelujah* as a risk, socially and financially. Initially, MGM rejected Vidor's idea for an all-Black cast film, especially so early in the new sound era. At that point, MGM had only begun producing one all-sound musical and was unwilling to center its next film on a Black story involving "authentic" Black characters—not overly stereotypical or harmful characters portrayed by white actors in blackface. To the studio's relief, MGM managed to release *The Broadway Melody*, a musical with a white cast, just two months before *Hallelujah*.[5] MGM had allowed King Vidor to proceed with *Hallelujah's* production only after he offered to help finance the film, deferred his $100,000 salary in exchange for 25% of the ticket sales, and convinced producer Irving Thalberg that it would be a worthwhile experiment, even if it might not be successful at the box office (Weisenfeld 20, 249; "Hallelujah"). Vidor directed *Hallelujah* and wrote the spine of the story. Other writing credits go to Wanda Tuchock for the scenario, Richard Schayer for the treatment, Ransom Rideout for the dialogue, and Marian Ainslee for the titles. Eva Jessye, an African American, was musical director and a background singer, although uncredited. Hugh Wynn and Anton Stevenson, both uncredited, edited the film. Shot in Tennessee and Arkansas, *Hallelujah* was one the first "on-location" films ever produced. Vidor and Thalberg produced both a silent version, apparently lost, and a sound version. MGM released the sound version, which opened in theaters on August 20, 1929 ("Hallelujah" Silent Version Suggested Deletions; "Hallelujah").

Regarding race and representation, the production and post-production of *Hallelujah* illustrate the careful consideration of race at major studios such as MGM. Curiously, the production attempted to maintain the social status quo while eliminating some of the elements that might be offensive to some audiences, including Black audiences, in terms of religion, decency, and race. The contradictions might reflect the delicate balance between reception and profit.

One of the most significant aspects of the production of *Hallelujah* in October 1928 was Colonel Jason S. Joy's frequent correspondence with the Motion Picture Producers & Distributors of America (MPPDA), Incorporated, also known as the Hays Office. The retired United States Army Colonel served as Director of Public Relations for the MPPDA from 1922 until 1926 and served as Director of Studio Relations for the Association of Motion Picture Producers (AMPP) from 1926 until 1932 (Colonel Joy Memo; Col. Jason S. Joy; Grieveson 321). The MPPDA secretary, whose name is not typed and whose signature is difficult to decipher, sent Col. Joy a letter asking him whether he had contacted MGM about its "proposed production" that would have "an all colored cast with the exception of one white actor" (MPPDA Letter to Col. Jason S. Joy). Concerned about how Christian viewers might react, Col. Joy sent a memo to the MPPDA regarding the role of Zeke as a preacher in the film. Col. Joy stated that after he read the "sequence synopsis" for the film, he advised MGM as follows:

It might be less objectionable if the negro preacher and evangelist was not portrayed as a weak character, succumbing to temptations in various forms. The story as now written makes the preacher's son [Zeke] the weak character and

> I have advised M.G.M. that I believe too much prominence
> is now given to the religious impotance [sic] of the son; that
> this criticism may be avoided by making it evident in the
> picture that the father [Zeke's father] is the real leader and
> minister and that the son is merely a zealous convert used by
> the parson as part of his shown [sic]. (Colonel Joy Memo)

Even more surprisingly, Col. Joy continued, warning MGM about its use of the word "nigger" and the use of stereotypical crap shooting scenes (Colonel Joy Memo).

The MPPDA letter is dated October 5, 1928, while Col. Joy's memo is dated October 4, 1928. Both are photocopies found in the *Hallelujah* clippings file at Margaret Herrick Library of the Academy of Motion Picture Arts and Sciences. Initially, Col. Joy had read an older version of the film's treatment. His memo answered the question found in the MPPDA letter, and he sent a letter dated October 6, 1928, to George Kann at MGM, in which he explained that after reading the "synopsis of the new continuity" of *Hallelujah*, Col. Joy was pleased to see that Zeke would be the weaker of the two preachers in the story. He explained that he still wanted to see Zeke's father as a more "prominent" character, clarified his suggestion that "the censors invariably eliminate the word 'nigger,'" and continued to caution against the crap shooting (Col. Jason S. Joy Letter to George Kann at MGM). Two handwritten notes appearing in the left margin of the letter read "changed," but based on the cut the studio eventually released, the changes were minor and probably intended only for appeasement. Perhaps MGM toned down Zeke's portrayal from the original treatment or script, but evidently, MGM felt confident enough to maintain Pappy, his father, as a minor character, even though he does appear to be the true leader of the church. The studio kept a crap shooting scene and other stereotypical content in the final cut, but it did remove the word "nigger." It is unclear as to whose decision it was, but they also removed the lone white character. The aforementioned correspondence does not specify how much input King Vidor had in any of these final changes.

An inter-office memo at MGM from Lamar Trotti, Colonel Joy's assistant at the AMPP Studio Relations Committee, to an executive only referred to as "Mr. M. McKenzie" summarized that *Hallelujah* might have been a revolutionary story if the characters were white instead of just another insignificant "nigger" story, based on its status as a Black cast musical. Trotti stated, "I hardly know what to say about 'Hallelujah' by King Vidor. If the characters were white, I would think very definitely that Vidor is treading dangerous ground" (Trotti's Inter-Office Memo; "Lamar Trotti"). He went on to state that the story was realistic and that he would compare Zeke to Elmer Gantry from the satirical 1927 Sinclair Lewis novel but only if Zeke was also white. Yet, Trotti stated that instead of painting Zeke as a hypocrite, the film simply presented him as "a weak nigger in the toils of a Black Deborah" (Trotti's Inter-Office Memo). He boldly added: "I don't think it matters whether the negroes like the picture or not, but I do wonder whether whites are amenable to such realism. Personally I rather fancy the idea,—except I can't think of being especially interested in an all-negro cast" (Trotti's Inter-Office Memo).

Trotti stated that he could foresee the portrayal of Zeke offending some people who believed in "the advancement of the negro race," but he explained that he harbored no concerns about it. Trotti blamed his views on his upbringing in the South, but his sentiment reflected the Hollywood majority at the time (Trotti's Inter-Office Memo).

Trotti's main concerns were with the much more "gruesome" demise of Hot Shot, whose name apparently was "Slickum" in the early drafts, and the apparent reference to Zeke as "Black Jedus" [probably misspelled intentionally], both of which were issues with the pre-release version of the story. Originally, Zeke kills Slickum/Hot Shot by breaking his back on a tree stump. Trotti mentioned that he agreed with Col. Joy that toning down Zeke's role as a preacher would prevent potential problems, and he explained that he wanted to see the "Black Jedus" reference removed or replaced with "Black Prophet" (Trotti's Inter-Office Memo). The film that was released complied with Trotti's suggestions.

Col. Joy addressed similar concerns with King Vidor on February 22, 1929, and with George Kann at MGM on July 11, 1929. Col. Joy explained that after viewing the most recent cut of *Hallelujah* available at the time, he discussed the project with King Vidor over lunch. Shortly thereafter, he viewed another edit with Irving Thalberg and listed nine concerns, some of which seem less reasonable than others: (1) His first comment was worded unclearly, but he recommended that Vidor and Thalberg tone down the "animalistic" scene in which Zeke kisses Missy Rose but that he should retain Chick's passion as "a small negress" due to "its treatment" (Colonel Joy's Resume). In the final cut, Zeke still kisses Missy Rose against her will early in the story. (2) Col Joy advised that the camera focuses on the actual crap shooting, not the money on the table, claiming that "this form of amusement is indigenous to negro life" (Colonel Joy's Resume). A contradiction of his comment about the scene in his earlier correspondence, this final assessment demonstrates a conditioned form of racial prejudice, even among whites who were supposedly well-meaning. (3) He advised that censors were likely to remove one of Chick's dances because of what he referred to as "vulgar and suggestive body movements" (Colonel Joy's Resume). If such a scene existed, the studio apparently removed it by the final cut. (4) He advised that the gun close-up before Spunk's shooting be edited. In the final cut, the audience sees the gun clearly, but there is no extreme close-up shot.

(5) Col. Joy advised that religious people might be offended. He stated that the comments Chick and Hot Shot hurl at Zeke are too scornful. In the final cut, they still mock Zeke and call him a phony, but it might have been toned down from the previous cut. Moreover,

since Col. Joy had warned that people might interpret the scene as a reference to Jesus going to Jerusalem, Zeke's robe is no longer white in the film's release. (6) Col. Joy's next comment suggested that people might be offended by the opening of Zeke's sermon because it seemed too authentic, too similar to the procedure of ministers in real churches. The studio concluded, in all likelihood, that the scene was realistic for some churches and was unlikely to be offensive in itself. The scene remains intact in the final cut.

(7) Col. Joy urged MGM to delete the "vulgar and suggestive" fight on the floor between Chick and 'Hot Shot,' name change noted, to avoid offending anyone with an extended fight between a man and a woman (Colonel Joy's Resume). Perhaps, in the final cut, the studio shortened the scene while preserving its essence. (8) Col. Joy also advised them to delete the scene in which Zeke rubs the "full length" of Chick's leg and (9) the close-up of the revolver pointed at the camera after Chick runs off with Hot Shot and tries to leave Zeke behind (Colonel Joy's Resume). Neither of these shots appears in the final cut.

In Col. Joy's letter to George Kann nearly five months later, he talked about five scenes that censors were likely to question, including (1) the "short shot of Chick's legs" the first time she dances and (2) the voice that cries out, "She could make a preacher lay his Bible down," during the same scene (Col. Joy's letter to George Kann, 1929), even though Vidor and the other writers might have merely intended that line as foreshadowing (Col. Joy's letter to George Kann, 1929). Other concerns included (3) the close-up shot of Zeke opening his knife after he confronts Hot Shot, (4) the idea that "English speaking censors outside the United States will want" shots of the American flag removed, and (5) the close-up shot of Chick after she dies (Col. Joy's letter to George Kann, 1929).

Handwritten "X" marks are found beside comments two through five. The studio compromised regarding the first concern but changed the last four. A Censorship Report dated October 15, 1929, and an Inter-Office Memo dated October 25, 1929, both complain that most of the "questionable" scenes were still intact (Censorship Report; J. B. M. Fisher Memo to Mr. McKenzie at MGM). The studio did not make the changes immediately but either fully or partially accommodated most of Col. Joy's concerns in time for the film's release in theaters.

Regarding MGM's final assessment of *Hallelujah* before its release, an MGM secretary whose initials were "ABK" completed a form, entitled "Secretary's Report for Review Committee," which is dated September 9, 1929. In the report, the "Action Taken by Committee" section is marked (with an "X") "Passed without change" (Secretary's Report for Review Committee, Sept. 1929). Rating options (blanks) for several categories under the "Secretary's Constructive Report" are "Excellent," "Good," "Fair," and "Poor." "Art of Production" is marked "Excellent," "Entertainment Value" is marked "Good," and "Instructional Value" is marked "Poor" (with the word "None" typed in parentheses. The "Moral Effect" category has the words "None" and "Doubtful" typed in, and "None" is marked. Under "Suitable for," "Family Audience including young people" is marked instead of "Family audience including children" or "Mature audience." The last marking on the form is "No" under "Recommended for: Photoplay Guide" (Secretary's Report for Review Committee).

Hallelujah opened on August 20, 1929, in the United States. It also screened in countries such as Brazil, Argentina, Spain, France, Italy, Finland, Portugal, Switzerland, Greece, and Poland soon afterward ("Hallelujah"). It might have eventually showed in British Columbia (Canada), but it was initially rejected there due to "objectionable scenes at incidents in religious gathering" according to John V. Wilson's Western Union telegram to MGM on December 12, 1929 (John V. Wilson Telegram to MGM). Wilson urged MGM to appeal to theaters there by claiming the need for a "sincere portrayal [of] Negro religious rituals" (John V. Wilson Telegram to MGM). Unfortunately, such a comment reinforces the stereotypes of African Americans as being hypersexual, sexually immoral, and both emotionally and mentally inferior to white people. Still concerned about the success of the film at home, MGM had created a new print by March 1930 (Letter Re: MGM's New York Exchange).

The MGM cinema press book copy on file at the New York Public Library includes an article entitled, "'Hallelujah' is Vidor Triumph: All-Talking Negro Epic Unusual, Stirring Picture." The following caption appears beneath the title: "IMPORTANT—Delete reference to the all-talking version in this article if theatre is not equipped" (MGM Cinema Press Books; emphasis theirs). Due to the poor condition of the press book copy used for the microfilm, the specific date is missing, but of course, the film itself was released in 1929. Evidently, the silent version of the film screened in some theaters that were not yet equipped for talkies at the same time the sound version was playing elsewhere. Unlike the sound version, which was released by MGM/UA Home Video on VHS in 1993 and by Warner Bros. on DVD in 2006, the silent version has not been released on video or DVD. It is likely that no surviving print exists.

MGM reissued *Hallelujah* in 1939. The MPPDA approved it again on August 11, 1939, but still required the elimination of several scenes afterward. These scenes were as follows: Zeke placing Chick on the bed and holding her after the baptism, Chick biting Zeke's hand (and the close-up of her face afterward) before she lures him out of the church, and the shot of the "disheveled" bed (MPPDA Letter to Louis B. Mayer at MGM; MPPDA Report: *Hallelujah* Re-issue Approved Without Limitations; MPPDA Deletions Report). To preserve authenticity, the 2006 Warner Bros. DVD release of *Hallelujah* presents the previous version from 1929.

Regarding racial representation in *Hallelujah* and allegations of discrimination, some critics have argued that King Vidor was no better than openly racist whites in the industry. Despite Vidor's claim that he desired to tell an authentic tale about "the Negro" and despite the overall quality of the film, unfortunately, *Hallelujah* is saturated with stereotypical depictions of Black characters. Zeke's huge family sings while picking cotton. Black children and adults sing and dance as if they do not have a care in the world, despite how tough times are or how hard they must work. For this reason, before the film begins in the 2006 Warner Bros. DVD release, a notice viewers cannot bypass appears on the screen and explains that while it is regrettable that such racialized content existed in early film, it would be a disservice to viewers if presented in an edited version to avoid acknowledging the past.

Hallelujah uses names and endearing terms that are a throwback to American slavery, such as biblical names and the names Mammy and Pappy, even though it had been uncommon for African Americans to use those terms to address their mothers and fathers. Although Chick, Zeke, and Hot Shot speak English that is easy to understand, minor characters use exaggeratedly "broken" English. As stated earlier, the film also shows Black people shooting craps, which supports the notion that Black people would rather seek ways to obtain easy money than work hard.

The film also plays on Black religious stereotypes and the notion that Black people conduct themselves according to a loose sense of sexual morality. Religious depictions of Black people include shouting, falling out, and "holy rolling" in church in addition to the inappropriate conflation of religious fervor and sexuality. The story hints toward incest in a figurative sense (Zeke's desire for his adoptive sister, which is relevant even though they are not blood relatives), and the story relies on the stereotype of the Buck, a physically aggressive, oversexed Black male who cannot control his emotions or sexual urges. In addition to Zeke's weakness, a seemingly middle-aged Black couple, Adam and Eve, come to Pappy early in the story to be married, after they have already procreated seven children.

Furthermore, the *Pittsburgh Courier* asserts that too many Blacks prematurely called Vidor "a friend of the Negro" and that musical director Eva Jessye deserves most of the credit for the film's success, despite the film being a "masterpiece of burlesque, travesty, lechery and Negro gutter life" ("King Vidor Exposed"). The article blasted Vidor, labeling him a "Negrophobe" who failed to illustrate in *Hallelujah* that "the Negro has a soul" and simply relied on aspects of Black life that white audiences and critics would enjoy ("King Vidor Exposed"). According to Eva Jessye, MGM paid Black employees, including the actors, a fraction of what it paid white employees, and their lunches were segregated (Cripps 250; "The Truth About '*Hallelujah*,'" 26 July 1930). An update to Jessye's story explained that the Black cast and crew were not accommodated well. She stated, "Many days we were called out to work [and when we arrived, they] had no place for [us] to await the call" ("The Truth About '*Hallelujah*,'" 2 Aug. 1930). Furthermore, the set of *Hallelujah* was allegedly no vacation for the Black cast and crew from white racist attitudes. According to a rumor, Nina Mae McKinney almost quit after a white grip called her a "nigger" (Cripps 250).

While white privilege dictates that numerous white people, both racist and nonracist, ignore racial injustice to varying degrees, one must question whether Vidor truly felt superior to Black people. Consider how hard he fought for *Hallelujah* at MGM. It would seem that only a liberal would have conducted such a high-profile experiment during the nadir of race relations in the United States. In terms of story and cinematography, it arguably was a superior production to Fox's *Hearts in Dixie*. Similar to President Lyndon B. Johnson (1963-1969), a white Southerner who much later also claimed to value Black culture in his own way and later signed the Civil Rights Act in 1964 against the advice of many of his staff, King Vidor claimed to have understood the sensibilities of Black people, having lived around large Black populations in Texas and Arkansas (Dowd 98). His father had initially been in the cotton business in Galveston, Texas (Dowd 1). A Black woman worked for his family, and most of his father's sawmill employees were Black men. Vidor often witnessed their interaction in groups independent of whites. In an interview with Nancy Dowd for the Directors Guild of America, Vidor stated, "I was very impressed with their music, their feelings, their attitude toward life, their feelings about religion, and their feelings about sex and humor. As long as I can remember I wanted to make a film about them" (Dowd 98). Vidor also stated that he wanted to dedicate a film to the memory of the Black woman who had worked for his family, but MGM repeatedly rejected the idea altogether. In 1928, Vidor pitched the idea as an all-Black cast "musical," though not a musical in the modern sense. The film was to be a drama with musical elements. MGM, stating box office concerns, resisted but agreed to proceed after Vidor offered to defer his salary, offered to help finance it out of pocket, and compromised with MGM President Nicholas Schenck. Focused on the alleged "sexual depravity" of Black people, Schenck declared, "I'll let you make a picture about *whores*" (Robinson 283). Based on the final cut, Vidor tried to balance his intended "homage" with Schenck's position.

One must also consider the argument that Vidor was a liberal who intended to produce a landmark film for Black actors and Black audiences. He and his supporters claimed that he fought for inclusion, and although flawed, *Hallelujah* was an important effort, considering such an early time period. Furthermore, consider *The Big Parade*, which is briefly discussed earlier in this chapter. When the news of the forthcoming *Hallelujah* began to spread, the Black press covered the story succinctly. The *California Eagle* stated that according to Vidor's assistant, referred to only as Mr. Rose, the yet-to-be-named film would be "an ordinary story of Negro life in the South" and that it would have "no ludicrous exaggerations to offend the Black race, nor any silly racial comparisons to antagonize the white race" ("Reel - Previews and Reviews"). In other words, viewers might consider the film anthropological in a sense.

On the other hand, Vidor's comments indicate that he might have admired certain aspects of African American culture while holding that these people were too different from whites to ever be accepted as equals in society. This contradicts his belief that he had fought for a production that would represent and benefit African Americans, presenting them as "real" people. Understanding that Southern whites might interpret the film as an attempt to promote racial equality, he was careful to explain that there was no "connection between his film and campaigns for civil rights for African Americans" (Weisenfeld 21). Perhaps Vidor included the stereotypical depictions as a compromise to appease the racist white audience.

Hearst newspaper gossip columnist Louella Parsons compared Vidor's self-proclaimed desire to present an authentic depiction of African American life to Robert Flaherty's *Nanook of the North*, stating that "he wants to show Negro life as it really is and without a mission or problem to solve" (Weisenfeld 21). Although Flaherty represented Nanook as a documentary or an anthropological travelogue film that showed life "as it was," the film was a commercially and racially biased depiction of the Inuit that manipulated reality through the staging of supposedly natural events and careful editing to present them as exotic and exaggeratedly primitive people. For example, in this silent film, the subtitles in one scene read that Nanook and a few others are "going to the white man's igloo" instead of just telling viewers that they are sailing to the trading post. Furthermore, in real life, the Inuit were using more advanced hunting tools than viewers see Nanook use in the film (*Nanook of the North*). Another negative issue of the film, whether intentional or not, is exploitation. If Flaherty's intentions seem noble, the issue of whether he cloaks the objectification of non-whites with the ideas of simplicity and innocent observation is debatable. More obviously, exploitation occurs because the funding and production of this film represent the interest of a fur company, Les Frères Revillon. For example, the film even includes a strange scene in which furs are hanging inside of an igloo. The scene resembles furs hanging from large department store racks.

The timing of *Hallelujah*'s release corresponded with the New Negro Movement. According to Vidor, the most authentic "folk Negro" was the Southern Negro. Hence, Vidor states, "the Negro of the North always wants to see himself as a poet. He is not content to see himself as he is pictured in '*Hallelujah*.' Even the Negro of Carl Van Vechten possesses, under the surface, the rhythm and abandon, the love song and laughter of those in a primitive state" (Weisenfeld 26, 252). Marguerite La Caze's chapter in *Racism in Mind*, entitled "If You Say So: Feminist Philosophy and Antiracism," argues that the dominant group determines political identity and that the oppressed group has no say in it. Thus, whites determine when race matters just as men determine when gender matters (La Caze 266). Similar to La Caze, Judith Weisenfeld states in *Hollywood Be Thy Name: African American Religion in American Film, 1929-1949* that Vidor believed "African Americans had little agency in formulating their culture and identities and instead were the products and property of white men like the author and photographer Carl Van Vechten and himself. In Vidor's view whites were more authorized than blacks to adjudicate the authenticity of blackness" (Weisenfeld 26).

Although the accusation of racial discrimination based on Vidor's perception of Black people certainly is not out of the question, it is also possible that Vidor simply accepted racial conditions as they were at that time, while on set, to avoid ruffling any feathers at MGM. Note that despite the discrimination on set, Black cast members were able to interact freely with whites at social gatherings. For example, Nina Mae McKinney attended actor Marion Davies' birthday party, which Vidor hosted at his Beverly Hills home. Also in attendance were the likes of Charlie Chaplin, Gloria Swanson, and Samuel Goldwyn (Dancer 1). According to notable film scholar Donald Bogle's *Bright Boulevards, Bold Dreams: The Story of Black Hollywood*, beginning on the last night of shooting *Hallelujah*, Nina Mae McKinney and other Black actors also partied at the mansion of Davies' niece Pepi Lederer for three days and ultimately, had to leave because of a complaint from Lederer's racist white neighbor (Bogle 93). The second party scenario might be an exaggeration of the lavish, carefree Hollywood lifestyle, especially since it is doubtful that racist neighbors would have waited until the third day to complain. Yet both stories show striking contradictions to strictly enforced segregation and are difficult to explain.

Under the studio system, an actor worked under contract, typically seven years, with a particular production company. The "option" contract, which ensured an actor's availability to appear in prospective films, forbade said actor to seek higher pay, work for other studios, or refuse to accept a role (Carman 35). Typically, the work year consisted of 40 weeks with 12 unpaid vacation weeks, and the duration of the contract was either five years or seven years. Although the actor was not allowed to voluntarily exit the contract before the full duration of the contract, the contract usually included a six-month option period, after which the studio could release the actor if it "decided that the actor's potential value was not substantial" (Jewell 255). Hence, the studios "owned" the actors, most of whom had little say in the productions. The studios also owned "the screens." In other words, they could control when and where their films were played by purchasing the theaters. It was such a lucrative and successful system that companies in other countries such as China and Japan imitated it (*1918-1928: Triumph of American Film and the First of its Rebels*).

However, "Independent Stardom: Female Stars and Freelance Labor in 1930s Hollywood" by Emily Susan Carman explains that by the 1930s, several of the most successful white actresses were able to bargain for themselves as free agents under the contract system. This refutes the longstanding argument that white males in the film industry completely dominated the careers of white actresses, with no exceptions. White women's drive for independence had already begun by the 1930s, not in 1944 with Olivia de Havilland's court victory against Warner Bros., in which the California Supreme Court established the right of all actors to become free agents (Carman 2). She sued Warner Bros. for attempting to add the time she spent under suspension to the end of her contract. In the 1930s, elite white free agents—such as Miriam Hopkins, Barbara Stanwyck, and Carole Lombard—worked with independent producers and pioneering, "maverick" talent agents to increase their earnings, attain the perks associated with star power, enjoy the freedom to work with multiple studios, manipulate publicity to control their own personas as modern working women ahead of their time, and enjoy varying levels of creative control that enhanced their career choices and allowed them the experimentation necessary for career growth (Carman 20).

Initially, Hopkins and Lombard had signed long-term contracts by 1930, but they chose not to sign new contracts in favor of the independence that freelance work could provide. Stanwyck, on the other hand, had avoided the long-term option contract altogether, and by 1930, she had only signed limited contracts. Through the mid-1930s, Stanwyck acted for several different studios (Carman 5). Hopkins, Lombard, and Hopkins also worked sporadically with United Artists, a small studio dedicated to independent production (Carman 20).

Select actresses bargained for star treatment and greater profit and perks: top billing, private dressing rooms, opportunities for special creative and financial provisions such as percentage deals, and even personalized wardrobes and stylists. Regarding top billing, they could ensure that their names appeared in a larger font than, and set apart from, the rest of the cast, or even set above the film title (Carman 28, 38, 48). Working with independent producers provided distribution deals, flexible schedules, and the freedom to work with multiple studios within the same time frame, unlike actors who were locked into a seven-year contract with one studio (Carman 60). Talent agents, the film industry's "middlemen," bargained with studio executives to gain for their clients improved working conditions and nonexclusive contracts in the 1930s, before this became standard practice in the 1940s. Given the moniker "ten percenters," as a reflection of their compensation from their clients, these early Hollywood talent agents were loved by actors and loathed by the studios (Carman 67).

The percentage deal, which paid the actor a bonus if her film exceeded an established box office gross, was one of the most lucrative rewards, and it is best illustrated by Clara Bow's Hollywood comeback after her bitter departure from Paramount. As a brief introduction to Bow's situation near the end of her long-term Paramount contract, note that the two most frequent comparisons to Nina Mae McKinney on screen were Greta Garbo and Clara Bow, both of whom were studio commodities who crossed over from the silent era into the sound era and enjoyed extensive filmographies. Greta Garbo worked steadily through 1942. Although her biography *Greta Garbo: Divine Star* by David Bret does not discuss her business savvy, she did not need to be as shrewd a businesswoman as the white actors who freelanced. Her star power was sufficient to sustain her career under a long-term contract with MGM. At first, Clara Bow did not have to be either. She only became a free agent late in her career. In the 1920s, Bow was Paramount's top star, and arguably Hollywood's first sex symbol, but the studio neglected her in the 1930s by simply taking advantage of her star power to sell mediocre films. This is incongruous treatment since Paramount accommodated her after she almost quit acting during her difficult transition to sound movies, according to *Clara Bow: Runnin' Wild* by David Stenn.

Unlike some actors who transitioned from silent movies and actors like Nina Mae McKinney who got their start in talkies, Clara Bow struggled. More than anything else, Bow feared that she would let down her fans, who eagerly anticipated her "talkies" debut. According to Stenn, only Greta Garbo's debut in talkies was more anticipated than Bow's. Yet, Garbo had two years to prepare at MGM. Bow only had two weeks at Paramount (Stenn 157-58). In silent films, as a pantomime actor, Clara Bow had become a star.

Of course, she feared that her success would not carry over into the sound era. Bow was at the peak of her popularity, receiving about 45,000 letters from eager fans in 1929 as the release of her first talkie, *The Wild Party*, approached (Stenn 159). As Stenn notes, the 1952 film *Singin' in the Rain*, starring Gene Kelly and Debbie Reynolds, parodies the film industry's crucial and tense transition from the silent era to the sound era (Stenn 157). The makers of this popular film might have loosely modeled the character Lina Lamont after Clara Bow during Bow's uneasiness about Paramount's sound transition, even though there were some significant differences between Bow and the character Lina. According to Louise Brooks, a fellow actor who looked up to Bow, Bow did not take herself too seriously. To her, Bow seemed oblivious to her beauty and talent (Stenn 158). Although Bow was more than capable of acting, she struggled with everything from her voice to microphone placement on set (Stenn 157). Similar to the character Lina, Bow was uncomfortable around microphones. Most importantly, Bow was also conscious of her Brooklyn accent and her high-pitched voice, which became even higher when nervous or under stress. She would also speak too rapidly when nervous and make errors (Stenn 157).

Furthermore, hearing gossip about the likelihood of her failure in talkies broke her confidence (Stenn 158). Fearing Paramount's plans for a multi-city series of public appearances to promote *The Wild Party*, Bow asked to be released from her contract. Paramount was also concerned about how well she would speak in front of crowds and decided to compromise, limiting her to just one appearance. In a clever move, Paramount held it in Brooklyn, where Bow's accent would fit right in and where she would not be as nervous (Stenn 162-3). Regarding her acting and emoting, "talkies required a restraint she had never developed and rendered useless the abandonment she had" in silent films (Stenn 160). In all fairness to Clara Bow, Nina Mae McKinney did not make her debut in silent films as Bow had. McKinney sang and danced on Broadway, skipped the pantomime style of silent film acting, and made her debut as a leading lady in one of the earliest sound films. Nevertheless, in sound films, McKinney was more of a natural. Unfortunately, cross-references between Bow and McKinney do not discuss any interaction between them.

Bow also suffered damage to her reputation and her professional standing in 1931 as the result of the civil suit against her former secretary Daisy DeVoe, who revealed Bow's "off-screen antics and personal life," and Bow faced an insurmountable obstacle with securing a comeback role at Paramount (Carman 107).[6] After her films *No Limit* and *Kick In* flopped, she had a chance to get back into a "plum lead role" in an "A-class" film, entitled *City Streets*. However, B.P. Schulberg, Paramount's production head, ensured that his mistress Sylvia Sidney received the role instead. Afterward, Schulberg, implying that Bow's career was all washed up, "undermined" her future at Paramount (Carman 107-8).

Bow and Schulberg "mutually agreed" not to renew her contract, which freed her to work with independent producer Sam Rork, who negotiated a one-film deal with Columbia for $100,000 (Carman 107-8). The studio revised its offer to pay $75,000 each for two films. Bow never signed, but by 1932, she accepted a different deal that was on the table for a two-film contract with Fox, where she made her "triumphant" comeback in 1933 in *Call Her Savage*. Bow wisely chose the film herself as it was sure to make money since it adapted a best-selling novel. Her contract included the following provisions: film selection; a $75,000 salary; a percentage deal requiring a $25,000 bonus if the film exceeded $800,000 gross earnings; approval of the script, director, and co-star; and shooting on a closed set (Carman 108-9). Working as a free agent with an independent producer allowed Bow to prove she could still be one of Hollywood's biggest box office draws and "restored her professional reputation" (Carman 109). Bow enjoyed a career of more than 50 films spanning 1922 to 1933. They include *Wings, Parisian Love*, and *Call Her Savage* ("Clara Bow").

While Clara Bow's percentage deal helped regain her Hollywood prominence, Miriam Hopkins used it in 1935 to protect herself while pursuing risky creative ventures such as *Becky Sharp*, which was produced in three-color Technicolor. Hopkins' agent, Myron Selznick, justified the percentage deal, arguing that it was only fair since nobody could accurately predict viewers' reactions to this new technology upon seeing it for the first time. Hopkins was granted director approval and a $60,000 salary plus 10% of the film's profit. Another clause allowing her accountants to verify the film's earnings provided her additional protection (Carman 109-10).

Aside from increased income and star perks, Hopkins, Stanwyck, and Lombard benefited from the publicity campaign, an instrument not only valuable to the studio as a marketing tool but also indispensable to the construction of the star's persona; hence, the freelance actor manipulated publicity to manage her own public image. Similar to fanzine culture, publicity campaigns included movie news and brief biographies. They were also vital to a star's longevity since remaining relevant and in the public eye prolonged box office popularity (Carman 62, 66). Most studios, including MGM, ran their own publicity departments, headed by a publicity director and organized in a similar fashion to a newspaper office. Akin to a press editor, a publicity director supervised a team of publicists and served as the fanzine contact person. The publicity director was usually a woman who focused on glamour, fashion, health, and movie stills (Carman 63-4).

Carole Lombard, the "ultimate publicity hound" of the 1930s, according to *Carole Lombard: A Bio-Bibliography* by Robert D. Matzen, appeared in more fanzines than anyone else. Seemingly, she took advantage of every opportunity to take photos, take interviews, and submit press releases (Carman 64-5). For example, the "complicated, blond, funny" Lombard (Burr 118) worked with publicist Russell Birdwell at Selznick-International Productions in the late 1930s on "various hoopla and ballyhoo campaigns" to create a buzz prior to the release of her films *Nothing Sacred* and *Made for Each Other*. First, their two-pronged approach arranged for her $500,000 freelance salary, of which she paid half in taxes, to be publicized in *Motion Picture* magazine in 1937, a year in which she was the highest-paid actor in Hollywood. In the story, Lombard explained that she only kept 13 cents on the dollar and that she felt a civic duty to pay taxes since movie stars "don't starve" and since tax dollars build new schools and "maintain all the public utilities we use" (G. Hall 67-68; qtd. in Carman 65). Of course, it was a "publicity goldmine" that not only prompted special thanks from President Franklin D. Roosevelt but also led to the most fan mail at Paramount in 15 years (Carman 65). Then, Lombard replaced Birdwell as Selznick-International's publicist for one week in 1938 and arranged for *The Hollywood Reporter* to print the story (Carman 66).

In addition to control of their public personas, successful white freelance actresses secured varying measures of creative control, pertaining to rights and career growth. For example, in 1932, Barbara Stanwyck's Warner Bros. contract included "sole star billing," the right to approve her roles and stories, and the right to decline any film or change her mind about a film within 30 days (Carman 47).

Carole Lombard's one-year Warner Bros. deal in 1938 for the film *Fools for Scandal* stated that the studio would employ the personal wardrobe designer of her choice and her own cameraman. It also allowed her to approve the sign and font of her billing, and it limited her workday to eight hours, ending no later than 6:00 PM (Carman 47).

In a calculated risk, Miriam Hopkins secured a deal with Warner Bros. in 1938 that provided for her approval of the script, director, and co-star of two "A-class" films. In return, she agreed to accept $150,000—half her normal four-film salary. Hopkins perceived this as a reasonable sacrifice while attempting her big screen comeback after having been absent for a year (Carman 48).

The creative control that Stanwyck, Hopkins, and Lombard attained as free agents working with independent producers also afforded them career growth by providing them opportunities for experimentation that the major studios would have been reluctant to take risks on. For example, Samuel Goldwyn initially thought Stanwyck was too young for the lead role in *Stella Dallas*, but he gave her a chance after she "campaigned" for it. The gamble paid off as the role demonstrated Stanwyck's range as an actor and earned her first "Best Actress" nomination at the Academy Awards (Carman 60).

Hopkins' aforementioned *Becky Sharp* deal in 1935 not only illustrated the value of the percentage deal but also granted her the freedom to work on Broadway or go on an "extended" leave of absence. Right before accepting the role, she set up a new two-year contract as Goldwyn's lead actress that outlined these terms (Carman 60-61). Two years later, critics raved over Carole Lombard's film *Nothing Sacred*, which she secured with David O. Selznick in 1937. It provided Lombard with the opportunity to work with Selznick on an "A-class" film, to work with Fredric March—the top free-lancer at the time, and to work with a script written by Ben Hecht, who had previously won the prestigious Oscar (Carman 61).

Despite Nina Mae McKinney's efforts, she was denied the agency of white actresses in Hollywood such as Carole Lombard because of her race. The experiences of McKinney and other non-white actresses illustrate that even as gender and class discrimination became less severe for first-rate actors, racial discrimination remained firm. Similar to McKinney, Chinese American actor Anna May Wong and Mexican actor Lupe Vélez struggled to maintain their careers (Carman 6). Wong and Vélez began their careers in the 1920s and had garnered critical acclaim by the 1930s as "feature players," and even though European companies made them offers, Hollywood studios refrained from signing them to long-term contracts. In Susan Emily Carman's "Independent Stardom: Female Stars and

Freelance Labor in 1930s Hollywood," she uses the term "forced independence" to describe the freelance work of Wong and Vélez (Carman 139-40). McKinney's experience at MGM falls somewhere between the instability of possessing a long-term contract that was not fruitful and the limited options associated with the forced independence of Wong and Vélez.

Although McKinney's contract, a first for Black actors, might have been part of the aforementioned *Hallelujah* experiment that King Vidor and Irving Thalberg convinced the studio to undertake, the length of McKinney's contract may or may not indicate discrimination. MGM only signed her to a five-year contract when seven-year contracts were also common at the major studios. However, clear discrimination is reflected in the fact that MGM only offered McKinney limited work for the duration of her contract. McKinney had broken the mold of being relegated to purely stereotypical roles in which Black characters were merely allowed to exist in the white man's world, and playing a maid was out of the question for her. Roles, especially leading roles, for Black actors were further limited because, between 1927 and 1956, the Hollywood Production Code or Hays Code prohibited depictions of miscegenation (Courtney). Race-mixing or interracial relationships could not be directly shown or implied in movies. MGM did not foresee that its little experiment, *Hallelujah*, would have such a profound impact and realized afterward that promoting McKinney's career and even allowing her a measure of control over it was a risky move that suggested racial equality. Hence, MGM execs limited her access and chose not to promote her or cast her as a lead again.

After *Hallelujah*, McKinney appeared in the feature films *They Learned About Women* (1930) at MGM and *Safe in Hell* (1931) at First National Pictures, which Warner Bros. owned. MGM never exercised the option to release McKinney from her contract. Instead, MGM would "loan" her out to other companies such as Warner Bros./First National. At any rate, the studios had utterly demoted McKinney from a leading lady (*Hallelujah*) to an uncredited singer who appears in only one scene. That scene was in *They Learned About Women*, a comedy centered on baseball. The *Hawaii Tribune-Herald* states that in the film, "Nina Mae McKinney, star of 'Hallelujah,' is featured in an all-colored revue called 'Harlem Madness,' in which she gives a number of barbarian dance routines" ("Famous Vaudeville Team Appears Tonight in Talkie at Empire"; *They Learned About Women*). Despite MGM's obvious demotion and the unflattering latter part of the *Hawaii Tribune-Herald's* scene description, the paper's coverage shows that even an uncredited appearance by Nina Mae McKinney was still noteworthy. Her next role was a supporting role in *Safe in Hell*, the story of Gilda (Dorothy Mackaill), a "lost woman" who flees the United States for a tropical island after she kills her lustful boss. In the role of the hotel manager, Leonie, McKinney steals the show in several scenes: Leonie's singing scene, the private conversation scene in which Leonie gives Gilda advice, and the scenes in which Leonie holds her own against the white men at the bar—refusing to accept being disrespected, talked down to, or bossed around. McKinney sings "When It's Sleepy Time Down South," written by Clarence Muse, who also appears in the film (Wollstein 134). McKinney and Muse insisted on playing their roles "their way"—without subservient or stereotypical shenanigans. Surprisingly, they got their way.

Nevertheless, Nina Mae McKinney would soon be relegated to appearing in musical shorts and uncredited roles. McKinney appeared in MGM's *Manhattan Serenade* as a singer/dancer in 1929; starred in the Vitaphone/Warner Bros. musical short *Pie, Pie Blackbird* with Eubie Blake, Noble Sissle, and the Nicholas Brothers in 1932; appeared as an uncredited dancer in MGM's musical short *What Price Jazz* in 1934; and appeared as an uncredited dancer in Republic Picture's *The Lonely Trail* (a John Wayne feature) in 1936. McKinney also had a cameo as a singer in MGM's feature *Reckless* in 1935. As she appears in the film's official trailer, the caption reads, "Nina Mae McKinney: Remember *Hallelujah*?" That is a testament to her name recognition and star quality even though Hollywood denied her any opportunities to reach her full potential ("Nina Mae McKinney"; "Reckless").

In 1933, to keep working, she accepted the role she dreaded—an uncredited maid role—in 20th Century Pictures, Inc. and United Artists' *Blood Money* ("Nina Mae McKinney"). *Safe in Hell* would be McKinney's last credited, feature-length Hollywood role until 1945 when she appeared in *Dark Waters*, a Benedict Bogeaus Production film distributed by United Artists. Unfortunately, the character Florella was a maid in *Dark Waters*. It was the type of role McKinney had tried hard to avoid early in her career, and it was the only role she could land for the remainder of her Hollywood career. In 1949, she had few lines in her portrayal of the maid, Rozelia, in Twentieth Century Fox's *Pinky*. It was a popular film but was by no means the resurgence of her career.[7]

While McKinney's Hollywood career declined after her appearance in *Hallelujah*, Anna Mae Wong and Lupe Vélez found themselves working in movie deals that ranged from only a few weeks to a year in length and with no creative control (Carman 140-41). Unfortunately, being chosen by Douglas Fairbanks to appear in *The Thief of Bagdad* in 1924 did not lead to better opportunities for Wong. She found herself trapped in stereotypical "Orientalist" and "exotic other" roles (Wollstein 250-51; Carman 141). Similar to McKinney, Wong ventured to Europe seeking better opportunities. After two successful British-German collaborations, *Pavement Butterfly* in 1928 and *Piccadilly* in 1929, Wong returned to Hollywood only to find that nothing had changed other than Paramount being willing to pay her $1,500 per week, which was more than the $300 per week that Warner Bros. had paid her previously. At Paramount, she still worked short-term deals and was restricted to the same stereotypical roles. After she was unable to parlay a successful Broadway debut in *On the Spot*—which enjoyed a prosperous 30-week run in 1931—into better opportunities in Hollywood, Wong explained to Los Angeles writer Doris Mackie that she had considered never acting in another movie. Wong stated, "I was so tired of the parts I had to play. Why is it that the screen Chinese is always the villain? And so crude a villain—murderous, treacherous, a snake in the grass! We are not like that. How could we be, with a civilization that is so many times older than the West?" (Wollstein 252). Nevertheless, to keep working, Wong accepted the role of Ling Moy, the "vengeful" daughter of *Dr. Fu Manchu* in Paramount's 1931 release, *Daughter of the Dragon* (Wollstein 252). Wong returned to Britain in 1934, but this time, the only available roles were similar to the roles she was trying to escape in the United States, and low production values ensured small profit. Thus, she returned to Hollywood again and continued to work sporadically with Paramount and Warner Bros. (Carman 141).

Meanwhile, Lupe Vélez, who had previously acted in Mexican theater, worked for MGM, Universal, RKO, and Warner Bros. at different times. She worked under the same conditions that Wong worked and without a long-term contract. At RKO, Vélez earned $2,500 per week, which was more than Wong earned per week at Paramount, but Vélez only worked three to four weeks at a time. Vélez was also reduced to racially stereotypical roles that merely evolved from the exotic sex object to the "ignorant comic" by the 1930s and the "Mexican Spitfire" by the 1940s. While denied "white" roles, despite her racially ambiguous appearance, she played roles that were non-white and non-Mexican (Carman 141).

On the other hand, a contrast between the careers of Lupe Vélez and Delores del Rio illustrates the complicated nature of racial discrimination in Hollywood. Vélez and del Rio, both Mexican but racially ambiguous in appearance, started their careers earning similar salaries. However, when del Rio went to Warner Bros. in 1934, she not only signed a three-film deal that paid her $25,000 for the first movie and $35,000 for the second and third, but the studio also allowed her some creative control; she approved the first two stories (Carman 146). *The Invention of Dolores del Rio* by Joanne Hershfield argues that the difference between studios' treatment of del Rio and Vélez was what may be referred to as "coding." In other words, the studios always took Vélez to specifically represent Mexico and Mexican immigrants' cultures. However, they labeled del Rio as "Spanish" or more generally as "Latin." Hence, the fact that studios coded del Rio as "quasi-European" afforded her better treatment than Vélez and other non-white women such as Nina Mae McKinney, but inferior treatment to white women (Hershfield 13-15; Carman 147).[8]

This coding even freed del Rio, unlike other non-white actresses, from the restriction of being forbidden any casting alongside white men, per the anti-miscegenation clause in the Hollywood Production Code (Carman 147). Therefore, del Rio would at least be considered for more roles than other non-white actresses, especially actresses who could not pass for white. This is representative of Marguerite La Caze's argument in her chapter in *Racism in Mind*, entitled "If You Say So: Feminist Philosophy and Antiracism." In the studios' contrasting treatment of Vélez and del Rio, indubitably, the dominant group determined their political identities, and members of an oppressed group had no voice in the matter. Whites "control membership in that privileged group [whiteness]" (La Caze 266). Even though European Jewish studio executives had assimilated and encoded themselves as white, La Caze's argument still holds true.

Through relative independence, select white actresses shaped and controlled their own public personas, but it was impossible for non-white actresses such as Wong, Vélez, and McKinney to do the same since racial discrimination excluded non-whites from the types of fanzines and studio publicity that for white actresses served to balance topics such as glamour, romance, and the "modern working woman"—topics that "endeared" white actresses such as Carole Lombard to female moviegoers (Carman 7). If Nina Mae McKinney had been allowed to attain the same kind of professional independence that the aforementioned white actresses attained, it would have unearthed a "goldmine" of positive publicity for McKinney, in general, and the Black press could have promoted her more effectively. Such independence would have provided McKinney with a path to superstardom. In addition, it would have been more difficult for the white press to dismiss McKinney as a naive little Black girl whose Hollywood days were numbered. "Chapter Five: Personal Struggles and the Press" will discuss this at length.

Discrimination against women of color stood in stark contrast to the increased opportunities for white female actors created by the studios' understanding that women were the "primary consumers" of movies during the 1930s. The movie industry patterned after the Broadway stage's "age of heroines," according to historian Ethan Mordden. Bolstered by the birth of sound, the studios began producing numerous stories centered on women protagonists in the genres of the fallen woman, screwball comedies, and women's melodramas (Carman 8). According to *Photoplay*, women comprised 75% of moviegoers in 1924, and *Motion Picture World* estimated an increase to 83% by 1927 (Smith 36; Brown 34; Carman 9). A 1931 *Variety* article argued, "Women are responsible for the ever-increasing public taste in sensationalism and sexy stuff. Women who make up the bulk of the picture audiences are also the majority of readers of tabloids, scandal sheets, flashy magazines, and erotic books" ("Dirt Craze Due to Women" 1; qtd. in Carman 9). Not only must this perspective be balanced against the longstanding belief that the white male gaze was one of the dominant factors in promoting female actors and their films, but it certainly supports the studios' financial motivation to be more inclusive of women. White men determine when sex matters (La Caze 266). This power is central to both racial and gender discrimination. Considering the potential of such an empowering door opening for women, it is clear that race inhibited the career growth and career longevity of Anna May Wong, Lupe Vélez, and Nina Mae McKinney.

Unlike the aforementioned freelancing white actresses such as Carole Lombard, a non-white woman was unable to attain star treatment or greater profit and rewards. Although McKinney refused to speak exaggeratedly "broken" English in most of her Hollywood roles and even insisted on portraying maids "her way," with dignity, it was the only creative control she ever possessed. For example, as alluded to earlier in this chapter, she and Clarence Muse were adamant about only speaking formal English in *Safe in Hell*. She did the same even as the switchblade-hiding maid Rozelia in *Pinky*, and she portrayed her role as nightclub maid in *Together Again* as a witty and eloquent glamour girl who just happened to be wearing a maid outfit. Nina Mae McKinney and other non-white actors were afforded meaningful but modest gains while denied significant career growth and advancement in Hollywood.

Richard Caves' theory regarding creative contracts argues that contracts reflect actor rankings according to an "A" list and a "B" list and that studios normally will only consider "special provisions" for "A" actors. Although "A" actors or A-listers cost the studios more money, A-listers' films earn more money. Audiences are even willing to pay more to see these actors. Therefore, studios can charge theaters higher rental costs. On the other hand, "the B-list artist might find it difficult to sell her services at any price. No matter how cheaply she works, the resulting film revenue might not cover its other costs. Or, given infinite variety, she may face long waits between films in which her services can be a cost-effective substitute for an A-list artist" (Caves 8; qtd in Carman 144). Of course, Caves' theory is logical. Nevertheless, no explanation other than race exists for why Hollywood studios did not give non-white actors, including Black actors, opportunities to at least become "B" actors. No one begins a career as an A-lister; it takes time to attain that status.

It is also relevant that smaller studios such as RKO, Columbia, and Universal were more open to working with free agents than MGM. It was cost-effective for RKO while Columbia and Universal could not afford to sign A-listers to long-term contracts. Yet, MGM had always made a profit during the Depression years and was secure enough to maintain a "stable" of stars who held long-term contracts (Carman 54). According to *Gods Like Us: On Movie Stardom and Modern Fame* by Ty Burr, MGM "specialized in quality as well as quantity, for MGM's [stars] were the most inarguably godlike," having "three queens" in Greta Garbo, Norma Shearer, and Joan Crawford as well as a "king" in Clark Gable (Burr 121). Gable was "the dominant star in Hollywood during the Classical Period" (Jewell 271-73). The "King" appeared on the "top 10 most popular actors" list every year between 1932 and 1942, and as John Wayne would in later years, "he represented the ideal American male, a figure of strength, resilience, savvy, humor and values" (Jewell 271-73). MGM's list of contracted stars in the 1930s "reads like the Pantheon," including Jean Harlow, Spencer Tracy, Judy Garland, and Mickey Rooney (Burr 121). "Everything at MGM was about the proper care, grooming, positioning, and sale of stars" as Louis B. Mayer and company saw stars as "the studio's primary products and movies only the boxes they came in" (Burr 123). Thus, MGM did not feel it was imperative to compromise its stances on the contract system or MGM's dealings with non-white actors such as McKinney.

Numerous Black actors such as McKinney possessed more than enough talent and charisma to at least become "workaday stars," if not megastars, at Hollywood studios such as MGM. Ty Burr describes a workaday star as an actor whose consistent work helped keep a studio in business since it was difficult, if not impossible, for studios to create and "mass produce" megastars such as Clark Gable and Greta Garbo (Burr 116). Although it is Eurocentric to place the word "Black" in front of the name of a famous, extraordinary white person because it implies that whiteness is required for relevance, some European audiences called McKinney "the Black Clara Bow" and later "the Black Garbo" out of respect and appreciation for McKinney's talent. Yet Hollywood denied her the opportunity to truly become "the Black Garbo." Race is the only reason Hollywood studios denied McKinney and other non-white actors opportunities to even become "workaday" stars.

Elevating Nina Mae McKinney or any other non-white actor to any degree of stardom would have been utterly destructive to the nation's prevailing notion of white supremacy, especially since the media—or "the press" back then—has held the power to either alter or perpetuate negative stereotypes in American society. Thus, MGM and other studios were more likely to engage in master scripting, which "silences multiple voices and perspectives, primarily legitimizing dominant, White, upper class, male 'voicings' as the 'standard'" (Parker 21).

In addition, according to Bill Nichols' *Ideology and the Image*, "ideology" is the picture that a society paints of itself in order to sustain itself, and "it is the "fabrication of images in the processes of representation to persuade us that how things are is how they ought to be and that the place provided for us is the place we ought to have" (Berry vii). Similar to Nichols and stardom theorist Barry King, cultural critic Stuart Hall argues that the media provides "the framework for perceiving reality," which allows twentieth-century capitalism to reign supreme ideologically (*Television's Influence on Cultures* 5; Berry vi). Furthermore, Richard Dyer and Paul McDonald argue that stars can make a political impact if they influence the values and attitudes of their audiences while Barry King argues that stars have "major control over the representation of people in society" in general, and by mass media (Dyer 7-8). Therefore, stars "have a privileged position in the definition of social roles and types, and this must have real consequences in terms of how people believe they can and should behave" (Dyer 8). Hollywood producers in the early twentieth century must have believed that as they delayed the dawn of Black Hollywood stardom, a threat to the social order, even though inclusion would have been good for business. There is no explanation other than race for a studio the size of MGM not taking a chance on signing a non-white actor such as McKinney to a long-term contract, honoring her contract, and actively promoting her as a star.

McKinney, despite her talent and charisma, was unable to overcome the social forces that suppressed Black actors in Hollywood. Since race and gender overlap, it is important to note that McKinney avoided the pitfalls of "service girls" (*Moguls and Movie Stars*), Hollywood hopefuls who were willing to do *anything* for a break. Instead, McKinney refused to bow down to "wolfish producers," as stated decades later in a short report published in the February 13, 1958, issue of *Jet* magazine ("Ex-Movie Actress Nina Mae McKinney"). Her statement holds much credence. Incidents of sexual harassment and exploitation have been uncovered in Hollywood from the early twentieth century to the present—including the "Me, Too" movement that gained a more massive following after multiple allegations were made against producer Harvey Weinstein in 2017.

Shirley Temple Black, former child actor and top box office draw, gave a notable example at MGM. When she appeared on CNN's *Larry King Live* on October 25, 1988, to promote her autobiography, *Child Star,* she discussed going with her mother to meet the executives at MGM to work on a film: "one picture, thank goodness, only one!" ("Larry King Live with Shirley Temple Black"). She had left Fox, and she was only 12. When she and her mother arrived at MGM, they were separated and directed to different offices. She met with Arthur Freed while her mother met with Louis B. Mayer. Regarding her meeting with Freed, Temple Black stated, "I thought he was a producer, but instead, he was an exhibitor. And I'd never seen anyone naked before except myself. So I had no clue about what was happening. And, um, so it struck me so funny, I laughed at it. And I laughed gloriously. I had tears, you know. And he got infuriated, and he said, 'Out, out, out, go!'" ("Larry King Live with Shirley Temple Black"). She said that she rejoined her mother in the lobby of the administrative building and that they walked to their car quietly. She said that when she told her mother what happened in Freed's office, her mother was quiet for a moment before telling her about what she had just experienced in Mayer's office. Temple Black explained, "Louis B. Mayer wasn't as bad as Freed was to me, but he came on to my mother. And so we both decided that we didn't like MGM much!" ("Larry King Live with Shirley Temple Black").

Although the white male gaze initially helped Nina Mae McKinney to receive recognition for her talent, which led to her opportunity in *Hallelujah*, it was not enough to sustain her career or to allow her to progress—especially since she refused to "cooperate" behind the scenes. Audiences, white and Black, found McKinney beautiful. However, her light-to-medium-brown complexion (without makeup) and her natural hair texture—thicker than a white woman's—represented a type of beauty that did not fit the dominant white standard.

According to *The Stars* by Edgar Morin, capitalism and audiences' "anthropological" need for myth and worship create stars (Morin 116). Morin argues that audiences worship stars because stars represent audiences' idealizations of personality and beauty. Hence, the early star system in the film industry promoted beauty, youth, and sex appeal (Morin 6). Of course, Hollywood studios in the early twentieth century privileged such worship to white actors. After the release of *Hallelujah* in 1929, MGM realized that King Vidor and Irving Thalberg's little experiment might make a much deeper impact than anticipated. Despite McKinney's breakthrough role and laudable performance, MGM failed to promote her. Continuing to praise her long after *Hallelujah* and advancing her career would have suggested that a Black woman could be equal to a white woman not only in social status but also in terms of ability and beauty.

While several white actresses became freelancers and worked with independent producers and talent agents to increase their profits, attain star treatment, control their own personas, and enjoy varying levels of creative control, most white actresses lacked such control. Only a small number of the elite white actresses did, and even they were not guaranteed longevity. In the 1930s, the estimated number of freelancers was 40 while the estimated number of contract actors was 500 (Carman 50). To further illustrate how difficult it was for white actresses to assert independence as free agents, note that, unlike Barbara Stanwyck, Miriam Hopkins eventually found herself unable to maintain her stardom after she realized that her freelance film with independent producer Samuel Goldwyn lacked the distribution of Paramount in 1937, appeared in no films in 1938, and found it difficult to find a suitable "comeback vehicle" with Warner Bros. (Carman 113).

Unfortunately, aging causes stars to eventually lose their luster as well. At the studios, "a premium would always be placed on youth" (Jewell 250). Younger stars, ultimately, have always replaced older stars in major roles. Actors may remain stars in the twilight of their careers but not at the same level as their youth. For example, Mary Pickford, the first major movie star, and Douglas Fairbanks did not successfully transition to the sound era partly because they were aging, not necessarily because they could not adapt to a different style of acting. It can be difficult for aging actors to deviate from the types of roles their fans have grown accustomed to. Yet, eventually, youthful roles are no longer open to them (Jewell 250-51). Of course, this is less relevant to actors of Nina Mae McKinney's era who, based on the color of their skin, were denied opportunities to become stars to begin with.

If Miriam Hopkins struggled to attain stardom and longevity, it was even more challenging for most other white actresses and impossible for non-white actresses such as Nina Mae McKinney. As James Baldwin argues in "The Devil Finds Work," unlike white stars who enjoyed successful careers of varying lengths, the major studios reduced a Black actor to a single "indelible" moment which she or he "created, miraculously, beyond the confines of the script" (Baldwin 554). Certainly, this was the case with McKinney's breakout role as Chick in *Hallelujah*, which is discussed at length in Chapter Six: The Groundbreaking Role as Chick in *Hallelujah*.

Chapter Three

Overseas Performances

Racism and sexism prevented Nina Mae McKinney's career growth in Hollywood, despite the success of *Hallelujah* (1929), but she refused to give up on her dream. While actively seeking new Hollywood roles in the 1930s but being forced to wait, she sang in American nightclubs such as the famous Cotton Club in New York, where she was well-received. Journalist Ted Yates stated that she was a "dramatic song stylist" and "a brilliant performer as an exponent of perfect entertainment in the current smash hit revuesical at the Swank Cotton Club" (Yates). Unfortunately, the only Black people allowed at the Cotton Club were the performers. Although segregation and exclusion did not sit well with McKinney and some of the other performers, at least it was a way to make a living doing what they loved. Wealthy white patrons only allowed the best performers to have longevity there, which Yates emphasized (Yates). Fortunately, other doors would open for some of them. McKinney found opportunities overseas, where she performed on the stage (music and theatre), in movies, on the radio, and in experimental television shows.

McKinney returned overseas multiple times. She performed in dramas and vaudeville acts, and she sang with a jazz band. Her tours included Paris, Nice, Cannes, and Côte d'Azur (the French Riviera) in France; Berlin, Germany; Prague, Czech Republic; Budapest, Hungary; Athens, Greece; various locations in Australia; and London, England. In London, she performed at the Alhambra, both a theatre and a music hall (Bourne 5, 16, 30, 33-34, 47). The *Pittsburgh Courier* does not specify the date or venue, but it states that McKinney also "gave a command performance before King George

V in London" (Nina Mae McKinney, Obituary, *Pittsburgh Courier*). The October 4, 1930, issue of the *Indianapolis Star* announced that McKinney had wed Douglas Daniels and that she would give an unnamed stage performance in Berlin after their honeymoon ("Negro Film Star, Dancer Married at Crown Point").

In the 1930s, she toured Europe with Garland Wilson, a jazz pianist. They recorded two critically acclaimed songs in Paris in 1932: "Minnie the Moocher's Wedding Day" (written by Harold Arlen and Ted Koehler) and "Rhapsody in Love" (written by Clarence Williams and also recorded by Cab Calloway and His Orchestra in 1932). In the jazz journal *Storyville*, Laurie Wright states: "He [Garland Wilson] is indeed a superb accompanyist, sensitive to both the lyrics and the singer's needs and Nina Mae is an above-average vocalist with a pleasantly husky delivery, dropping into a growl for effect, but who makes use of some odd pronunciations; more often than not, the word 'rhapsody' comes out sounding like 'rhapsoday'" (qtd. in Bourne 16). The description seems reminiscent of her performance in *Hallelujah*. Between the 1930s and 1940s, her vaudeville and cabaret performances included "jazz numbers," and audiences appreciated her style and delivery. Despite her popularity, the two aforementioned songs seem to be her only verified recordings, even though the *Pittsburgh Courier* (via the Associated Negro Press or ANP) reported on April 27, 1935, that McKinney (also a cornet player) recorded "four victrola records for Parlophone" and released two of them—"You Bring Out the Savage in Me" and "It Had to Be You" ("Nina Mae Makes Four Parlophone Records"; Bourne 16).

Garland Wilson also accompanied McKinney in *Chocolate and Cream,* a revue that featured a racially integrated cast in London on February 13, 1932. This performance made McKinney a star in London. Producer Charles B. Cochran had helped McKinney's idol Florence Mills attain similar success in London in the 1920s. Next, McKinney's performance in Cochran's "Revels in Rhythm" at the

Trocadero Restaurant in 1933 "exposed her to the rich and elite of London's high society" (Bourne 30). McKinney sang "Bring Back the Charleston" and "Stormy Weather," which Harold Arlen and Ted Koehler wrote for Ethel Waters' Cotton Club performances. As part of an "elite" Black group of rich nightclub and general-audience vaudeville entertainers, McKinney was part of what historian Jeffrey Green coined "the Negro Renaissance in England" ("Revels in Rhythm"; Bourne 31).

McKinney also appeared on the big screen. She filmed her first British movie, *Kentucky Minstrels*, released in 1934. It is a comedy starring the African American variety show duo of Scott and Whaley, who gave a minstrel performance. McKinney sang "I'm in Love with the Band." Debroy Somers and his band, in blackface, performed with her. According to the May 24, 1934, issue of *Film Weekly*, McKinney was "the best thing in the picture" (qtd. in Bourne 32).

The following year, alongside Paul Robeson she starred in *Bosambo*, renamed *Sanders of the River* (1935). *Sanders of the River*—directed by Zoltan Korda and starring Paul Robeson, Nina McKinney, and Leslie Banks—is a film produced by London Film Productions in London. It was initially distributed between 1935 and 1936 by United Artists in the United Kingdom and the United States and by several other distributors in Austria, France, Sweden, Finland, Belgium, and Portugal (*Sanders of the River*).

Along with Earnest Trimmingham (leading man in *Jack, Sam and Pete* in 1919 and *Where The Rainbow Ends* in 1921), McKinney and Robeson were among the first Black actors to have leading roles in a British film (Ogidi). Paul Robeson signed on first, and when he insisted on bringing Nina Mae McKinney in to play the female lead, the production company "immediately cabled the William Morris Agency," and she was "aboard the first steamer that sailed for the Continent" (Yates).

Set in Nigeria under British colonial rule, the film is a pro-colonization story that was advertised as "Alexander Korda's spectacular epic of the jungle" (*Sanders of the River*). The film celebrates the colonizers as the courageous keepers of the peace and the protectors of the "primitive" natives. It supports the notion that colonization was for Africans' own good or that was in their best interest, including underlying factors such as "the colonized mind" and paternalism, the idea that Africans were like children under the British. The film also illustrates male chauvinism in terms of the male characters' dominant attitudes toward women, in general. To be fair, one must note that McKinney and Robeson felt tricked after completing the film. "When he discovered that the film's message had changed during editing and it presented a deeply racist interpretation of African history," Robeson "famously disowned" it (Eschner). Either this substantial edit was the production company's plan all along or they later decided to make a sociopolitical or racialized concession so the film could be released in the United States with less resistance.

However, the film pretends to tell a moral tale. For example, Commissioner R. G. Sanders (Banks), the King of Britain's representative in Nigeria, declares to a slave-raiding African king that slavery would not be allowed in the territory that Sanders oversees. Sanders also disapproves of polygamy, lying to nine young women who all want to marry Bosambo (Robeson). In addition, the importation of gin and rifles is forbidden in the territory. The "people of the river" are obedient to Sanders. Bosambo, the Ochuri (Bosambo's people), and several other chieftains of the river affectionately refer to Sanders as "Lord Sandy" even though they speak English very clearly. Bosambo is the unquestionably loyal chieftain appointed by Sanders after African King Tofolaba (Tony Wane) and his soldiers come from the south and "threaten the peace." Sanders, accompanied by Bosambo and their men, goes before Tofolaba. Sanders threatens to overthrow Tofolaba if he attempts to harm anyone under the British king's command. Tofolaba backs down. Feeling disgraced, he blames Bosambo for bringing Sanders to him. Soon, Sanders takes leave and returns to Britain. After greedy white gin traders lie about the death of Sanders, Tofolaba plans to attack Bosambo's people and sell them into slavery. For revenge, he wants to kill Bosambo, and he kidnaps Lilongo (Nina Mae McKinney), the wife of Bosambo, as bait. Sanders returns from Britain just as Bosambo attempts to rescue Lilongo. Sanders overthrows the king and installs Bosambo as King of the River.

In the role of Bosambo, Robeson stands and walks in a manner that is supposed to illustrate to white audiences that he is a "noble savage" but still primitive compared to Sanders and the other white people. Despite the subservient role, one of the film's strengths is the power of Robeson's voice as both an actor and a singer when he is not shrinking himself down in front of Sanders. Unfortunately, his songs are tributes to Sanders.

For the role of Lilongo, McKinney has been darkened around the eyes and wears dark lipstick, probably to make her eyes and lips look bigger. McKinney, neither dark-skinned nor light enough to pass for white, was beautiful to Black audiences and white audiences. Although Hollywood's limitations on Black actors were worse, this British production demonstrates that London was neither ready to shed racist colonization themes nor promote an on-screen Black beauty queen as equal to white starlets either. This was the case despite the success and popularity of Josephine Baker in Europe in the 1920s and 1930s.

Lilongo looks quite different from the other African women, some of which are topless or half nude and all of which are dark-skinned. Not only is Lilongo fully clothed, but McKinney also portrays her as intelligent and strong-willed. Unfortunately, this film insinuates that Europeans considered light-skinned Black women more beautiful than dark-skinned Black women and that both a predominantly white society and Black men prefer them.

Notwithstanding the dominant male chauvinistic theme, Lilongo has power over Bosambo and overcomes Sanders' initial objections to her marrying Bosambo. She also insists that she will be Bosambo's only wife. Bosambo eagerly agrees and also says he will practice her religion, which she refers to as Mohammedan (or Muslim). In one scene, McKinney sings a beautiful lullaby to put her two children to sleep. This is the best shot scene in the film, which is fitting because even with the larger-than-life presence of Robeson, McKinney more than holds her own. Critics recognized McKinney's solid performance, but the highest praise belonged to Robeson. Film critic P. L. M. (initials available only) of *London's Daily Herald* states, "This film is a landmark for British studios. It impresses and amuses; it is boldly triumphant as colorful drama and manages to be patriotic without flag-waving. Above all it gives Paul Robeson the part of his life" (qtd. in "Describes Robeson Film as Best British Hit").

In the United States, *Sanders of the River* screened for a full house on Broadway. An unnamed critic with the *Pittsburgh Courier* states, "The film which brings to Broadway all the thrill and color of native Africa, has been rated as one of the best flickers to come from the other side in some time and gives McKinney and Robeson, unequaled chances to display their superb acting ability" ("Starring in Broadway 'Pic'"). Despite the film's toned down but ever-present pro-colonization theme, notable historian and author J. A. Rogers adds, "One of our truly great accomplishments of the motion picture is Robeson's singing of the African war-songs, spear in hand, in the midst of his African warriors, is unforgettable" ("'Sanders of the River' Screens at 2 Theaters"). The film was a moderate success in the United States, but the British highly regarded it. The Institute of Amateur Cinematographers awarded its annual gold medal to *Sanders of the River* as "the most significant talking picture of 1935" ("Robeson Film Wins High English Honor;" "Robeson-McKinney Film Wins Coveted Annual English Award").

On February 17, 1933, Nina Mae McKinney became the first Black person and the first Black "artiste" to appear on television after John Logie Baird invited her to appear in one of his "experimental television programmes" in London (Bourne 46). Although television was a young medium with limited viewership, McKinney was famous enough for *The Times* to announce her appearance, in advance, "for 11 to 11:30pm: 'Television transmission by the Baird process (Vision): Nina Mae McKinney (song and dance)'" and to later announce her first BBC radio broadcast for May 10, 1933, which preceded her fellow international star Josephine Baker's appearance in another Baird experimental show on October 4, 1933 (Bourne 46).

In late 1936, BBC launched its television programming at Alexandra Palace aka Ally Pally, and Nina Mae McKinney was among the first entertainers selected to star in their own variety shows. On Saturday, February 27, 1937, BBC's live broadcast of McKinney's *Ebony* showcased McKinney, Johnny Nit—a Black tap dancer who had also performed in Lew Leslie's *Blackbirds* in the 1920s, and the BBC Television Orchestra presented by Dallas Bower. As Black pianists Kirby Walker and Ruby Smith played, McKinney sang "Papa Tree Top Tall," "Harlem Moon," and "Why Am I So Blue?" according to a program log preserved at the BBC's written archive. The *Radio Times* "published a full-page portrait of Nina Mae, taken by the London photographer 'Cannons of Hollywood,' in its television supplement," but unfortunately, the production company did not yet possess the technology to record the show (Bourne 47-48). McKinney also appeared in producer Dallas Bower's *Dark Laughter* on Saturday, June 5, 1937, alongside Leslie Thompson, a Jamaican trumpeter. Black pianists Kirby Walker and Yorke de Souza played as McKinney sang "Copper Coloured Gal of Mine" and "Big Boy Blue." Both shows reflected Black Broadway and the Harlem Renaissance (Bourne 46-48).

In 1937, McKinney appeared in BBC's *Television Demonstration Film*, a "film survey of BBC television programmes during the first six months of operation (November 1936 to May 1937), intended for manufacturers and retailers" (Bourne 48). Most of the documentaries about the history of British TV—including BBC's *Salute to A.P.* (1954), *This Was the Future* (1957), *The Birth of Television* (1977), *Magic Rays of Light* (1981), and *That's Television Entertainment* (1986) as well as Channel 4's *The A to Z of TV* (1990)—have featured McKinney's performance in *Television Demonstration Film* (Bourne 48).

In 1937, as the star of the vaudeville revue *Hello Harlem*, McKinney also toured Australia (Anae 123). Her experience there illustrates how her talents and presence were more appreciated abroad than in the United States, which she had told the Black press in America. In Australia, McKinney's performances were well-received, and her aura, glamor, fashion, and words off-stage were extraordinary. Perhaps, despite her unfortunate historical erasure or mitigation, the clearest instances of her voice are found in her tours of Australia. She controlled her image as a Black woman, and even "against the backdrop of the 'White Australia' policy," she spoke assertively and candidly about the people of Harlem, race in America, and Black internationalism (Anae 123, 142). In her chapter in Keisha N. Blain and Tiffany M. Gill's *To Turn the Whole World Over: Black Women and Internationalism*, entitled "'They Will All Be My Color': Nina Mae McKinney and Black Internationalism in 1930s Australia," scholar Nicole Anae focuses mainly on McKinney's press interviews (Anae 123). Anae acknowledges that McKinney's own words "contrast historical accounts about McKinney that tend to silence her own voice, offer relatively limited examples of her own articulations, or underplay the scope and significance of her international fame" (Anae 123).

According to Anae, "McKinney asserts control over the discourse of black representation not simply by controlling what she is saying but also by controlling the contexts in which she herself is saying it: remote from the American context but proximate to the growing awareness of black internationalist activity in Australia" (Anae 136). In a *Sydney Mail* interview, "Music and Drama: Nina Mae McKinney" by Kerwin Maegraith (October 20, 1937), McKinney explained, "The modern coloured people of America live mostly the same existence as the whites. We have our doctors and our lawyers in Harlem, many of them very talented men, and on the stage there are many great coloured performers" (qtd. in Anae 134).

In the same *Sydney Mail* interview, McKinney upheld the civil rights activism of her *Sanders of the River* co-star Paul Robeson. McKinney stated, "There is not a finer man living than Paul Robeson, and his gifts to charity have been enormous. He is like a big brother to me, and he numbers among his close friends some of the most highly respected notabilities of the old world" (qtd. in Anae 135). In "Paul Robeson: Artist and Man—An Interview with Nina Mae McKinney" by Lesley Williams in the *Inverell Times* (November 26, 1937), McKinney added, "To artists, both black and white, who work with him, he is a tower of physical, mental, and artistic strength" (qtd. in Anae 135).

During the aforementioned *Sydney Mail* interview, McKinney also clarified her religious beliefs and spoke on the religious natures of Harlem, New York, and Paul Robeson. McKinney stated, "The publicity I see all over the world about the preachings and teachings of 'Father Devine' and the glorified reports about his 'heaven' do not typify our people. The folk in Harlem are not fanatics in their beliefs, and many are deeply religious. I am a devout Catholic and Mr. Robeson is a church-going man" (qtd. in Anae 134).

McKinney also addressed the "threat of race mixing implicit in the Joe Louis versus Tommy Farr championship prize fight in 1937 and the concerns about race mixing that surrounded the abandoned project to release a cinematic version of David Belasco's play *Lula Belle*" (Anae 140). The titular role would have been McKinney's (Anae 140). In "Drawing the Color Line: Lovely Negro Actress Gives Example," by Ian Smith in *Labor Daily* (August 27, 1937),

McKinney explained, "A negro can fight a white man for the championship of the world, and American audiences will cheer both men. But . . . it is different when it comes to a negro actress appearing in a love scene with a white man" (qtd. in Anae 140). In another interview, "Gentleman Jo Louis Will Win, Says Actress" in the *Daily News* (Perth, August 25, 1937), she stated, "It was not Hollywood's fault. . . . In the Southern States such a film would never have been tolerated. But there's no color bar in boxing" (qtd. in Anae 140).

Black entertainers, including African Americans discovered by producers at London nightclubs, made notable contributions abroad until the onset of World War II in 1939. Nina Mae McKinney fit right in among these multitalented and amazing actors, singers, dancers, and musicians, including Paul Robeson, Eunice Wilson, Garland Wilson, Valaida Hall, Adelaide Hall, Fats Waller, Alberta Hunter, Elisabeth Welch, and the Mills Brothers. We will never know what would have come next for Nina Mae McKinney abroad if World War II had not arrived and brought with it an air of uncertainty. Inevitably, McKinney returned to New York.

"Chapter Four: Choosing Race Films and Returning to the American Stage" will discuss the next phase of Nina Mae McKinney's entertainment career.

Chapter Four

Choosing Race Films and Returning to the American Stage

Around 1937, Nina Mae McKinney tried her hand at "race" films. Although race films lacked the production values of Hollywood films, they pleased Black audiences. McKinney remained a star despite being shut out by Hollywood. Yet she was not content to simply find work in race films. In her attempt at agency, she did not accept just any role. In terms of her professional status, she secured leading roles, and she chose roles that were non-stereotypical or at least balanced. During and shortly after this cinematic run, she made a well-received but short-lived return to the American stage (music and theatre).

During her transition from Hollywood films to race films, McKinney was overly concerned that audiences might conflate her characters with her real-life persona. McKinney said she wanted to play "the well-bred woman in films, and not a hell cat" (Yates). She felt that she did not receive that opportunity in her roles in *Safe in Hell* and *Hallelujah*, which "took away the poise and gentility that the actress had inherited from birth" (Yates). The idea that her "character of hypocrisy" in *Hallelujah* "stuck to her for a long, long time" was something that "got on her nerves" (Yates). Instead, desiring to "appear as an actress at ease," she wanted her characters to be "attractive," but she was not interested in being portrayed in Hollywood like the "flaming Latin Lupe Valez [Vélez] type" (Yates). In race films, she held on to her artistic integrity/ideals, accepting leading roles that portrayed balanced, self-determined, and independent characters.

Nina Mae McKinney starred in three documented race films. In Million Dollar Productions' *Gang Smashers* (1938) and *Straight to*

Heaven (1939) as well as in Sack Amusement's *The Devil's Daughter* (1939), McKinney was still a believable actor. McKinney's level of productivity demonstrates her drive to keep working and fight for the survival of her entertainment career. Note that *The Devil's Daughter* and *Straight to Heaven* were released by two different production companies during the same month and year: Sack Amusement on December 7, 1939, and Million Dollar Productions on December 12, 1939, respectively ("The Devil's Daughter"; "Straight to Heaven").

In *Gang Smashers*, McKinney portrayed Laura Jackson, one of the first Black detectives—if not the first—to appear in a movie. The film, rereleased by Toddy Pictures as *Gun Moll* in the 1940s, was written by the "Dark Gable" Ralph Cooper—a race film star and the male lead of *The Duke is Tops* alongside Lena Horne in 1938 ("Gang Smashers," IMDb). As the story begins, the opening graphic states that the film seeks to pay tribute to the Black members of the Intelligence Service who fought against organized crime. In the first scene, Jackson attends a cabaret where she sings, "That's not the kind of love that I've been dreaming of, and I just can't see it your way" (*Gang Smashers*). A "no settling for just any old thing or anybody" song that illustrates the character's self-sufficiency is a fitting opening.

Club owner Gat Dalton has an altercation with Bowers, a local businessman. Afterward, Bowers' dead body is found inside his ransacked business. The police suspect Dalton and show up to question him. They know he is lying about not having left the club, and they accuse Jackson of lying to cover for him. When the police question Jackson and Dalton separately at the station, the audience learns that Jackson is working undercover. She wants her boss to ease up on Dalton for a while, especially since the people who pay him are afraid to talk, but her boss is determined to break Dalton's "protection" ring, in which Dalton and his henchmen have been forcing local business owners to pay him for "damage insurance."

Regarding the cast, Mantan Moreland portrays Gloomy, one of Dalton's lackeys. Moreland displays his typical brand of comedy, a stereotypical "coon" figure, but the character's presence is less harmful since he is the only character of this type in the movie. Moreover, McKinney received top billing. The film's opening credits read, "TODDY PICTURES CO. presents NINA MAY McKINNEY [sic; emphasis theirs] in GUN MOLL" [emphasis theirs]. McKinney was not the same bright-eyed, bubbly persona whose on-screen exploits seemed nearly effortless in *Hallelujah* nine years earlier, but she was still more than impressive enough to be the highlight of the film.

McKinney's once effortless charisma and natural spring in her step are not quite the same as before, but her acting is still convincing, which is crucial. Note that although this film and numerous other race films are entertaining, they are often dialogue-driven because their budgets were much smaller than those of the major studios. Staging fewer action scenes saved money, and of course, Black audiences rarely complained about films that ranged in quality because the films fulfilled their need to see balanced portrayals of themselves on screen. McKinney's physical appearance is also somewhat different in *Gang Smashers*. Her hair is straightened and slicked down, and her skin tone is lighter. Her nose also appears to be slightly less round and more pointed. These differences first become noticeable in *Pie, Pie Blackbird*, which was released three years after *Hallelujah*. After being met with resistance after her breakout role, she might have gradually changed her appearance to keep working. It still was not enough to boost her career in Hollywood. She remained resistant to stereotypical Black roles until late in her career, and apparently, she still refused to demean herself behind the scenes. She was still far too resilient and talented to be shut out of show business altogether.

In *The Devil's Daughter* (1939), also known as *Pocomania*, Nina Mae McKinney co-stars as Isabelle Walton, a woman who tries to scare off her sister Sylvia Walton (Ida James) to gain full control of the family business in Jamaica after their father's death ("The Devil's Daughter"). To accomplish her goal, Isabelle pretends to practice Obeah, which is similar to Voodoo and also derived from particular West African religious roots. Its representation as witchcraft solely used to harm people reflects typical Western distortions about Africans and people of the African Diaspora. Yet, the film attempts to balance the strengths of the performers against the story's stereotypical images that include Isabelle's buffoonish servant Percy and his exaggerated dialect, irrationally superstitious Black people, and of course, witchcraft—the fear and use of it. For example, to keep Percy in line, Isabelle convinces him that she has the power to transfer his soul to the body of a pig. Although *The Devil's Daughter* does contain stereotypical images of Black people, the portrayals of the leading roles, Sylvia Walton and her scheming but later penitent sister Isabelle, offset these images. McKinney's performance as Isabelle lacks the exuberance of her earlier role as Chick, but she is quite convincing in her role as a slightly older woman who is willing to cheat her family to get what she wants. McKinney plays out the character arc and its conflicting emotions well. Standout performances and the theme of forgiveness are the film's redeeming factors.

In *Straight to Heaven*, McKinney played the role of Ida Williams, the mother of singing prodigy Jimmy Williams and the wife of Joe Williams, a chemist who tries to expose both the company that knowingly distributes spoiled canned food and the racketeers who force local stores to sell it. After co-worker George Elliot causes Joe to lose his job, John "Lucky" Simon, local club owner and secret head of the racketeering ring, frames Joe for George's murder. Joe is wrongfully arrested and convicted.

Then, the audience learns that Ida will immediately take action to clear her husband's name, with or without anyone's help. She is intelligent enough and determined enough to do so, but fortunately, Joe's friend Stanley Jackson is an attorney. Stanley eagerly assists in solving the case and clearing Joe's name. Meanwhile, a naive Jimmy finds himself kidnapped by the racketeers after Lucky hears him singing outside with his friends and hires him to sing without consent from Ida. While Jimmy's life is in danger and Joe's freedom hangs in the balance, Ida and Stanley rush to solve the case.

Somehow, McKinney had either managed to maintain her popularity with Black audiences since the release of *Hallelujah* or triumphantly regained it by 1938. Despite the absence of critical reviews, her race films—especially *Gang Smashers*—were popular in Black theaters. According to the *California Eagle*, the number of people who went to see *Gang Smashers* increased daily after it opened. By the second week, Million Dollar Theater in downtown New York had to turn away moviegoers because it could not accommodate all of them ("Million $ Pic Held Over Second Week"). *Gang Smashers* also broke Million Dollar Theater's house records ("Million $ Pic Enters 3rd Big Week"). Its success there prompted RKO's theater chain to obtain the film for release in its three Harlem theaters the following month ("RKO Theater Chain to Present 'Gang Smashers': Picture Has Been Booked for Three Harlem Theaters"). The film was well-received in RKO's Harlem theaters, especially at the 116th Street Regent Theater, as management stirred fanfare by arranging an appearance by the film's cast at one of its showings ("Harlemites Go 'First Nighter' for Sepia Film; 'Gang Smashers' Opened with Pomp of Hollywood's Best"). The *Pittsburgh Courier* lauded the film as a major part of the race film industry's stellar year in 1938, which also included films such as Lena Horne's *The Duke is Tops* (Morris 21).

As an entertainer, McKinney continued to fight hard to remain in the forefront. By 1938, McKinney had not given up on Hollywood, but she was wise enough and versatile enough to put forth tremendous effort in race films while simultaneously forming a jazz band in 1939. McKinney managed to book the band (official name unknown) for the World's Fair in New York City (Handy 46; "Nina Mae McKinney," *California Eagle*). In 1939, it also must have been exciting for McKinney to return to a *Blackbirds* stage production as a headliner for a prolonged tour after she had been a chorus girl in the 1928 production only briefly. According to flutist and author D. Antoinette Handy, Gertrude Eloise Martin—a concert violinist based in New York—conducted the "twenty-five-piece orchestra" for the 1939–1940 version (Handy 46). In its December 23, 1939 issue, the *Chicago Defender* stated that "America's No. 1 Swingheart, Nina Mae McKinney, vivacious star of stage and screen" and her orchestra would debut (qtd. in Handy 46). The show opened in Columbia, South Carolina, on December 28, 1939, and it ran on Broadway from February 11, 1940, until February 18, 1940 (*Blackbirds*, 1939). McKinney left the tour early, around April 1940, to headline the *Gay New Orleans* production at the World's Fair in New York City (Handy 46).

McKinney performed in *Tan Manhattan*, which ran in 1941 at the Howard Theatre in Washington, D.C. in January and at the Apollo Theater in Harlem in February. Her castmates included Flournoy Miller, a comedian, and Avon Long, a singer and dancer. In this all-Black musical comedy scored by jazz musician Eubie Black and lyricist Andy Razaf, McKinney sings "Say Hello to the Folks Back Home" and "I'll Take a Nickel for a Dime" (Bourne 55).

From there, McKinney joined Pancho Diggs and his Orchestra in 1942. McKinney became the lead vocalist and the headliner, securing more dates for the group. "Black audiences across America knew and idolized her as a beautiful but wacky screen star on the order of Carole Lombard," and "in New York, she was a favorite at the Apollo Theater, where she teamed with the top male comedians of the day in an act similar to that of the old-time entertainers Butterbean and Susie" (Bourne 56). The orchestra benefited from McKinney's name as she still was a draw, leading to a name change: Nina Mae McKinney and her Orchestra. Its tour lasted for a year. The orchestra lost "its identity" as most audiences focused on McKinney, and it disbanded when the Army drafted Pancho Diggs (Bourne 55-56).

"Chapter Five: Personal Struggles and the Press" will include more of McKinney's entertainment ventures.

Chapter Five

Personal Struggles and the Press

An overview of the personal struggles that Nina Mae McKinney endured as she fought to maintain her acting career helps establish the importance of rediscovering her and restoring her legacy. Although McKinney possessed an "it" factor that led to her discovery at such an early age, beginning and maintaining her career in Hollywood was a tremendous challenge. During and after the production of *Hallelujah*, racism in the white press and occasional negative publicity in the Black press were major stress factors for McKinney. When vital details about historical figures are missing, it is useful to draw comparisons to similarly situated historical figures. To help us arrive at meaning, this chapter discusses the latter portion of McKinney's life and draws relevant comparisons to entertainers Eartha Kitt and Josephine Baker as well as schoolteacher Essie Washington-Williams, the secret Black daughter of Strom Thurmond, a well-known senator and southern white segregationist.

Landing a leading role in a major motion picture was a remarkable accomplishment for a 16-year-old Black female in 1929. As if the era's pervasive racism and sexism were not stressful enough, of course, Nina Mae had to adapt to the rapid pace, taxing workload, and grand expectations of a major studio production. Note that *Hallelujah* was released in August 1929. They had finished filming by May 1929, but they reconvened to reshoot the cabaret scene because "dissatisfaction was expressed with a preview shown at the Hollywood Theatre" ("'Hallelujah' Star Overcome by Heavy Movie Tasks"). Such a statement does not indicate exactly who was dissatisfied, but the audience likely included the top execs at MGM. Thus, Nina Mae faced longer work hours than usual. It was a "program of early morning till midnight of strenuous acting before the cameras" ("'Hallelujah' Star Overcome by Heavy Movie Tasks"). Despite the late hour, around 7:00 PM, she and the rest of the cast were enjoying the scene. So was her mother Georgie, who was allowed on set to watch her ("'Hallelujah' Star Overcome by Heavy Movie Tasks"). Note that in the beginning, Nina Mae and Georgie were so close that Nina Mae insisted that she could not accept the role unless MGM agreed to bring Georgie along with her ("Didn't Raise My Daughter to Be an Actress"). Nina Mae was working beyond exhaustion, but no one could tell. Everyone on set was caught by surprise when she passed out while singing and dancing. The directors and cast carried her outside to get some air, and shooting ceased for the night ("'Hallelujah' Star Overcome by Heavy Movie Tasks").

Nina Mae McKinney likely endured tremendous stress and fought bouts of depression for various reasons. First, racial barriers in her career prevented a level playing field in Hollywood and the entertainment industry in general. McKinney's career and lifetime fell within the nadir of race relations in America. Not only were the major Hollywood studios reluctant to imply racial equality by promoting McKinney as a star, but racist critics in the white press also helped ensure that her career did not advance. White columnists deliberately shifted attention away from McKinney's talent in favor of presenting her as a Jezebel figure and a useless actor whose Hollywood career could not possibly last.

One of the most devastating examples is "Black—and Potentially Blue" by Elizabeth Goldberg in the April 1930 issue of *Motion Picture Classic* magazine. Goldberg implied that all-Black cast films would not be around much longer, and she claimed that there was no buzz at all in New York upon McKinney's return for the premier of *Hallelujah* there: "The press agent was nonplussed. Even newspaper men, it seems, observe a color line" ("Nina Mae McKinney Libeled in Nasty Magazine Article"). Goldberg also stated, "Nina is a Cleopatra for sure. She wants to be a siren and a heartbreaker. Crazy for men. Crazy for money. Crazy for admiration. No wonder she has accepted the illusion of Hollywood's friendliness" ("Nina Mae McKinney Libeled in Nasty Magazine Article").

According to Goldberg, "Nina Mae imagines that she has made the big jump from the Black world to the white. Poor little Nina. Colored people no longer appeal to her fastidious taste. She has been in the homes of John Gilbert and Gloria Swanson. In her illusory success, she has drawn away from her own race, cut herself off from friends among her people, for what she imagines are better things" ("Nina Mae McKinney Libeled in Nasty Magazine Article"; Regester, *African American Actresses*). The *Afro-American* (Baltimore) quoted this openly racist excerpt. Insisting that McKinney had turned her back on Black people, Goldberg added a statement that she claimed McKinney made publicly: "If you start going out with them, pretty soon they [Black people] think they're just as big as you are" ("Nina Mae McKinney Libeled in Nasty Magazine Article"; Regester, *African American Actresses*). If McKinney spoke those words at all, it is likely that Goldberg merely extracted one short line, not McKinney's complete statement. One must also consider Goldberg's use of the word "them." McKinney's words could have been taken out of context easily. It is illogical and improbable that someone who relied on publicity to help keep her career alive would have erred and made such negative statements regarding racial politics or even degraded other Black people publicly. The *Afro-American* might have been defending McKinney by deliberately misspelling Goldberg's name as *Elisabeth Goldbeck* when it introduced her article (Regester, *African American Actresses*) but spelled her first name correctly later in its own article. The *Afro-American* would not have felt the need to defend McKinney if its staff had any reason to believe the statement Goldberg attributed to McKinney was authentic. McKinney, who soon filed lawsuits against Goldberg and *Motion Picture Classic* for defamation of character, responded: "It is not true. I don't know why they should write such a story about me unless it is to destroy the faith of my people in me and ruin my career" (Regester, *African American Actresses* 53; "Nina Mae McKinney Libeled in Nasty Magazine Article"). Goldberg's tone and mockery seem to suggest just that. McKinney's public persona also contradicts Goldberg's attempt to discredit her. For example, McKinney and fellow *Hallelujah* cast members Daniel Haynes and Fanny Belle DeKnight sent telegrams to the Regal Theater in Chicago to express their gratitude for showing the film ("Bakay, Garbage, Armstrong, Hudgins, and 'Hallelujah' on Dazzling Regal Bill").

Later, in February 1932, Nina Mae McKinney entered the "race" to become the NAACP's "Miss Olympic" to represent the organization's "Greater New York Area" at the Olympic games in California the following summer. She stated that she had "always wanted to make some worthwhile contribution to the work of the N.A.A.C.P." and saw this "venture" as a "splendid opportunity" ("In Race for 'Miss Olympics'"). Records of who won this honor seem to be missing. Although one may only speculate about the balance between McKinney's desire for publicity as she struggled to maintain her career and her desire to do something to benefit "the race," her effort is noteworthy. She was likely sincere, considering her support of Paul Robeson's activism (discussed in "Chapter Three: Overseas Performances").

Unlike the white press, articles by the Black press sometimes worked in McKinney's favor, even if the publicity was not always positive. For example, the Black press, including the *Chicago Defender* and the *Afro-American*, reported on another source of McKinney's struggle: her love life, including her failed marriages and alleged marriages. Details about why her marriages did not work out are missing, and none of her husbands were wealthy or held high social status. There is no apparent reason to believe that McKinney was a vixen or that she married for materialism and to advance her career.

According to the *Chicago Defender*, her first marriage was a brief union to Jimmie Marshall in 1929. Marshall, manager of the Lafayette Theater in New York, confirmed that he and McKinney "quietly married" after the *Hallelujah* Premiere ("Reported Wed"). However, neither a confirmation from McKinney nor any records of marriage, annulment, or divorce are available.

The following year, according to the *Chicago Defender*, McKinney, age 19, allegedly married vaudeville dancer Douglas Daniels, who was 16 or 17, only to seek annulment soon afterward. The *Afro-American's* reference to Daniels as McKinney's "boy-husband" and the *Chicago Defender's* failure to state his exact age and its reporting that both he and McKinney claimed that the other left them alone seem to sensationalize this news ("Negro Film Star, Dancer Married at Crown Point"; Regester, African American Actresses 54; "Nina Mae Seeks Annulment of Marriage"). Talk of Daniels' age was likely nothing more than juicy gossip. There is no evidence that Daniels was only 16 or 17, and based on McKinney's previous residence in New York, a person had to be at least 18 to marry without parental consent in New York ("Information on Getting Married in New York State").

However, according to Indiana Marriage registration records, the two were married on October 23, 1930, in Lake County, Indiana. This was near Chicago, where they resided at the time ("Negro Film Star, Dancer Married at Crown Point"; Indiana, U.S., Marriages, 1810-2001). Indiana was the home of marriage mills—especially in Crown Point, Jeffersonville, Lawrenceburg, and Valparaiso—that were well-known to celebrities between the 1920s and 1940s. Other celebrities who got married there included Rudolph Valentino, Tom Mix, Red Grange, Red Skelton, and Ronald Reagan. At the time, Indiana neither required residency nor a waiting period. It was similar to 'getting hitched quick' in Las Vegas as "Indiana marriage laws at the time were not only fuzzy, but they were also virtually nonexistent," according to Dawn Mitchell's *IndyStar* article entitled "Indiana Was a Scandalous Marriage Mill and Valentino Took Advantage" (Mitchell). The justice of the peace was available 24/7 and did not have to report this income. The justice of the peace accepted all manner of payments, $2 to $15 in cash, depending on how elaborate the couple wanted the wedding to be. It was a "one-stop shop, offering rings, flowers and clothes for sale at all hours of the day for those couples who opted for the spur-of-the-moment nuptials" (Mitchell).

Many of the marriages performed by these marriage mills easily ended in annulment or divorce, especially since couples often admitted they had visited local taverns right before their weddings took place. The marriage mills began to decline after Indiana passed a law in 1938 requiring the bride to be a resident of the county where the wedding took place. Unfortunately, no record of McKinney and Daniels' annulment or divorce is available.

McKinney's next marriage was to jazz musician Jimmy Monroe, who was her manager at the time. The details are sketchy, and there are conflicting stories about when the marriage took place. They were married on November 25, 1931, in Portsmouth, Virginia, according to Virginia marriage records (Virginia, U.S., Select Marriages, 1785-1940). In 1931, news of her wedding made front page news in the *Chicago Defender*, which reported that McKinney and Monroe had dated for several months and entered nuptials shortly before the premiere of McKinney's film *Safe in Hell* ("Nina Mae McKinney Reported Married;" King, "Film Pioneers"). When World War II began, McKinney left Europe, where she had performed in major cities such as London, and she returned to New York. According to another story, this is when she married Monroe and began touring with a jazz band (Pettus, "Nina McKinney"; Pettus, "Lancaster Brick Wall Pays Tribute to Notable Citizens of That Area"; Pettus, "Nina Mae McKinney: Deserving of a Place in History"). McKinney and Monroe had known each other since the 1930s (also a vague time frame) when he first served as her manager, and their marriage only lasted for a year, between 1940 and 1941 (Bourne 56). Her reasons for marrying or remarrying Monroe in 1940 are uncertain, considering what happened between them in 1937: McKinney collapsed on a London stage due to a stomach ailment and remained hospitalized at London's Duchess Nursing Home for two weeks. A few days before McKinney's release, Monroe allegedly left London for Paris with a white woman. McKinney stated that he left with all of her money and many of her belongings ("Nina Mae Collapses on Irish Stage").

McKinney's next two marriages were also brief. She allegedly married Melvin Wolfolk, a ship steward. The date of the marriage is unverified as corroborating records are unavailable, but one week after McKinney allegedly divorced Wolfolk, she married civil engineer Frank Mickey, supposedly on April 8, 1949 (Wollstein 137). New York marriage license records confirm the marriage but contradict the marriage date, listing it as April 7, 1951 (Index to Marriages, Nina Mickey). Yet the 1950 U.S. Federal Census lists them as a married couple (U.S. Federal Census, 1950. Nina Mickey). How long the marriage lasted is unconfirmed because neither a divorce record nor a death certificate has been found for Frank Mickey.

Tragically, Nina Mae became pregnant and had a miscarriage, according to a letter dated July 5, 1950, from her mother, Georgie, to Hedda Hopper, actress and 1930s-1960s *Los Angeles Times* entertainment columnist (Maynor). No records of the child's name or death certificate have been found. Losing her child must have been an extremely difficult time for Nina Mae. Whether Frank Mickey was the child's father is unverified, but he was living with Nina Mae and Georgie in New York City according to the 1950 U.S. Federal Census (U.S. Federal Census, 1950, Nina Mickey).

McKinney allegedly had three other marriages: to boxer William "Gorilla" Jones in 1930, to Joel Fluellyn in 1938, and to Robert "Charleston" Montgomery in 1939. The September 13, 1930, issue of the *Pittsburgh Courier* only identifies Jones as McKinney's husband in a sports blurb stating the fans' disappointment with the outcome of the Harry Smith–Gorilla Jones fight ("Smith–Jones Go 'No Contest'"). According to the October 15, 1938, issue of the *Pittsburgh Courier*, Joel Fluellyn—McKinney's fellow member of "the film colony"—stated that he and McKinney traveled to Ensenada, Mexico, to be married in September 1938 ("Flash! Flash! Flash!"). The September 23, 1939, issue of the *Pittsburgh Courier* states that an "exclusive source" reported that McKinney had just wed Robert Montgomery, a former Apollo Theater errand boy also known for supposedly doubling (standing in) for Stepin Fetchit at a court date. According to the article, this marriage was unexpected news because McKinney was rumored to marry her theatrical agent as soon as her divorce from Jimmy Monroe was finalized and because McKinney allegedly had been "romantically linked to any number of theatrical and professional men" (Smith, "Movie Star Weds 20-Year-Old Youth"). Note that the Fluellyn and Montgomery dates are only one year apart and that the Montgomery date is also questionable, considering the Jimmy Monroe dates discussed earlier in this chapter. McKinney might have been in relationships with Jones, Fluellyn, or Montgomery at some point, but no marriage records are available. Furthermore, although Joel Fluellyn's name is spelled differently— *Fluellen*—in *Dorothy Dandridge: A Biography*, he could be the same person whom film historian Donald Bogle confirmed as a platonic mutual friend and "consort" of Nina Mae McKinney, Louise Beavers, Billie Holiday, Josephine Baker, and Hattie McDaniel (158-59). In short, these Nina McKinney marriage stories were most likely sensationalism, publicity stunts, gossip, or misreported information.

Rumors of substance abuse point to another possible factor in McKinney's struggle. Although unsubstantiated, drug use or alcoholism could account for the notable change in her physical appearance from her role in *Hallelujah* (1929) to her role in *Pinky* (1949). She looked older than 37, her age at the time. High stress levels and a difficult life, personal and professional, could either serve as contributing factors or provide an alternative explanation. Nevertheless, it is likely that McKinney's husband, James Norman Monroe aka Jimmy Monroe, introduced her to drug abuse at some point when he was her manager or husband. Rumors that Monroe was a pimp and a hustler are unconfirmed. What can be confirmed is that he was the brother of Harlem nightclub manager Clark Monroe, that he became an entertainment manager, and that his marriage to Nina Mae McKinney made him more well-known.

Monroe introduced his next wife, Billie Holiday, to heroin use, according to Holiday—whom he married in Elkton, Maryland, on August 25, 1941. Holiday did not place all the blame on Monroe, but she acknowledged his role in her initial drug use and stated that it became something they did together to help save their struggling marriage. Monroe mostly associated with white women when he was in London, where he met a white performer, and he returned to New York as her manager. Their relationship was also romantic. That was when Holiday first met Monroe. "The Monroe/Holiday marriage was doomed from the start" because Monroe continued his other relationship (Bourne 56). Holiday's finding out about his betrayal led her to write the popular song "Don't Explain." Monroe and Holiday eventually divorced after he served a nine-month prison sentence for "smuggling marijuana between Mexico and California" (Bourne 56-57). McKinney had also experienced Monroe's unfaithfulness during her marriage to him.

McKinney attended parties and social gatherings, but there has been no documentation of drug abuse or misconduct of any sort. There is one alleged party incident with actress Marion Davies' niece Pepi Lederer, who was a cocaine user according to *Flapper: A Madcap Story of Sex, Style, Celebrity, and the Women Who Made America Modern* (Zeitz 255). Yet the story does not mention McKinney using drugs there. If the story about Lederer's party is true, the worst thing that happened was when Lederer's white neighbor objected to McKinney and other cast members from *Hallelujah* being present (Bogle, *Bright Boulevards, Bold Dreams* 93). Herein lies an important contradiction and a tremendous source of McKinney's stress. McKinney was able to interact with white people of high status while denied public stardom in Hollywood. She was excluded when it mattered most: when studios considered actors for greater opportunities and career development.

Nina Mae McKinney died of a heart attack at Metropolitan Hospital in New York City on Wednesday, May 3, 1967. She was only 54. Her funeral was held on May 8, 1967, at "the actors' church" aka the Little Church Around the Corner—whose formal name is the Church of the Transfiguration—on the corner of 29th Street and Fifth Avenue. Her funeral was attended by "many actors from the 'Golden Age' of the colored theater," including fellow Negro Actors Guild members (White, *Afro-American*; Bourne 90; Church of the Transfiguration). After "hundreds of people" attended the viewing at Odessa M. Bailey Funeral Home, she was cremated at Ferncliff Cemetery on May 9 (Bourne 90). However, her remains are currently interred in Plot Cosmos Section 196/197 Lot 47NW at Woodlawn Cemetery in the Bronx, New York (*African American Legacy of the Woodlawn Cemetery*; Nina Mae McKinney, 12 Jun 1912 – 3 May 1967).

Sadly, McKinney's passing was relatively quiet. Although overlooked by *Variety* and other major sources, the *Daily News* (New York) and several Black newspapers reported her death. The *Daily News* covered it on May 8, 1967, the *Amsterdam News* on May 13, 1967, the *Washington Afro-American* on May 16, 1967, and both the *Afro-American* (Baltimore) and the *Pittsburgh Courier* on May 20, 1967 (Nina Mae McKinney, Obituary, *Daily News*; Nina Mae McKinney, Obituary, *Amsterdam News*; White, *Washington Afro-American*; White, *Afro-American*; Nina Mae McKinney, Obituary, *Pittsburgh Courier*; King, Susan). At the time, even if Hollywood did not acknowledge her death, at least some of "her own" remembered her.

Nina Mae McKinney's death certificate (City of New York Vital Records) does not mention that she had been a famous entertainer. It only states that she was "widowed" and that she was working as a "domestic" for "private families" (Bourne 90). Whether Nina Mae had married again after her marriage to Frank Mickey and had become a widow is unknown but unlikely because a search for additional marriage records yields no results, and the only confirmation of her profession comes from a *Hallelujah* technician who said that he attended a New York dinner party and was surprised to see an overweight Nina Mae McKinney working as a maid there (Bogle 94).

A discussion about Nina Mae McKinney's later years is warranted, although little is known. Dorothy Kilgallen's "The Voice of Broadway" in the July 20, 1960, edition of *The Coshocton Tribune* and the *Longview News-Journal* edition of the same date lacked details but reported that Nina Mae had become seriously ill and was in a hospital in Harlem (Bourne 89-90; King, Susan; "One-Time Movie Star Nina Mae McKinney Is Seriously Ill in Harlem Hospital"). She recovered and returned to performing whenever she could, but greater sorrow followed. Georgie's death—in New York on June 11, 1962—must have also been an extremely challenging time for Nina Mae (White). Losing her mother left Nina Mae alone. According to the *Afro-American*, Nina Mae was divorced at the time of her mother's death (White). She had brought Georgie to live with her after her stepfather, a postal service worker of 27 years, died in 1949—on the day she reported to the *Pinky* set for work ("Heading for Paris").

Still relatively young, Nina Mae struggled to find consistent work in the 1940s and 1950s. Racism, sexism, and industry politics had been factors throughout her career, and rumors of her drug addiction and alcoholism had resurfaced. She had been known as the "Queen of Night Life" in Athens, Greece, where she toured in the 1950s and 1960s, but details are scarce. Ultimately, she returned to New York, and her days as a performer seemed to be over (Pettus, "Nina Mae McKinney—Deserving of a Place in History"). She had stopped performing by the 1960s, involuntarily and heartbreakingly. She bitterly resisted maid roles early in her film career. Unfortunately, she had to accept a few maid roles in the 1940s or be denied work as an actor. Nina Mae insisted on playing these roles her way, with more dignity than the traditional representation of mammies and Black maids. Nevertheless, such a compromise must have been demoralizing, and to eventually work as a maid in real life would be a tragic ending to her story.

Nina Mae made her last "recorded professional performance" in 1951 at the Apollo Theatre in Harlem. In *Rain*, a drama by W. Somerset Maugham, she portrayed Sadie Thompson, a jazz enthusiast whom Gloria Swanson and Joan Crawford had previously portrayed in the movie adaptations. Sadie drank, smoked, and was a prostitute. The role was a departure from Nina Mae's preferred roles, which seems to indicate that she was in dire need of work. This dramatic play did not fare well since the Apollo's audience thought it was overpriced and was more accustomed to musical acts (Bourne 88). However, the *Brooklyn Daily Eagle's* review of *Rain* praised the overall acting quality of the cast. In particular, it stated, "Nina Mae McKinney, rather more buxom than some others who have essayed the role, was most effective in the part of Sadie Thompson, and her impersonation grew steadily in power until the final curtain" ("Curtain Time: Negro Cast Presents Well-Acted Performance of 'Rain' at Bedford").

Sadly, Nina Mae McKinney's final attempts at making a comeback—starring in Manhattan Paul's Revue at Small's Paradise in 1953, forming a "new act with ex-Count Basie guitarist, Jimmy McLin" in 1954, and playing the guitar in a USO tour of Japan—fell short (Bourne 89).

Unfortunately, no further details are available about McKinney's later years. In the era of modernism that upheld the city as being more sophisticated than the country and in light of the seemingly inescapable racism, it is possible that McKinney never wanted to return to the South—especially during the chaos of the early and modern civil rights eras. She had no surviving children, and it seems that she died alone. It is uncertain whether McKinney was merely separated from relatives by miles or whether she had remained distant for some other reason. One might also question whether shame was a factor in her unwillingness to return to the South and whether relatives, during her lifetime, either believed the drug abuse and alcoholism rumors or possibly confirmed them.

One might also wonder if a family secret existed, as questioned in Chapter One, which discusses the inconsistencies regarding the identity of Nina Mae's father. Additionally, could Nina Mae have done something terrible before leaving Lancaster, South Carolina? Keep in mind that she was only about 13 years old when she left Lancaster permanently to join her mother in New York. More likely, had something terrible been *done to* Nina Mae, Georgie, or Aunt Carrie before Nina Mae left? This is possible, to reiterate this book's discussion in Chapter One, given an era in which some white people harassed Black people and in which some white men molested and raped Black females and usually went unpunished by the law, especially in the South. Voluntary sexual encounters between Blacks and whites in the South existed, but certainly, they were rare or at least secretive, given the time period. Regarding sexual abuse, white men would kidnap young Black girls and "discreetly" return them to their neighborhoods. They often "secretly" abused young Black girls, sometimes for sexual experimentation before openly courting white females for marriage. Maids working in white households and other types of female employees of white employers often felt powerless, having no protection and no recourse. These were the types of stories that elderly Black women in the early twentieth century told the younger members of their families both to illustrate how race relations were even worse during their youth and to serve as warnings to be careful around whites. White males often took advantage of their own privilege, young Black females' low socioeconomic status and subordinate position in society, and the racist as well as sexist laws of the Old South that were still in practice (Bass 33-35).

Regarding race, lineage, and secrecy, a striking similarity exists in the story of performer Eartha Kitt, who was also from South Carolina. Born in St. Matthews, Calhoun County, in 1926, Eartha never knew her biological father. She only knew he was a white man who had raped her mother. Eartha's daughter, Kitt Shapiro, held an interview with *The Observer*, in which she explained that Eartha died in 2008 still not knowing the identity of Eartha's father, despite a legal battle to gain access to Eartha's birth certificate. In 1998, after waiting about six months, officials finally allowed Eartha and her daughter just fifteen minutes to view the records. To Eartha's devastation, someone had blacked out her father's name. Shapiro stated, "My mother was 71 at the time and it was approaching the 21st century, and yet they were still protecting the name of the father even though he was clearly dead. They were protecting the white man because they would not have gone to that trouble to protect a Black man. The courts still held it as legal to withhold the documentation. We were amazed. My mother assumed it was their dirty little secret" (Luck). Evidently, Eartha's father was not only a white man but was also someone of prominent status in the community. *America's Mistress: The Life and Times of Eartha Kitt* by British journalist John L. Williams names local doctor Daniel Sturkie as Eartha's father. Shapiro said she did not recall whether anyone had ever suggested this particular man before, even though she recognized the name Sturkie as that of a local white family. She stated, "There were a lot of names" (Luck).

In a similar vein, United States Senator Strom Thurmond kept his Black daughter, Essie Mae Washington-Williams, a secret. She was born in 1925 to Carrie Butler, Thurmond's 16-year-old Black maid (Bass 33). Thurmond only acknowledged Washington-Williams secretly, providing financial support and even putting her through college at South Carolina State University, a historically Black university. He never met her until she was 16, and, afterward, he only visited her on occasion, in secret (Bass 61). Thurmond, who was born in Edgefield, South Carolina, in 1902, was a champion of segregation during the modern civil rights era. Washington-Williams waited until Thurmond's death in 2003 to reveal that he was her father. Although Washington-Williams had known her father's identity for most of her life, she needed a greater sense of freedom that could only come with telling the world (M. Thompson; Bass 33, 61). This was similar to Eartha Kitt's dire need to know her father's identity.

It is also possible that McKinney simply did not want to return home after having her entertainment career fall well short of her hopes and aspirations, especially if she wound up working as a maid. Here, considering similar experiences, a comparison to Josephine Baker is useful since Baker avoided returning to her hometown of St. Louis, Missouri. Born into poverty, Baker was the daughter of washerwoman Carrie McDonald, who had given up her own dreams of becoming an entertainer, and vaudeville drummer Eddie Carson, who abandoned her and her mother (J. Baker 68; "Josephine Baker Biography"). According to *Josephine: The Hungry Heart* by Jean-Claude Baker and Chris Chase, "Her fears cost her. Because the pattern was set; once she started running from her past, she couldn't stop. The best show that had ever happened for Black people, and she was not part of its debut in her own hometown" (Baker 68). Baker's mother came looking for her when the *Shuffle Along* stage show came to St. Louis in 1923, and fellow cast member Adelaide Hall informed her that Josephine simply did not come with them on the trip from Chicago to St. Louis (Baker 66-7).

Similarly, Nina Mae McKinney did not seem fond of returning to the South—and would only venture there as briefly as possible for a performance—certainly due to her childhood memories of the South but also due to her adult experiences. For example, she and her band were traveling from Jacksonville to New Orleans, and they stopped in Lake City, Florida, on January 11, 1940. There, she was "brutally assaulted and injured by a white soda fountain attendant" when she asked for a cup of coffee and was refused service. She was "struck on the shoulder and about the face, with a heavy instrument." She immediately left for New Orleans, where she received medical care, and then headed for the band's next stop in Jackson, Mississippi ("Wanted Coffee, Is Given Beating").

Race was an all-encompassing factor in Nina Mae McKinney's life, from her ancestry to her personal life and her acting career. Comparisons to entertainers Eartha Kitt and Josephine Baker as well as Senator Strom Thurmond's secret daughter Essie Washington-Williams are relevant since similarities in their stories illustrate probability, or at least possibility, where details about McKinney's life are missing. While wrestling with personal issues, McKinney fought for survival in a racist social and political climate.

Racist journalism in the dominant white press might have been a factor in MGM's refusal to promote McKinney after her breakout role in *Hallelujah* while McKinney seemed to have a love-hate relationship with the Black press. Perhaps the criticism and gossip were mere sensationalism for the sake of selling papers. Black newspapers, especially the *Pittsburgh Courier,* often attempted to aid in her battle to remain in the public eye and maintain her career. They promoted her by reporting her prospective projects, public appearances, photo shoots, glamour, and fashion.

Nina Mae McKinney disappeared from the screen, and later, her death went virtually unnoticed. Ending her life as a real-life domestic worker after she tried so hard to avoid such a role on-screen makes her story even more heartbreaking.

Chapter Six

The Groundbreaking Role as Chick in *Hallelujah*

After briefly reviewing the events that led Nina Mae McKinney to Hollywood and summarizing her film *Hallelujah*, providing important context and perspective, this chapter will establish McKinney as the archetype for the Black leading ladies in Hollywood who came after her and establish McKinney's role as Chick in *Hallelujah* as an archetype for roles that rebelled against the stereotypical Hollywood treatment of Black characters, in general, and Black female characters, in particular. Although the actor McKinney and the character Chick are two different people, they share an important trait: the spirit of independence and self-determination. Each was a modern woman ahead of her time. This chapter will discuss how *Hallelujah* came to be and how Nina Mae McKinney landed the role of Chick. To place the role of Chick and the film *Hallelujah* in perspective, it will also discuss how the film was received. Then, it will discuss the reception of McKinney's performance as Chick and interpretations of the role. Readers who have not yet viewed *Hallelujah* may wish to do so before proceeding with this chapter.

Since Nina Mae McKinney's film career began after King Vidor discovered her in *Blackbirds* on Broadway, it is useful to begin with a brief description of that performance. Having delivered 518 shows between May 9, 1928, and June 15, 1929, Lew Leslie's *Blackbirds* (1928 version) became one the longest-running shows on Broadway. McKinney was a young hopeful in the chorus line, but the cast included several well-known Black entertainers such as Adelaide Hall, Bill Robinson, and Mantan Moreland.

McKinney was a dancer, singer, and actress who danced in *Black-birds* when she was only 16. By that time, she had taken "Nina Mae" as her stage name. This was when King Vidor discovered her (Williams, Francis 19). McKinney stood out from the rest. Vidor recalled McKinney in *Blackbirds* as "third from the right in the chorus" (Dowd 99).

Ethel Waters, although 16 years older than McKinney, was Vidor's original choice for the role of Chick in *Hallelujah*. Unable to reach Waters, Vidor considered Josephine Hall and Honey Brown (Regester, *African American Actresses* 42). He initially cast Brown; however, after watching McKinney in *Blackbirds*, Vidor brought McKinney on set and would soon replace Brown with McKinney. He had no regrets about casting McKinney. In his biography, *A Tree is a Tree* (1953), Vidor reflected, "She was beautiful and talented and glowing with personality," later adding, "She just had it, whatever you wanted, whatever you visualized, she could do it. Nina was full of life, full of expression, and just a joy to work with. Someone like her inspires a director" (Vidor 176; qtd. in Bourne 12). McKinney was still 16 during the filming. That calls into question the appropriateness of her rather adult role. She carries it well, and the questionable scenes are suggestive, not explicit. Furthermore, it was common for people her age to be treated like adults in the early 1900s.

Since *Hallelujah* is Nina Mae McKinney's most important film, this section will provide a substantial summary instead of a brief synopsis. Shot in Arkansas and Tennessee, *Hallelujah* is a drama that presents the theme of fast, city life versus simple, rural life as well as the themes of going home and temptation versus salvation. It is not a musical in the traditional sense, as it does not use song and music continuously to tell the story or to handle its exposition. Instead, it sporadically integrates its musical sequences to serve as an extension of the narrative and to authenticate the culture it seeks to emulate. The music, used almost as anthropological evidence, also offers occasional comic relief to offset the more serious and tragic events.

Nina Mae McKinney, Daniel L. Haynes, and blues singer Victoria Spivey sing solo selections throughout the film. The Dixie Jubilee singers also supply much of the film's music ("Hallelujah").

McKinney plays the role of Chick, a cabaret singer who cons country newcomer Ezekiel Johnson aka "Zeke" or "Zekiel" (Haynes) out of his money at a nightclub. The main arc of the story begins by introducing the protagonist Zeke, his mother Mammy (stage actress Fanny Belle DeKnight), his father/minister Pappy or Parson (real-life minister Harry Gray), his brother Spunk (Everett McGarrity), and his unnamed small siblings (Milton Dickerson, Robert Couch, and Walter Tait). Another child appearing in an uncredited role is Matthew "Stymie" Beard of *Our Gang* aka *The Little Rascals*.

Zeke teases his adoptive sister, Missy Rose (Spivey), about the two of them getting married. After a long day of picking cotton, his large family sings and dances outside. Later that night, Zeke approaches Missy Rose, who seems to be close to his age, when she is all alone. True to the stereotype of an animalistic Black male who cannot control his lustful urges, Zeke kisses her by force. Here, his behavior is both disturbing and ludicrous. Yet, it is but a fleeting "Jekyll and Hyde" moment that occurs ten minutes into the story. Zeke tells Missy Rose that the devil got into him, and he apologizes. Oddly, Missy Rose smiles and accepts his apology; she is unable to hide her romantic interest in him.

The moment that propels the story forward is when Zeke and Spunk leave the countryside to sell their cotton as it will lead to Zeke's first encounter with Chick. After selling the cotton, Zeke passes a group of crapshooters, but he pays them no mind. Here, the story introduces a beautiful dancer whose performance captivates a crowd and captures Zeke's attention. This is Chick. Zeke now begins to make decisions that will have irreversible consequences. At first, under the assumption that Zeke is a poor "country bumpkin," Chick rejects him. Then, he flaunts his cotton money, and Chick is suddenly interested. Brilliantly acted through her facial expressions and body language, McKinney flashes her gorgeous, doll-like eyes.

Zeke walks off with Chick, and he forgets about his brother Spunk, who is on the wagon looking for him.

Later, at the nightclub, Chick sings "Swanee Shuffle" and performs a dance routine. Afterward, Chick enthralls Zeke as they share a slow dance. Gradually, stroking Zeke's ego, she sets him up for a rigged craps game. Then, Chick introduces him to her con partner, Hot Shot (William Fountaine), who insults Zeke's pride so he will keep playing. Zeke falls for the ruse and gambles his money away. Angry about losing all his money, Zeke suspects weighted dice and confronts Hot Shot. In the ensuing shootout, a stray bullet hits Spunk, who has finally found Zeke. Spunk dies, and Zeke is devastated.

When Zeke returns home with Spunk's body, his parents grieve, but they forgive Zeke and do not hold him responsible. Soon, Zeke becomes a preacher of the gospel like his father. He then shares with his parents his intentions to marry Missy Rose. Zeke travels and preaches, drawing large crowds. One day, Zeke, dressed in a robe and riding through the street on a donkey, mimics the biblical story of Jesus traveling to Jerusalem as King (John 12; Matthew 21; Mark 11). Zeke passes Chick and Hot Shot, who snicker and mock him mercilessly. He tries to ignore them and travels on.

However, after considerable time passes, Zeke faces his greatest temptation. Down by the riverside, Zeke preaches a sermon in front of a large crowd, and people come forward to be "saved" and baptized. Chick is sitting in the crowd, but her sudden return is unexplained. Hot Shot is not with her. At first, she mocks Zeke. She challenges him to make her cry like some of the other people in the crowd, although he cannot hear her. Then, as she listens to Zeke's "Train to Hell" sermon, her demeanor changes, and Zeke's sermon overwhelms her. Chick comes up to be baptized. Suddenly, passion and lust overcome Zeke, which director Vidor juxtaposes with religious frenzy. Zeke lifts Chick out of the water and carries her to a small tent nearby. Missy Rose and Zeke's mother have been watching the interaction between Zeke and Chick. Missy Rose frets, but Zeke's mother enters the tent right behind Zeke. She arrives just in time to prevent Zeke from having an opportunity to act upon his lust. Ashamed, Zeke walks out of the tent, leaving Chick and his mother behind.

After an unspecified length of time, Hot Shot tracks Chick down. He shows up and tries to take her back to the city. She insists that she has cast her sinful life behind her, but Hot Shot argues that she will never stop sinning. When she refuses to leave with him, he tries to force her. Chick beats him repeatedly with a fireplace poker, and then, she rushes off to the church where Zeke is preaching that night.

Zeke preaches an energetic sermon, swinging his fists and pantomiming his beating up the devil for leading God's people to sin. Chick gazes upon him and rocks back and forth on her seat. The scene is well-acted by McKinney and Haynes, whose characters seem to have sincerely tried to reform only to remain torn between two desires: salvation and worldliness. Again, Vidor juxtaposes the religious frenzy of feeling the Holy Spirit with the sexual tension between Zeke and Chick. People sing and shout while others "fall out" onto the floor. Two men even dump water on a woman who loses control during the service. Although Chick has appeared to be quite sincere about her religious conversion until this point, she lures Zeke out of the church, and he carries her off into the night. After they disappear into the woods, Missy Rose sings a song of lamentation.

Months later, Zeke and Chick are living together in a small house out in the country. No longer preaching, Zeke works in a sawmill. Foreshadowing the climax, Chick sings lines from a variation of the song "St. Louis Blues." Chick pretends to be happy, but Zeke grows suspicious when he comes home and sees an unattended wagon nearby. Chick comforts Zeke momentarily, but as soon as she thinks Zeke is asleep, she sneaks out with Hot Shot. This is Hot

Shot's first appearance since Chick fought him off with the fireplace poker earlier. His return and the reason Chick would join him again are not explained. At any rate, Chick and Hot Shot ride off in a horse-drawn wagon. Zeke, rifle in hand, chases after them. After he fires at them, the wagon loses a wheel, and Chick falls out. She lands in the mud. Soon, the wagon turns over, and Hot Shot flees on foot. Zeke catches up with Chick and chastises her for trying to leave.

Still enraged, Zeke exclaims, "Don't you know you can't quit me like that? Before I let you get away from me, I'll break you in two" (*Hallelujah*).

In pain, Chick replies, "I'se broke in two already, Zeke" (*Hallelujah*). She continues, "I ain't two-timing you, Zeke" (*Hallelujah*).

After Zeke argues that she has done just that, Chick replies, "I never knowed what I wanted. Don't be sore with me" (*Hallelujah*).

Just before they left in the wagon, Hot Shot told Chick how difficult it was to find her, which indicates that leaving Zeke was indeed spontaneous, not something Chick had planned far in advance. In Zeke's arms, a repentant Chick's last words are, "I's scared, Brother Zekiel. I'se scared to meet the Lord. So scared" (*Hallelujah*).

Hot Shot begs for his life, but Zeke chases him down and chokes him to death. Soon afterward, Zeke serves a prison sentence of hard labor, and he is released on probation. First traveling by boat and later by train, he plays a guitar and sings a song entitled "Going Home" (*Hallelujah*). In the end, his family welcomes him back and accepts him. So does Missy Rose.

Although scholars have noted the importance of *Hallelujah* primarily as King Vidor's early sound and on-location film experiment, the film should also be remembered for Nina Mae McKinney's performance and for the precedent that the character Chick set. In Hollywood, McKinney became the archetype for Black actresses, and Chick became the archetype for Black female characters in leading roles: characters who deviated from the dominant mammy and maid roles of early film. A complicated character, Chick represents the independent, modern woman who lives on her own terms and seeks to control her own destiny. McKinney's portrayal of Chick gives her both adult and girlish qualities, and except for the scenes in which Chick is torn between worldliness and salvation, McKinney seems to be naturally and genuinely having fun. Although it is not a comedic role, McKinney takes the stage inside the club and begins Chick's "Swanee Shuffle" routine with a comedic flair.

McKinney's physical attractiveness and her believability in the role of Chick showcase her sass and spunk, highlighted by her body language—including mannerisms such as delivering the "whatever" finger snap in the air. To accentuate her figure, McKinney also holds her hands at her waist and slightly exaggerates her switching when walking. In addition, McKinney uses her charming eyes to sell the role effectively. Her "eye acting" is just as convincing as the delivery of her lines. For example, her eyes demonstrate Chick's instant recognition of an opportunity to con Zeke out of his money when he flashes it for the first time. Once she has successfully baited Zeke, her eyewink to Hot Shot appears similar to the "always up to something" antics of the children in *Our Gang* aka *The Little Rascals*. Other notable examples include Chick's religious conversion scenes: her being baptized at the river and finding herself absorbed by Zeke's sermon inside the church during a night service. In these scenes, Chick is torn between worldly desires and salvation.

Chick knows when to be sincere, and she knows when to play a particular role to her advantage: sweet and playful or cunning and sultry. Note how Chick lightly skips over to Zeke after her first singing performance inside the club. She turns her back to him, and then, she falls into him gently. It comes across as playful, not whorish. Then, she gives him a quick peck on the cheek before she returns to the stage for her next number, an extended dance routine. Just before conning Zeke into gambling his cotton-picking money (no pun intended), she slow-dances with him. Here, Chick's seduction is more girlish and playful than lustful.

Chick establishes other important characteristics for Black female leading roles: She "gets her man," experiences a downfall, and introduces the physical appearance that Hollywood would find suitable in appealing to both white and Black audiences. Chick gets her man, and the pursuit is where the fun is. Once she finally gets what she thought she wanted, she is no longer sure about what she really wants. Regarding her tragic downfall, like the titular character in *Carmen Jones* (1954), Chick is similar to the tragic mulatto. However, Chick and Carmen (Dorothy Dandridge) are clearly coded as Black. Carmen's physical appearance in 1954 is similar to Chick's in 1929, from her hairstyle to her complexion. Like Chick, Carmen's skin color falls between light-skinned and dark-skinned; neither is "high yellow," which, of course, is a Black cultural reference, not something intended in a derogatory sense here. Similar to MGM's treatment of Chick, Carlyle Productions and Twentieth Century Fox made no attempt to "whiten" Carmen in terms of complexion or hair texture, and Carmen's style of dress is similar: sexy but not scanty. Furthermore, her behavior follows the pattern set by Chick, even though Carmen is a less complicated character than Chick since Carmen's inner struggle is less clearly defined than Chick's.

Unlike similar white characters, Black females—including "mulattas"—typically are denied their redemption or must die, literally or figuratively, to receive it. This applies to the roles, not McKinney's or other actors' portrayals of particular roles. The difference is Chick's strong will to control her own destiny. She is an agent, not a practically helpless figure. Yet, in general, "the powers that be" must put the independent woman in her place according to the male-dominant standards of society. Gilda in *Safe in Hell* is a rare example of a similar white female lead who faces a tragic end. Factoring race in makes such a rule even more unbreakable.

Additionally, Chick's physical appearance corresponds to Nina Mae McKinney's early physical appearance on film. Like actress McKinney, of course, Chick is neither dark in complexion nor light enough in complexion to pass for white. In *Hallelujah*, her hair is thick and natural. It is not relaxed, but it is styled, not unkempt. She straightened her hair only after she was demoted from Hollywood leading lady to minor roles. Her style of dress is often sexy but just enough to show off her figure. Natural sex appeal is not substituted for a getup befitting of hookers. Instead, Chick embodies womanly yet girlish qualities.

Physical appearance was a critical issue in casting the first Black leading lady in Hollywood. Hence, the casting of Chick in *Hallelujah* was more complicated than explained earlier in this chapter. Nina Mae McKinney was not as dark in complexion as the women who had typically been cast as slaves and servants in Hollywood films, but she was not light enough in complexion to pass for white, either. This was important in the studio's effort to appeal to both white and Black audiences. King Vidor avoided talking about his previous choices for the character in interviews. It is true that Vidor was blown away by McKinney's performance in the chorus line of *Blackbirds* in 1928, but when he first brought her on set, she was on standby. Honey Brown, a Club Harlem dancer, was Vidor's choice after his nationwide search (Weisenfeld 38). Head of Production at MGM, Irving Thalberg overturned Vidor's decision after he saw Honey Brown in the initial prints of the film's first days of shooting. Thalberg argued that Brown was not sexy enough, especially since he believed that Chick's "unrestrained sexuality" was integral to the story and perfect for Hollywood. Even though he felt that Brown possessed a comedic flair appropriate for certain scenes, he felt that her scenes of sexual tension appeared ludicrous or silly. Vidor attempted to justify his decision to cast Brown, at first, but Thalberg clarified his objection from a particularly Eurocentric assessment of beauty. Thalberg bluntly and vulgarly stated, "My chief objection to Honey Brown is certain ugliness particularly around her mouth, her flat chestedness, and her upper lip has very outstanding hair line" (Weisenfeld 38). Thalberg approved of Vidor's replacement, Nina Mae McKinney, a woman he found more attractive in terms of physical features. Compared to Brown, McKinney was lighter in complexion, had smaller lips, and had a curvier figure. Thalberg was convinced that McKinney was ideal for the role but placed emphasis on ensuring that McKinney did not "appear too white" on screen (Weisenfeld 38).

Despite Vidor's alleged resistance to replacing Honey Brown, it seems that he simply tried to give Brown a fair chance. He already knew that Nina Mae McKinney would be perfect for the role, in terms of talent and physical appearance, after she stood out to him in *Blackbirds*. Since Vidor already had McKinney waiting in the wings, he must have seen in her what Thalberg saw long before Thalberg spoke up about it. Like Thalberg, Vidor knew McKinney would appeal to white and Black audiences. The rumor that Honey Brown had to be replaced because she fell ill all of a sudden was likely started by someone at MGM to cover up Thalberg's true reason and possibly to help Brown save face after losing the role.

Regarding complexion and hair texture, a comparison to actor/dancer Fredi Washington and a discussion about the descriptions of McKinney found in articles are particularly relevant. Fredi Washington possessed the complexion and hair texture to "pass" for white. Some Black people who could pass for white did so in order to escape the bitter, pervasive racism that darker-skinned people faced on a daily basis while others "passed" only when convenient, using it to help improve their socioeconomic status and secretly give back to the Black community. Nevertheless, some, like Fredi Washington, refused to pass and distinctively chose to only be Black in defiance of racial discrimination. Fredi Washinton's deep convictions on this matter limited her opportunities in the entertainment industry. Washington proclaimed, "Oh, for the color of Nina Mae McKinney!" ("Being Too White is the Problem of Fredi Washington"). She identified with McKinney's struggle as a Hollywood actress but wished she had McKinney's complexion. Makeup and lighting made her seem lighter, but black-and-white photos and color paintings of Nina Mae McKinney as well as her self-descriptions make her complexion unmistakable. McKinney was neither dark-skinned nor light enough to pass for white, and one must also consider her hair texture in *Hallelujah*. As Chick dances in her introduction scene, a member of her audience calls her "brown sugar" and exclaims, "What a brown-skinned bunch of sweetness she is!"

An August 21, 1929, *New York Times* review of *Hallelujah* describes McKinney as "chocolate-colored" (Hall). Even though this description might be an exaggeration since dark-skinned Black people have often been referred to as chocolate, often in a playful way, it still emphasizes that McKinney would not have been referred to as "high yellow" or "red," whether those terms were intended to be derogatory or endearing. Furthermore, Dean Glynn's "On the Spot" entertainment column in the Saturday, April 16, 1932, issue of *The New York Age* describes McKinney as having a "smooth brown complexion" (Glynn). J. B. (initials available only) interviewed McKinney and wrote an article entitled "Meet Nina of Harlem! – Amber Girl with Dancing Feet" for the British paper *Sunday Dispatch* on February 12, 1933. McKinney explained to J. B. that "high yellow is almost white," which hardly described her. J. B. states, "Nina is a brown skin, she explains, not high yellow, as some people think" (qtd. in Bourne 30).

McKinney had experienced color-based discrimination from white people numerous times, including being turned away by restaurants that falsely claimed to be full. Of course, racial conditions were worse in the South, but in this interview, she was talking about how badly Black people were often treated in New York. J. B.

also described McKinney's hair as "straight and wiry, curling at the ends" but "not kinky" (qtd. in Bourne 30). That might have been another way of saying that her hair was attractive although different from a white woman's.

To place the role of Chick and the film *Hallelujah* in perspective, this section will discuss the reception of the film, and then, it will discuss the reception of McKinney's performance and interpretations of the role. Today, film scholars recognize *Hallelujah* as a landmark film. Despite its stereotypical content, such as the Black male who is always overcome by his emotions and sexual urges, the film has its strengths. King Vidor shot the film on-location, despite the obvious challenges of the era, such as heavy equipment. Vidor's first sound film narrowly missed becoming the first all-Black cast musical film, as Fox's *Hearts in Dixie* was released just three months earlier, in May 1929 ("*Hallelujah*," "Hearts in Dixie"). Yet, it was MGM's first musical film with an all-Black cast. *Film Daily* and *National Board of Review* included *Hallelujah* among the 10 best pictures of 1929 (Weisenfeld 20). However, scholars such as Alexander Walker argue that *Hallelujah* was "better in intention than achievement" since it avoided the controversial topic of race relations (Wollstein 132). In other words, it entertained Black and white audiences but had no moral or social impact on the latter.

Despite the outstanding quality of acting in *Hallelujah*, there were no Black nominees in any category at the Third Annual Academy Awards in 1930. Nina Mae McKinney and Daniel L. Haynes delivered performances worthy of "Best Actress" and "Best Actor" Academy Awards respectively, but this was an era in which the Academy did not consider Black actors. Noting that some European audiences referred to McKinney as the Black Garbo, it is interesting that Greta Garbo received the Best Actress nomination for her roles as the namesake character in *Anna Christie*, her first talking movie, and as Madame Rita Cavallini in *Romance*, even though Norma Shearer won the Oscar for the role of Jerry in *The Divorcee*. George Arliss won "Best Actor" for the titular role in *Disraeli*.

King Vidor received the lone nomination for *Hallelujah*. Vidor was nominated for "Best Director," but Lewis Milestone won for *All Quiet on the Western Front* ("Academy of Motion Picture Arts and Sciences;" "1929-30 Academy Awards Winners and History"). King Vidor's nomination might have been either a token nomination or a nomination based on his lifetime of achievement, which arguably has become a pattern with the Oscars.

Hallelujah has been mistakenly referred to as the first all-Black cast musical, but as stated earlier, the film narrowly missed this distinction. *Hearts in Dixie*, featuring Stepin Fetchit and Clarence Muse, was released three months earlier. Black leaders, including ministers, criticized both films for their stereotypical representations of Black people (Knight 142). In terms of cinematic quality, however, *Hallelujah* was well-received in general. For example, according to the *Daily News* (New York), it premiered before segregated audiences on the same night at the Lafayette Theatre and the Embassy Theatre, and critics rated it three stars ("King Vidor's Colored Folk Movie Shows at Embassy, Too"). To put it in perspective, historically, most movies have failed to receive four or five stars, with one star meaning "poor" and five stars "excellent." Critics and writers such as Alain Locke and Sterling Brown preferred the "carelessness" and "superficiality" of *Hearts in Dixie*, despite its lack of plot. W. E. B. Du Bois preferred *Hallelujah* (Knight 140). Du Bois hailed *Hallelujah* as a great drama but criticized the film for emphasizing its Irving Berlin-penned theme songs, "The End of the Road" and "Swanee Shuffle," instead of the more authentic Black folk music that the story begins with. Du Bois considered Negro folk songs, such as the sorrow songs, to be the first truly American-born music in the United States, and he believed them to be part of the Negro's gift to all, transcending color (Knight 141). Du Bois's assessment of the music is particularly important considering King Vidor's later statement that he wanted to depict "the Negro" as accurately as possible. Vidor stated in an interview that he never liked the idea of using music that had a "Tin Pan Alley popular Broadway sound," but considering how difficult it was to convince MGM to produce the movie, he went along with it. "End of the Road," in particular, was Irving Thalberg's idea (Dowd 103). Although the film was collaborative, the moguls won in the end.

Hallelujah opened to a segregated premiere at separate theaters in New York, which led to protests and discrimination lawsuits from Blacks who were turned away from the Embassy on Broadway. Blacks were relegated to the Lafayette Theater (Regester, African American Actresses 50). Due to "flagrant segregation" in Los Angeles, Black audiences would not be allowed to see the film unless the Redwood Theater booked a special showing just for Blacks ("'Hallelujah' Shown to Whites Only in L.A."). Evidently, theaters throughout the West showed *Hallelujah* at least on a segregated basis. The *Chicago Defender* reported that the white press lauded the film as "a notable achievement" while there was a mixed reaction among Black people. Some Black preachers found it offensive to the Black church ("Prattis Gives 1930 Review of Theater: Says Race Has Made Great Strides"). Nevertheless, *Hallelujah* and Nina Mae McKinney's breakout role gave numerous Black viewers and Black actors a sense of hope for a day when racial discrimination would no longer limit Black actors to minor roles and stereotypical roles in Hollywood films.

Hallelujah received a mixed reaction in the South. Of course, some theaters did not show the film at all. As stated earlier, there was no mention of the film in McKinney's hometown newspaper at the time of release. In North Carolina, a theater polled its white patrons before agreeing to show the film ("NC Theater Takes Poll on 'Hallelujah'"). An October 1931 *Chicago Defender* article predicts and laments the end of race films, and it explains resistance in the South, despite the long theater runs of *Hearts in Dixie* and *Hallelujah* in the North ("Solid Souths Hand Seen in Race Film End").

Of course, director King Vidor and producer Irving Thalberg lauded the performances of both McKinney and Daniel L. Haynes (Bogle, *Dorothy Dandridge: A Biography* 135). Thalberg stated that McKinney was "one of the greatest discoveries of the age," and *New York Post* writer Richard Watts Jr. stated that McKinney was "assuredly one of the most beautiful women of our time" (Wollstein 131-32). McKinney received recognition for her talent throughout the film's run. Nancy Dowd of the Directors Guild of America stated that McKinney's performance "endures beyond any of the actors in the film" (Wollstein 132). Dowd continued, "Miss McKinney's great beauty, her arrogance, her ambiguity, and her determination to get some pleasure out of life, no matter who tried to stop her, make her seem more modern and interesting than her chic Flapper counterparts" (Wollstein 132). Indeed, Dowd made a bold comparison to McKinney's white peers. In terms of popularity among African Americans, Donald Bogle's *Heat Wave: The Life and Career of Ethel Waters* states that Nina Mae McKinney came in second place in the *Pittsburgh Courier's* poll as its readers' favorite female star three years later in March 1932 (Bogle 206). Vince Venturini, who wrote a play about McKinney's life, asserted that "McKinney was an idol for many white and black actresses" (King, "Local Resident's Play Features Pioneer Star"). He adds something with which film historians may also agree: McKinney "was the first woman actress to be sassy. She placed her hands on her hips and added sassy to her character. A tidbit many picked up from her from during the early talkies period" (King, "Local Resident's Play Features Pioneer Star"). All of this speaks to the immediate and long-term impact made by Nina Mae McKinney and Chick.

Prominent film scholars have discussed the life and career of Nina Mae McKinney laudably but arguably not at length. *Nina*

Mae McKinney: The Black Garbo by Stephen Bourne was the only book-length publication on McKinney before the publication of *Nina Mae McKinney: At the Dawn of Black Hollywood Stardom.* Charlene Regester's *African American Actresses: The Struggle for Visibility, 1900-1960* devotes a chapter to McKinney. Donald Bogle discusses McKinney in several publications and acknowledges that later actresses owe a debt to Nina Mae McKinney's performance in *Hallelujah.* However, he exaggerates Chick's "raunchiness," and one of his comments in *Toms, Coons, Mulattoes, Mammies, and Bucks: An Interpretive History of Blacks in American Films* about Chick's cabaret dancing scene seems unduly callous. Even though she performs "sensuous bumps and grinds," there is no valid reason to claim that Chick was "the movies' first Black whore" (Bogle 31). Charlene Regester agrees that although Bogle "does point out her undeniable sexuality," such a statement is a bit "harsh" (Regester 45-6). Critics and scholars have failed to acknowledge that despite the dominant social expectations for women during McKinney's era, she portrayed an independent character who was always in control—a reflection of McKinney's struggle to maintain her career on her own terms. Emphasis on this aspect of McKinney's portrayal of Chick seems more appropriate, especially for a Black woman in Hollywood in 1929.

One must also consider the clear double standard for racy women's roles in the late 1920s and 1930s, given the popularity of "fallen woman" and "gold digger" stories. There was sufficient variety in roles for white women to avoid their roles being viewed as generally negative depictions of white women. However, critical race theory (CRT) may explain how one negative characteristic, although exaggerated, has overshadowed McKinney and Chick's agency and rebellion against stereotypical Black images. CRT holds that a member of a minority race who is in the public eye often bears the burden of representing the race, especially in the absence of, or scarcity of, other members of the same group. Hence, any negative aspect of a

Black character becomes magnified in a manner that white privilege exempts white actors from. This theory might explain why critics have exaggerated the vixen characteristics of McKinney's Chick, in pursuit of Zeke, when there has never been any uproar over, or any significant condemnation of, white female characters of the same era such as Clara Bow's Betty Lou (*It*), who lies across her boss' desk to get his attention.

Hallelujah never implies that Chick is a whore, a prostitute, or even a promiscuous woman; some viewers have simply been conditioned to assume that she is such, based on the Jezebel stereotype of Black women dating back to antebellum slavery. A whore is ready and willing to perform various sexual acts when she stands to gain something or when she simply seeks pleasure. The film has no explicit scenes depicting sex or sexual acts, only an implied lead-in. Chick is an independent woman who is defiant of 1920s and 1930s social expectations. If one may interpret Chick as a Jezebel, it is only because she manipulates Zeke. The common assumption that a woman such as Chick must naturally be out of place in society makes the Jezebel stereotype relevant. At worst, one may logically refer to Chick as a temptress and a manipulator of men. She is similar to the femme fatale later found in film noir who often teases but rarely, if ever, fulfills the sexual fantasy of the men who gaze upon her. She feels that she must always be in control, and she uses her feminine wiles to her advantage. Chick is flawed, but she is only guilty of making her own decisions, right or wrong.

Chick is a cabaret singer/dancer, a tough city girl, a schemer, and a hustler. There is no reason to assume that Hot Shot is her pimp or her boss. It is always clear that she and Hot Shot are equals. She does not serve him or take orders from him. Chick always knows what role to play: sweet and playful or cunning and sultry. She also knows when to be sincere. Since Chick has "game," the white dice image on the front of her Black dress is quite appropriate. She is a "player." Always in control, Chick is a "boss."

Regarding the raunchiness of Chick, the only thing that can even be remotely interpreted as a prior sexual relationship between Chick and Hot Shot is a line that he delivers when she resists his attempt to physically drag her back to the city with him. He asks, "Since when did you not want my hands on you?" That could just as easily be interpreted as platonic, since they were partners in the con game, or it could be an indication that Chick and Hot Shot had been lovers at some point in the past. They never behave as if they might be lovers until the end of the story, but even then, such an idea is not convincing; this is when Chick attempts to leave Zeke, and she kisses Hot Shot just before they sneak out of the house. McKinney acts out the scene as if Chick is reluctant to kiss Hot Shot and as if she has only agreed to leave with him to escape her dull existence out in the country with Zeke.

The "love" scenes between Zeke and Chick are sexually charged but not graphic or boundary-pushing, even for a pre-Hays Code (or "Pre-Code") film. The Hays Code (roughly between the 1930s and 1960s) restricted, in the name of decency, what filmmakers could show in their movies. By the end of *Hallelujah*, Chick and Zeke are "shacking up" or living together, indicating that they have had a sexual relationship. Before this, however, McKinney and Haynes captured their characters' sexual tension without so much as a steamy kissing scene. Even if there had been a sex scene, it would not have necessarily made Chick a whore or even a raunchy woman.

Zeke represents the stereotypical Black male who cannot control his sexual urges and cannot find fulfillment. Each time he wants Chick, he finds himself separated from her. For instance, when Zeke carries Chick off in his arms, his suspicious and worried mother follows him and interrupts him before he has a chance to do anything, no matter how much he and Chick might have wanted to have sex.

Moreover, the physical attraction between Chick and Zeke is mutual. To refer to Chick as a whore under these circumstances is sexist, even if unintentional. It reinforces two disturbing assumptions. First, there is the assumption that a man must truly be behind the seemingly independent actions of a woman. Then, there is the age-old perspective in American society that for a man, it is understandable and even acceptable to be governed by libido. Yet, the woman who does the same, or the woman whom we misinterpret as such, must be a whore. The case is the same for a woman who relentlessly pursues a man, even when sexual activity is either absent or merely hinted at.

As a forerunner to similar Christian-themed films, beginning with Spencer Williams' *The Blood of Jesus* (1941), the dominant themes in *Hallelujah* are salvation, temptation, regression, and redemption. *New York Times* movie reviewer Mordaunt Hall labels the film's genre as "Melodrama" and "Religious Drama" (Hall). To label Chick, and McKinney by extension, as merely a vixen or a Jezebel ignores this important context. Each term would be misused in this case. Although "Jezebel" has a biblical context, the term also refers to the sexually promiscuous stereotype of the Black female that white men used to justify their sexual abuse of Black females during the American slave period. The myth became so widely used or expressed by white racists in the antebellum South that they found it necessary to amplify another Black female stereotype, the Mammy, to mitigate the discomfort of white women who felt powerless to "fight back" against their unfaithful husbands. Of course, the Jezebel stereotype has survived over time, especially considering its entertainment value on screen for whites who have traditionally enjoyed their "gaze" of the Black female—with or without an Old South fantasy world—and have enjoyed seeing Black stereotypes, in general. According to the *Oxford English Dictionary*, a vixen is "a she-fox" ("Vixen," Def. 1). In addition to stating the same definition, the *Merriam-Webster Dictionary* adds that a vixen is "a sexually attractive woman" ("Vixen," Def. 3). While one may attribute foxlike characteristics to a woman figuratively, and certainly to Nina Mae McKinney's Chick, the sexual connotation and the notion of the loose woman are absent from the word's definition. If one may interpret Chick as a Jezebel, it is only because she manipulates Zeke.

Even though King Vidor juxtaposes Black Christian religious frenzy, or "feeling the Spirit," with the sexual tension between Zeke and Chick, she appears to be sincere when she "gets saved." She even beats Hot Shot down with a fireplace poker when he shows up and tries to take her back to the city by force; she refuses to leave with him voluntarily. She does not leave with him at all. Instead, she leaves him lying helpless on the floor and rushes off to church. Here, her argument with Hot Shot reveals her overdependence on Zeke, but she still seems genuine about her religious conversion. Unfortunately, Chick later becomes a "backslider," a person who reverts to worldliness after being converted. Zeke's mother and Missy Rose have been suspicious of Chick's conversion all along, but McKinney acts out these scenes in a manner that could lead viewers to interpret Chick's behavior either way: as genuine or pretentious.

Another indication of the emphasis on religious themes deals with the contrast between religious music and secular music in the film. When Chick first appears, she is outside dancing to secular music, and she dances and sings secular songs in the club shortly thereafter. However, right before Hot Shot finds her and tries to force her to return with him, she is singing "Old-Time Religion," a gospel song. On her way to a nighttime service at Zeke's church, Chick sings:

> Gimme that old-time religion.
> Gimme that old-time religion.
> Gimme that old-time religion.
> It's good enough for me.

It was good for the Hebrew children.
It was good for the Hebrew children.
It was good for the Hebrew children.
It's good enough for me. (*Hallelujah*)

At the end of the story, she has been living with Zeke, but she attempts to leave him. Right before she sneaks out of their house, she is singing secular music again. Here, she sings a variation of a blues song, entitled "St. Louis Blues." Foreshadowing her escape, Chick sings:

I hate to see that evening sun go down.
My man done quit me and done left this town.
Feelin' tomorrow just like I feel today.
I'm gon' pack my trunk and make my getaway.
Easy Rider, I done lost this race.
With gin and gamblin', they gonna hide your face. (*Hallelujah*)

One might interpret the earlier baptism scene and the nighttime church scene as Chick's either being a cunning temptress or a woman who is truly torn between worldliness and her newfound salvation. Yet she is no longer a gold digger. She is more of a desperate woman trying to make sure she gets her man. The fact that Zeke has no money or material things to offer Chick no longer matters to her.

The film never gives any indication that Chick and Zeke get married after the church scene in which he carries her off into the night, but months later, they are living together at the end of the story. First, note that in Chick's absence, Zeke had become engaged to Missy Rose, but Chick reclaims him. Furthermore, Hot Shot and any reference to him are absent between the scene in which Chick beats Hot Shot down and the end of the story when she sneaks off with him, leaving Zeke and his little country house behind. It is feasible that

Chick had grown bored with her modest new life with Zeke, who then worked in a mill and was no longer a preacher. Chick's situation, at this point, presents the common literary, artistic, and cinematic theme of "city versus country," a parallel between simplicity and the fast life or between morality and immorality. Unfortunately, the temptation to return to her former lifestyle overcomes Chick.

"Going home" is also central to the story. Chick goes home spiritually; Zeke returns to his family. Ultimately, as Chick dies in Zeke's arms, she expresses her regret and repents. Metaphorically, after falling in the mud, she tells Zeke that she fears she is going to the devil, but Zeke sheds his anger long enough to assure her that it is not too late to find redemption. Of course, their conversation implies this, rather than stating it directly. Perhaps, Vidor was trying to avoid being too preachy. Instead of fearing the devil, her last words illustrate her uneasiness about death and meeting her maker. Typical of a sexist era, Chick pays for her self-determination with death and needs a man's forgiveness. Nevertheless, she dies not in the frantic state of her tragic wound, but in peace. Then, there is also the physical journey for Zeke. Folklore, literature, and film have repeatedly told variations of the prodigal son, or more broadly, stories about one's downfall and eventual redemption. For Zeke, after serving his time for killing Hot Shot, there is only one thing left to do: go home. Missy Rose and his family have forgiven him, and they eagerly welcome him back.

African American Actresses: The Struggle for Visibility, 1900-1960 describes Nina Mae McKinney and *Hallelujah*'s Chick as being one and the same, a girlish seductress/Jezebel figure. Yet, it offers no support other than quotes from one Black critic/reporter Ruby Berkeley Goodwin, who referred to McKinney as "beautiful and irresistible," "a child who wants the admiration of the world," "the seductive little cabaret dancer," and "the vampire" in the June 8, 1929, edition of the *Pittsburgh Courier* (Regester 44). However, it is the unsubstantiated opinion of one journalist, which may be biased. Another reviewer disagreed with the argument that McKinney's sexuality won her the role of Chick: "Rhythmically bowing and dipping, swaying, and turning with a troupe of seasoned chorus girls, she was unconscious of the critical eyes of the great director, King Vidor. She did not know that the pendulum had swung from mediocrity to stardom when he viewed her with unusual interest" (Regester, *African American Actresses* 43). Considering McKinney's talent and "it" factor, "obscurity" would have been a better word choice than "mediocrity."

Goodwin's claims that McKinney used her sexuality on stage to allure viewers and that her personality was the same in real life is similar to Elizabeth Goldberg's disparaging *Motion Picture Classic* magazine article, which is discussed in "Chapter Five: Personal Struggles and the Press." However, a few things need to be taken into consideration. First, King Vidor had already cast Honey Brown as Chick in *Hallelujah*. Although impressed by McKinney's performance in the *Blackbirds* chorus line, he did not replace Brown with McKinney until Irving Thalberg intervened. Furthermore, it has been common for some journalists or critics to either love or hate particular performers for whatever reason or for no apparent reason at all. No specific stories support the claim that McKinney was a seductress on stage and in real life. Perhaps, as stated earlier, sensationalism was just a means to sell papers. Considering the previously mentioned mixed opinions of McKinney, one must also consider the contradiction found in the fact that the Black press made much effort to keep McKinney in the public eye, hoping it would help her maintain her acting career in a discrimination-filled Hollywood.

Some critics have referred to McKinney's performance in *Hallelujah*, especially her dancing, as hypersexual or dirty. Disdain for a negative Black stereotype is understandable. However, McKinney's dancing is exaggerated, especially the part of her "Swanee Shuffle" singing scene, in which she performs dance moves that predate similar moves performed by, or arguably appropriated by, Elvis Presley in the 1950s. Black people had created these dance styles before *Hallelujah*'s 1929 release. Yet, to further illustrate the previously mentioned exaggeration, note that some older whites criticized Elvis's dancing as being too sexually charged when the truth was that they resented his imitation of Black artists.

When Chick is introduced, she is dancing for a small crowd. She is the object of the male gaze as Regester and others have asserted (Regester 45-6), but McKinney, despite wearing a short dress, seems careful to avoid revealing her undergarment, even as she performs the high-stepping part of her routine. While the pre-release cut of the film might have had a more suggestive dance scene, this particular scene in the film that was released is about as lustful and inappropriate as Betty and Veronica performing a similar dance in the animated "Sugar, Sugar" episode of *The Archie Comedy Hour* in 1969 ("Sugar, Sugar"). Here, my comparison is lighthearted but not absurd, even considering the notion that people generally upheld higher standards for public decency in the early twentieth century.

After her "Swanee Shuffle" performance, Chick shares a slow dance with Zeke and works her way up to conning him into gambling away his money. Here, Chick's seduction is more playful than lustful. The character Chick is quite comfortable with her sexuality, and the young actress Nina Mae McKinney may have been as well. However, neither their sexuality nor their slow dancing, or even "grinding," implies that these free-spirited women were whores.

According to *Bright Boulevards, Bold Dreams: The Story of Black Hollywood*, beginning on the last night of shooting *Hallelujah*, Nina Mae McKinney and other Black actors partied at the mansion of Marion Davies' niece Pepi Lederer for three days and only had to leave because of Lederer's racist white neighbor (Bogle 93). This scenario might be an exaggeration of the lavish, carefree Hollywood and wealthy Beverly Hills lifestyles, and it is also doubtful that a racist neighbor would have waited until the third day to complain. Unfortunately, unsubstantiated rumors and vague claims have always typified Hollywood gossip. According to actor Louise Brooks, a friend of Lederer, it was a weekend party that took place during the absence of Davies's sisters, Rose and Ethel. Brooks stated that Lederer visited the set of *Hallelujah*, was "struck by McKinney," and invited McKinney and other cast members over. Brooks stated that later, Lederer laughed and enjoyed telling Brooks, "And I shall never forget the expression on Ethel's face when she opened the door and saw me in bed with Nina May [sic]" (Bogle 93).

Even though Lederer's claim about McKinney may be true, Lederer's credibility must be questioned. It is unclear as to whether it is Bogle or Brooks who describes Lederer as "free-spirited," but, undoubtedly, Lederer was quite privileged, and she reveled in attention. Lederer drank frequently and used cocaine, according to *Flapper: A Madcap Story of Sex, Style, Celebrity, and the Women Who Made America Modern* by Joshua Zeitz (2006), which also recounts Brooks' story about McKinney and Lederer (Zeitz 255). Given Lederer's reputation as a lesbian (Zeitz 255) and the fact that drugs, alcohol, and sexual promiscuity/experimentation were part of the Hollywood-Beverly Hills scene, it is possible that something happened between her and McKinney. However, if that was the case, it would seem astounding that such a scandalous story remained a secret for so long, especially considering Brooks's own exploits and Lederer's well-known behavior. Zeitz states that although Brooks avoided drugs, she had slept with Lederer "for good measure" and that Brooks, a star in her own right, claimed to have also slept with other women, including megastar Greta Garbo (255-56).

According to friends and relatives, Lederer also enjoyed pulling pranks and doing things for shock value. For example, Louise

Brooks discusses an incident that occurred around noon on a different occasion: "Before Marion and Mr. Hearst were on stage, we were swimming in the pool when Pepi learned that a group of Hearst's editors solemnly outfitted in dark business suits, was sitting at the table, loaded with bottles of scotch and gin, in the dining room of Casa del Mar—the second largest of the three villas surrounding the castle. Pepi organized a chain dance. Ten beautiful girls in wet bathing suits danced round the editors' table, grabbed a bottle here and there and exited" (Zeitz 256). Brooks describes the reaction of these men as "stunned" and states that one asked another, "Does Mr. Hearst know these people are here?" (Zeitz 256). They sat in disbelief at Lederer's prank and the fact that it took place at Hearst's mansion.

If Lederer and McKinney really were in bed together, it could easily be taken out of context. Lederer's claim does not indicate what they were doing. It could have been completely innocent or platonic. They could have simply been exhausted from partying, or they could have passed out from drinking too much. Lederer's sister might have been shocked at the mere presence of a Black person in the house at all. The idea of sexual activity between Lederer and McKinney is mere conjecture when neither of them admitted that anything really happened that night. There is no confirmation that McKinney used drugs there, either. Around age 17, McKinney might have been more vulnerable when exposed to these environments where anybody could be tempted or make mistakes they regret. She and the people around her likely saw her as an adult, but her close relationship with her mother (who had been with her during the filming of *Hallelujah*) must have provided a moral compass to some extent.

McKinney's lavish lifestyle after the release of *Hallelujah* is also vague. According to *Bright Boulevards, Bold Dreams: The Story of Black Hollywood*, "In a town that prized excess, she was known to spend wildly: on clothes, on jewelry, on friends, on nights on the town, eventually, on drugs" (93). Bogle states that "such stories about McKinney ran rampant up and down Central Avenue—and perhaps up and down some of the plush boulevards in Beverly Hills" (93). While these statements might be true since McKinney was young and "hot," both in terms of her appearance and in terms of her Hollywood leading lady status at the time, they are too vague be accepted as absolute. The expression, "she was known to" is insufficient, especially in the absence of specific stories for support.

McKinney purportedly entered into a relationship with a maharaja and became a high fashion "movie goddess" (Bogle, *Bright Boulevards, Bold Dreams* 93). Hence, she was exactly what Black Hollywood wanted and needed, according to Floyd Covington of the Urban League's journal *Opportunity* (Bogle 93, *Bright Boulevards, Bold Dreams*). Although the Black press's attempts to help build and maintain McKinney's star status coincide with Covington's comments, Bogle's claim about McKinney and a maharaja is ambiguous. Here, Bogle does not state exactly who this maharaja was or exactly when this relationship allegedly occurred. However, an article in the June 1959 issue of *Ebony* magazine states that McKinney met Sir Jagatjit Singh, the Maharaja of Kapurthala, at a Hollywood nightclub in 1939 and that Singh "immediately took a liking to her" and "took her out several times," including a Hollywood party, before he returned to India. It was typical for Hollywood to "roll out the red carpet" for royalty, and Singh was "the third-richest man in the world" ("Darlings of Royalty"). According to gossip columnist Hedda Hopper, "every beautiful girl under studio contract was ordered to dress to the eyeballs" in anticipation of Singh's arrival at a party called "the social event of the season" ("Darlings of Royalty"). Imagine everyone's surprise when Singh arrived at the party with Nina Mae McKinney. Although McKinney's MGM contract had long since expired (1929-1934), she was still gorgeous, and she still possessed an unmistakable "it" factor or "star" quality. Singh treated her with a great deal of respect and enjoyed her company. Even though several of "Hollywood's most glamorous beauties" tried to gain Singh's attention and "favor," McKinney always had his full attention, and he left the party the same way he arrived: with McKinney ("Darlings of Royalty"). His preference for McKinney's company over entertainers who had attained a higher status than hers might indicate that his admiration had developed into a longstanding friendship.

According to "Indian Maharaja at Feet of Nina Mae," a short article published in the November 16, 1929, issue of the *Afro-American*, the two met in 1929 (ten years earlier) as the result of his seeking her out. He showed up after one of her exhausting rehearsals, presented her with fine jade and "Chinese brocaded satin," and offered to take her on a tour of Europe and India ("Indian Maharaja at Feet of Nina Mae" 10). Whether a romantic relationship developed is uncertain, and it is apparent that McKinney presented herself as "a lady," no matter how impressed she might have been with Singh's wealth and extravagance. There is no reason to believe that McKinney married or even entered romantic relationships for materialistic ends or to advance her career. As discussed in this book's chapter entitled "McKinney's Personal Struggles and the Press," her confirmed marriages to working-class men contradict the thought of such behavior.

Chapter Two of this book discusses an important parallel between the personal lives of Nina Mae McKinney and Eartha Kitt, and another parallel must be addressed here: critics' and powerful white people's dismissal of a Black woman by mischaracterizing or exaggerating her sexuality. Charles Revson, founder of Revlon cosmetics, had been one of Eartha Kitt's former lovers (Luck). That does not necessarily mean she was a loose woman only attracted to men of wealth and status. By the 1950s, the singer/dancer had captivated British and American audiences with her "suggestive and sensuous" performances (Luck). None of that necessarily made Eartha a

Jezebel whose screen and personal lives were identical. Eartha Kitt also portrayed Catwoman in the 1960s *Batman* television series, starring Adam West. Instead of focusing on a Black Catwoman's flirtation with Batman, which was still taboo because West was white, it is more rational to acknowledge her as arguably "the first Black woman to achieve mainstream television success in America," (Luck) which began when she debuted in *Batman* in 1967—one year before Diahann Carroll debuted as the titular character in *Julia*—even though Nichelle Nichols first appeared in *Star Trek* as Uhura in 1966 ("Star Trek"). Like the performances of Diahann Carroll and Nichelle Nichols, Eartha Kitt's should never be overshadowed by the racial climate of its time—including double standards for Black women.

Eartha Kitt, a 1960s civil rights activist, also spoke out against the Vietnam War. Not only did this end her career in the United States, but the CIA also probed into her personal life and drew the biased conclusion that she was "a sadistic nymphomaniac" (Luck). Similar to Nina Mae McKinney, early in Eartha's career, Eartha received acclaim overseas (in Britain) after leaving Katherine Dunham's dance company, and Eartha returned to Britain in the 1960s (Luck). Due to Eartha's white rapist father, she was neither dark-skinned nor light enough in complexion to pass for white—similar to Nina Mae, whose immediate ancestry likely included at least one white man on each side of her family between the late 1800s and early 1900s (as explained in Chapter One). In short, Eartha's experience illustrates that a convenient way for powerful white people or critics of any color to dismiss or discredit a Black woman or a woman of apparently mixed race was to portray her as a Jezebel figure. Whether their claims were gross exaggerations or outright lies has never mattered to them or their base.

The entertainment industry, especially as a visual medium, has always preferred women who could be sultry because that sells.

Women who could captivate audiences with their beauty, charm, and sex appeal have always been in demand. Therefore, the gaze is a built-in feature, especially for the non-white, exotic "other." None of these women, including Nina Mae McKinney, deserve to be automatically categorized negatively, even when they have portrayed vamps and seductresses on screen. There is no valid reason to project the Jezebel stereotype onto the entire career and personal life of a Black actor, especially when far more white actors have portrayed similar roles without receiving the same harsh treatment.

Critics have upheld a double standard for Black actresses then and now. As stated earlier, Clara Bow apparently did not receive criticism for the role of Betty Lou in the film *It* (1927), even though the character is manipulative and flirtatious. Instead, scholars acknowledge Bow as Hollywood's first sex symbol. Bow received praise from audiences and critics for being the embodiment of Elinor Glyn's definition of "it." Betty Lou uses Monty, whom she refers to as Cyrus Waltham's "office boy," just to get close to Cyrus (*It*). Later in the film, she lies across Cyrus' desk, which plays to a male office fantasy. Near the end of the story, Betty Lou plays a terrible joke on Cyrus just to get back at him for being reluctant to accept her. This happens after he thinks she has a baby because she has lied to Monty and the social workers to keep the child from being taken from her friend, the child's true mother. In Betty Lou's scheme, she uses Monty again, and she joins them on a yacht cruise. There, she seduces Cyrus into proposing to her, only to laugh in his face and leave him standing there. Similar to the girlish quality of McKinney's Chick, Betty Lou soon regrets her immature antics. Fortunately, Cyrus forgives her, they kiss, and they get together. *It* affords Betty Lou a happy ending, unlike Chick's tragic ending in *Hallelujah*.

Despite exaggerations that reduce Chick's significance to that of a mere temptress, Nina Mae McKinney's *Hallelujah* performance is not inherently degrading, and there is no evidence that McKinney and Chick were ever the same sexually and morally conflicted person. What they do have in common is their struggle for independence, which was especially audacious for a Black woman in the 1920s. Given the time period, it is imperative that we recognize McKinney for paving the way for future Black actors to play leading roles and shun the degrading roles to which Black actors had been relegated. This is not much different from the struggle of early Black stage actors who had to wear blackface in order to work, while hoping that one day, they or later Black actors would finally benefit from their struggle and find better opportunities. Nina Mae McKinney played her roles, even loosely or blatantly stereotypical ones, "her way" and with dignity. The spirit of self-determination that defines her role as Chick in *Hallelujah* and her failed attempt to maintain her career on her own terms was courageous and nothing short of revolutionary.

Chapter Seven

The First Black Star in Hollywood

As the first Black actor in a leading role in Hollywood, Nina Mae McKinney was the first Black star in Hollywood. Mel Watkins, author of *Stepin' Fetchit—The Life and Times of Lincoln Perry*, states, "On some levels, McKinney broke the colour line in Hollywood; before her no black performer had been courted with such uninhibited exuberance" (Watkins 129). Watkins adds that after *Hallelujah* was released, MGM's Irving Thalberg, "one of the most powerful and respected producers in Hollywood," called her "the greatest acting discovery of the age" (Watkins 129). This chapter discusses why McKinney was also the earliest precursor to Black superstardom in Hollywood. That requires an understanding of "who" and "why." Since it is impossible to name every possible alternative, this section will focus on those who seem most logical: several distinguished performers, beginning with Florence Mills and Josephine Baker, the entertainers whom McKinney named as her greatest influences, according to *Returning the Gaze: A Genealogy of Black Film Criticism 1909-1949* by Anna Everett.

In a June 6, 1929, *Pittsburgh Courier* article, "From 'Blackbird' Chrine to 'Talkie' Star," McKinney stated, "The phenomenal success of Florence Mills and Josephine Baker stimulated me. I longed to hold a place in the hearts of the world as they did" (Everett 165, 337). Florence Mills was a major draw as a stage performer on Broadway and in major European cities such as London and Paris, but she did not make the transition to movies.[9] Mills was a singer, dancer, comedian, and civil rights activist who "wanted to improve the state of her people" (Egan 269). Born on January 25, 1895, in Washington, D.C. to parents who were former slaves, Mills made her stage debut at the age of five under the name "Baby Florence." Mills, whom audiences called the "Queen of Happiness," is remembered for her hit song, "I'm a Little Blackbird Looking for a Bluebird" ("Florence Mills Biography"). Although the song's lyrics speak of loneliness and longing for happiness, it also held a racial uplift subtext for Mills, a vibrant personality of the Harlem Renaissance. Mills' big break was in the musical and comedic stage extravaganza *Shuffle Along* in 1921 ("Florence Mills Biography"). *Shuffle Along* was not a Broadway show, but it was an important opportunity for Black entertainers as it ran for 484 shows. Pianist Eubie Blake composed the music, and Noble Sissle wrote the song lyrics ("Shuffle Along").

Later, Mills headlined the 1925 and 1926/1927 Broadway musical productions of *Blackbirds* (Egan 139; Gavin 20; "Florence Mills Biography"). Nina Mae McKinney did not perform in these versions. She would have only been 13 or 14 at the time, but her appearance in Blackbirds of 1928 is even more interesting since Florence Mills was one of McKinney's influences as an entertainer. According to *Underneath a Harlem Moon: The Harlem to Paris Years of Adelaide Hall* by Iain Cameron Williams, director and producer Lew Leslie had intended to present the 1928 version as a showcase for Florence Mills (Gavin 20; "Florence Mills Biography"). Mills was perhaps the first African American international entertainment sensation, having enjoyed success in Paris and London before returning to Broadway. *Blackbirds* also had a successful run in Europe, most notably Paris and London, where Mills starred in the 250th show. Mills appeared in all of the previous shows (Egan 161, 175, 199). Even royalty such as Prince George, Duke of Kent attended the shows (Egan 182).

Sadly, Mills died of complications from tuberculosis in 1927 at the young age of 31 before the new *Blackbirds* production began (Gavin 20). The exhaustive schedule contributed to Mills' decline in health. She told friends she was "going to a health resort for a rest cure" (Egan 211). She only had a brief break during the Christmas holiday before having to return and learn new material (Egan 189). Leslie had frequently changed and added material for the show, and evidently, he relied on Mills so much that she never had a stand-in or an understudy (Egan 199).

As a performer, Mills liked doing things her way and was persistent, similar to the autonomy Nina Mae McKinney exhibited in her refusal to speak using unintelligible dialect in her film roles. According to *Florence Mills: Harlem Jazz Queen* by Bill Egan, "'Miss Mills say so den dat goes,' were typical remarks that one heard all the time when *Dover Street to Dixie* or *Blackbirds* was in rehearsal or running" (Egan 263). Mills' success on Broadway, her status as the first African American female performer to enjoy a measure of international success in the twentieth century ("Florence Mills: The Little Blackbird"), and her racial uplift ideals were impressive to young hopefuls such as Nina Mae McKinney. Nevertheless, similar to McKinney, Mills is underappreciated today.

Josephine Baker had become a star in Europe by the 1930s, but she did not enjoy the same level of success in the United States on stage or in film. Born in St. Louis on June 3, 1906, Baker used dancing to escape poverty and make a better life for herself ("Josephine Baker Biography"). Baker appeared in *Shuffle Along* in 1921 in New York and toured with the show (J. Baker 55), but since her opportunities as a Black entertainer were limited in the United States, she traveled throughout Europe. Baker became popular, especially in France, where she sang and danced, sometimes in semi-nude reviews.

Baker captivated audiences, and she became well-known for spectacle and exploitative performances on stage. On October 2, 1925, her opening night in *La Revue Nègre* sold out a 2,000-seat theater in Paris (J. Baker 3). Black jazz saxophonist Sidney Bechet performed as light-skinned Black chorus girls danced the Charleston (J. Baker 4). Then, Baker appeared. She was the headliner of the show, "darker than the other girls, a clown with rubber legs and rubber face" (J. Baker 5). In blackface, her yet-to-be-trained voice sang, "Yes Sir, That's My Baby," and she "pushes [pushed] her knees together, does [did] splits, her pants rolled high" (J. Baker 5). The audience, thoroughly enjoying her performance, could not tell whether she was white or Black until the finale: a "Charleston Cabaret." At this point, half-nude African dancer Joe Alex carried Baker onto the stage. She was nude, except for feathers attached to her ankles and waist. As the jazz music "begins [began] to pound," Baker "slides [slid] down Joe's body" and "seems [seemed] to be making love to him in front of everyone" (J. Baker 5).

While a few people were "muttering that jazz and Blacks are going to destroy white civilization," others were yelling for more (J. Baker 6). Most of the audience gave her a standing ovation. Theater director André Daven stated that "it was like the revelation of a new world" and that it was like "eroticism finding a style" (J. Baker 6). Singer Lydia Jones stated, "We were horrified at how disgusting Josie was behaving in front of this French audience, doing her nigger routine. She had no self-respect, no shame in front of these crackers, and would you believe it, they loved it" (J. Baker 6).

Afterward, Baker referred to her first performance in Paris as "savage" and she stated, "A frenzy took possession of me . . . seeing nothing, not even hearing the orchestra, I danced!" (J. Baker 6). The chorus girls believed the show's pianist Claude Hopkins had cheated on his wife with Baker. Jean-Claude Baker and Chris Chase, authors of *Josephine: The Hungry Heart*, state that Baker used the finale's dance to make Hopkins jealous, which is similar to a critic's allegation that Nina Mae McKinney used her dancing in *Blackbirds* to seduce King Vidor or anyone in the audience who could further her career. McKinney also knew how to exude sensuality in dance, and, while critics accused her of blurring the line between reality and her role as Chick, she was more in awe of Baker's international impact than her own impact in America. Furthermore, McKinney risked her career in Hollywood by refusing to compromise herself backstage the way some desperate Hollywood hopefuls were willing to do.

With her growing popularity, Josephine Baker also starred in several films in France, including the short film *The Fireman of the Folies Bergere* and features such as *Siren of the Tropics* (1927), *Zou Zou* (1934)—her first "talkie," and *Princess Tam Tam* (1935). Similar to some of her stage performances, her movies were exploitative, as her characters were underdeveloped caricatures of an exotic Black woman. These films included gratuitous semi-nude and nude scenes and were primarily designed to showcase her dancing. *Siren of the Tropics* was her feature-length debut, in which she displayed some of her best dancing, including the Charleston. There is partial nudity, but each of those performances is toned down compared to the aforementioned *La Revue Nègre* stage performance in Paris in 1925. Although Baker was the main attraction in her French films, she did not enjoy this level of success in the United States, where she appeared in *Shuffle Along* and only had one brief stint on Broadway.

Upon her brief return to the United States to perform in the 1936 edition of *The Ziegfeld Follies*—also featuring Bob Hope, the Nicholas Brothers, and Fannie Brice—Baker did not receive the same raving reviews that her other performances had received in Europe (Bogle 268). At this time, Baker allegedly "snubbed" both Ethel Waters and Nina Mae McKinney, refusing to see them (Bogle, *Bright Boulevards, Bold Dreams* 270). No specific stories or sources support this, but if it was true, it might not have been a simple matter of Baker not wanting to associate with them. It was more likely that Baker was "sulking" due to the harsh reviews that critics in the white press gave her (Bogle, *Bright Boulevards, Bold Dreams* 270). For example, a *Time* magazine article stated, "In sex appeal to jaded Europeans of the jazz-loving type, a Negro wench always has a head start, but to Manhattan theatergoers last week she was just a slightly buck-toothed young negro woman whose figure might be matched in any nightclub show, whose dancing and singing could be topped practically anywhere outside France" (Bogle, *Bright Boulevards, Bold Dreams* 269-70). Such a harsh critique was part of the "backlash" against her because she was able to escape the severe racism of the United States and enjoy success in Europe (Bogle, *Bright Boulevards, Bold Dreams* 269-70). The use of the word "wench" clearly indicates racist sentiment. White critics also resented Nina Mae McKinney's brief success in Europe, as well as her brief status as a Hollywood leading lady in much the same way. Some producers and executives likely harbored the same sentiment. "Chapter Five: Personal Struggles and the Press" discusses this topic further.

Like Florence Mills, Baker's courage and convictions were well-known and admirable. Baker was active in the civil rights struggle of the 1950s and 1960s in the United States. Yet, she is remembered more for her World War II French Resistance efforts, including her conflict with actor and alleged Nazi sympathizer Maurice Chevalier. He was a friend of Baker's Belgian-born competitor Mistinguett, who tried her best to "block Josephine's solo performances" because she was afraid that the "younger, exotic Baker would eclipse her popularity" (Jules-Rosette 63, 134). Baker's last performance in Paris during the French occupation was in May 1940, after she had opened at the Paris-Londres revue with Chevalier earlier that year. France had entered World War II in September 1939 after Germany attacked Poland. Later that month, Baker joined the French Counterespionage Services and Free France organization while maintaining her stage performances.

In 1941, Baker served as a counterespionage agent in North Africa until she became ill. After spending most of the following year recovering, she met U.S. Army Lieutenant Sidney Williams and agreed to perform for Allied forces in North Africa. Still struggling with health issues, Baker would make no recordings until 1944. In 1946, the French government awarded Baker the Medal of Resistance with Rosette (Jules-Rosette 289-90). Josephine Baker's state military funeral at La Madeleine in Paris gave her a 21-gun salute on April 15, 1975, which was three days after she died from a cerebral hemorrhage ("Josephine Baker Biography"). She had just given her final performance, a sold-out show at the Théâtre Bobino in Paris on April 8. Josephine fell into a coma two days later (Jules-Rosette 293). While Baker's performances and personal stances made her an international celebrity, she never attained Hollywood stardom.

Bert Williams and Charles Gilpin were important antecedents to Black stardom on the dramatic stage, and were arguably stars themselves; however, neither was able to transition to successful film careers. Bert Williams was arguably the first Black star in America, but most of his career preceded the notion of stardom, even for white entertainers, and it chiefly consisted of Vaudeville and Broadway acts, not movies. Scholars do not refer to Williams as African American since he was born in the Bahamas and identified himself more broadly as Black ("Bert Williams"). Williams, who spent most of his career in blackface, began his career as a comedian in the early 1890s as part of the Williams and Walker comedic duo with partner George Walker. They sold their act as "two real coons" to distinguish themselves from whites in blackface. Off stage, especially in photographs, Williams and Walker presented themselves as sharply dressed distinguished gentlemen (Forbes 356), which contradicted their "two real coons" act. Williams tried to separate himself from blackface, which he wore to find work, and tried to treat it as merely a mask (Chude-Sokei 31). Camille F. Forbes argues in *Introducing Bert Williams: Burnt Cork, Broadway, and the Story of America's First Black Star* that despite the burnt cork, the duo, unlike white actors, attempted to present Blacks as real people with real experiences (Forbes 59). *The Last "Darky": Bert Williams, Black-on-Black Minstrelsy, and the African Diaspora* by Louis Chude-Sokei agrees that Williams and Walker deconstructed the traditional darky and coon stereotypes found in minstrelsy. Chude-Sokei argues that most Black audiences could appreciate the duo's performances and that "it was the presence of Williams' Blackface mask that anchored the performance for the white audience" (Chude-Sokei 32). Yet, numerous Blacks criticized their act for failing to uplift the race, which is of particular interest since the 1890s predate the New Negro Movement in which increasing numbers of African Americans began to challenge their status in society.

The duo's most successful acts were *In Dahomey* (1902-1904), which also toured Britain, and *Abyssinia* (1906). Williams had developed a hard luck "Mr. Nobody" persona, and *Abyssinia* was such a hit that it led to successful musical recordings, such as Williams' most famous song "Nobody," which sold between 100,000 and 150,000 copies. Columbia continued to sell Williams' recordings through 1931. By then, Williams' total catalog had sold 1,866,300 copies (Brooks 144). As a solo act, Williams had become the most famous Black performer and was immensely popular. He became the first Black performer to appear in the *Ziegfeld Follies* (1910) and eventually the "highest paid principal" (Forbes 308). Even at that point in his career, Williams did not view himself as a star. Williams defined a star in the following terms: "When you are the star of the show and unable to appear, the company closes until the star can appear. If you can't come back, then the company stays closed" (Forbes 308). In context, Williams was referring to Charles Gilpin, even though Williams' quote on stardom, applied much more broadly, transcends their era.

Charles Gilpin played the dramatic lead as Brutus Jones in the play *The Emperor Jones* in 1920.[10] Gilpin had previously worked with Williams and Walker but went on to achieve a measure of dramatic acting success desired by, but denied to, Williams. Bert was happy for his friend Charles but disappointed at the same time, especially since so many Black viewers were proud to finally see a Black dramatic lead on stage instead of the subservient characters and stereotypical comedies Black actors were relegated to.[11] For example, according to James Weldon Johnson, "By his work in *The Emperor*

Jones Gilpin reached the point of achievement on the legitimate stage that had yet been achieved by a Negro in America" (Forbes 307). Gilpin later founded the Lafayette Players, a Black theatrical group ("Charles Gilpin").

Although most of Williams' career preceded the notion of stardom in Hollywood, the first white movie stars were born during the twilight of his career. As Hollywood was in its infancy, Williams was still primarily a stage performer, and his only film appearances were in four silent shorts. He acted in two in 1916, *Fish* and *A Natural Born Gambler*, which he also wrote, produced, and directed for the Biograph Company. He also appeared in two comedic shorts as himself, Vitagraph Company of America's *Actors' Fund Field Day* in 1910 and *Darktown Jubilee* in 1914 ("Bert Williams").[12] Since Biograph and Vitagraph were important silent film companies and the predecessors of the Hollywood system, it was simply a matter of unfortunate timing for Bert Williams.[13] On the other hand, Charles Gilpin's career would continue through the 1920s, and he appeared in the race films *Ten Nights in a Barroom* in 1926 and *Scar of Shame* in 1927 ("Charles Gilpin"). However, Gilpin would never enjoy Hollywood success, and neither Williams nor Gilpin would become an archetype for the Black leading man Hollywood would later accept.

Hollywood had always resisted Black male stars largely because of the popular perception that they were a threat to white male masculinity. The emasculation of Black males was deeply rooted in early twentieth-century American racism, from calling them "boy," no matter how old they were, to placing them in dresses or "one-pieces" like Buckwheat in *Our Gang*. In addition, the Black Buck draws frequent, unwanted sexual comparisons to white men and upholds white racist fears of needing to protect the virtuous, beautiful white woman from him. This ranges from the alleged rapist wearing blackface in *Birth of a Nation* to Hollywood's traditional, though modernized, resistance to pairing Black males with white females. Therefore, the closest Black males would come to stardom in the early twentieth century were the nonthreatening Bert Williams and Lincoln Perry, best known for his lazy and buffoonish Stepin Fetchit on-screen persona.[14]

Madame Sul-Te-Wan was arguably the first Black film actor white people in Hollywood recognized on the merit of acting ability. She made her film debut in 1913 and appeared in minor roles throughout the 1920s in films such as *Birth of a Nation* in 1915. She was the first Black actress to work under contract in Hollywood, but the leading lady door would remain closed to the dark-skinned actress who was born Nellie Conley in 1873, despite her lifelong friendship with director D.W. Griffith. Regarding her acting career, she stated, "I get bitter sometimes because I don't work long enough to buy a handkerchief" ("Madame Sul-Te-Wan Biography"). By the 1920s, other Black actresses, including light-skinned actresses such as Evelyn Preer—known for Oscar Micheaux's revolutionary race film *Within Our Gates* (1919)—and Lucia Lynn Moses—known for the influential race film *Scar of Shame* (1927)—would also be denied Hollywood leading roles and stardom despite their talent. Madame Sul-Te-Wan worked in stage, film, and television productions through 1958, but most of her roles were uncredited and were stereotypical characters such as African natives and servants to whites ("Madame Sul-Te-Wan Biography").

Hattie McDaniel's career serves as the best example of numerous Black actresses, especially dark-skinned women, who found themselves unable to break free from stereotypical roles in Hollywood. For her role as Mammy in *Gone with the Wind* (1939), McDaniel won "Best Actress in a Supporting Role," making her the first African American to win an Academy Award. McDaniel, who began her career in entertainment as a band singer in the 1910s, began her acting career in 1932, but her first credited role was not until 1934, when she played the maid, Aunt Dilsey, in *Judge Priest* ("Hattie McDaniel Biography"; "Judge Priest"). Her winning an Academy Award and mentoring younger actors (Jackson 146) during such a challenging time period makes her an important figure. For example, she encouraged Lena Horne when some of the older Black actors felt threatened by Horne's breakthrough in the movie industry (Bogle, *Dorothy Dandridge: A Biography* 96).

The white stars of McDaniel's day, including her *Gone with the Wind* co-stars, loved and respected her, but no studio ever promoted her as a star. Her Oscar victory in 1939 did not advance her career. Edward Mapp has compiled a filmography of seventy-one films (Mapp 122-24), but only twenty-four of them came after her Oscar. McDaniel appeared in at least 300 movies but only received a film credit for about 80 of them (Jackson xi). These roles seemed to always be a maid, a cook, or a mammy. McDaniel was, at least, able to make a comfortable living with this typecasting. Even if her characters are as bold in their speech as Mammy is in *Gone with the Wind*, they are still subservient to white characters and are reduced to being caricatures inserted for comedic effect. Of course, they were nonthreatening to racist white audiences.

The film career of Butterfly McQueen, known for her high-pitched voice and her role as the loyal slave Prissy in *Gone with the Wind,* did not advance either. Neither did the career of Louise Beavers, despite the major success of *Imitation of Life* in 1934, in which Beavers portrayed a maid. Unfortunately, cross-references to Nina Mae McKinney in primary and secondary sources on these actors appear to be unavailable.

Fredi Washington, who possessed the complexion and hair texture to pass for white, sacrificed her chance at stardom early in her acting career by choosing to be Black. Born Fredericka Carolyn Washington in Savannah, Georgia, in 1903, she was nine years older than Nina Mae McKinney. Like McKinney, she was born in the South and began her career on Broadway. Washington appeared as a chorus dancer in the off-Broadway musical *Shuffle Along* between 1922 and 1926 (Fredi Washington Papers). Her acting roles include Duke Ellington's love interest (uncredited) in the film *Black and Tan Fantasy* aka *Black and Tan* in 1929; Undine in the film *The Emperor Jones* (1933) opposite leading man Paul Robeson; Peola, a troubled Black woman passing for white in the Academy Award-nominated novel adaptation of Fannie Hurst's *Imitation of Life* (1934); and Lissa in the stage play *Mamba's Daughters* (1939–1941) starring Ethel Waters. Washington received the CIRCA award for "lifetime achievement in the performing arts" in 1979. She was also inducted into the Black Filmmakers Hall of Fame in 1975, three years earlier than Nina Mae McKinney (Fredi Washington Papers). Like McKinney's *Hallelujah*, Washington's *Imitation of Life* is listed in *Time* magazine's "The 25 Most Important Films on Race" (Corliss).

Green-eyed and "white-skinned" Fredi Washington was a Black entertainer who early in her career would have found more opportunities by passing for white. Yet she chose to be Black in both her personal life and in her career, in defiance of the notion of white superiority. Washington proudly proclaimed, "I'll pass for nothing but an artist," ("Uptown Fredi Washington Gives the Lowdown on Hollywood"). She continued, "I deplore sham and insincerity" ("Uptown Fredi Washington Gives the Lowdown on Hollywood"). She was also emphatic about separating her real life from her role as Peola in *Imitation of Life*, especially considering how convincing her character portrayal was. Washington explained, "Perhaps I have been able to show in the new picture how a girl MIGHT [emphasis theirs] feel under the circumstances, but I am not showing how I feel, myself" ("Part in 'Imitation' is Not Real Me,' Says Fredi."). Washington viewed being able to pass for white as an extreme disadvantage for herself as someone who had such a powerful sense of racial pride. Considering the 1930s racial climate, an Associated National Press article adequately summarized the circumstances of Washington's career: "Her skin is white. For that reason, she does not fit into many productions. She is too colored for white pictures and too white for colored. Thus her work opportunities depend upon the chance of something like Fannie Hurst's story coming along" ("Being Too White is the Problem of Fredi Washington").

Having become increasingly frustrated with her career, Fredi Washington retired from acting and became a prominent civil rights activist. She aligned herself with Walter White, NAACP president. In 1937, she joined Noble Sissle, Dick Campbell, and W. C. Handy in New York as founding members of the Negro Actors Guild of America. As Entertainment Editor, she also wrote for *People's Voice* (1942–48), which Adam Clayton Powell Jr. founded (Fredi Washington Papers).

The promotion of Hollywood stardom has always leaned toward women, partly due to the male gaze and partly because female moviegoers have always outnumbered male moviegoers. The first major stars in early Hollywood were women such as Mary Pickford. Of course, Black stardom in Hollywood would follow the same pattern. In addition, Black females such as Nina Mae McKinney had a better chance at reaching stardom than Black males since whites often perceived Black males to be a threat to white masculinity. For example, Sidney Poitier had only experienced a taste of stardom by the time he became the first Black male to win an Academy Award in 1963. Sidney Poitier's first leading role in a Hollywood movie occurred in 1950, in *No Way Out,* when he portrayed a doctor falsely accused of murder after treating the gunshot wounds of two robbers who happen to be white racists and one of them dies ("Sidney Poitier"; *No Way Out*).

Daniel L. Haynes was arguably the first Black male to land a leading role in a Hollywood movie. As the male lead, Haynes played Ezekiel in *Hallelujah* in 1929. Although unfair, it is easy to overlook Haynes because of his co-star Nina Mae McKinney's major impact. Haynes also received positive reviews. Two years after the film was released, the *Chicago Defender* referred to Haynes as one of the finest actors of his day when the paper announced his next role as Adam in *Green Pastures* ("Stars as Adam"). Apparently, the plans for that film fell through, and it was not released. Perhaps, the Black-cast Warner Bros. flick *The Green Pastures* was the same film or a replacement produced with editorial and casting changes. It was not released until 1936. Rex Ingram, who plays both Adam and "De Lawd," appears with Etta McDaniel (sister of *Gone with the Wind*'s Hattie McDaniel), Mantan Moreland, and Eddie "Rochester" Anderson ("The Green Pastures"). Haynes is absent from the credits. The worst obstacle Haynes faced was the fact that Hollywood was even less receptive to Black males than Black females in that era. His career stalled after *Hallelujah*, despite the film's reception and the quality of his performance, and he was never allowed to secure another lead role in a Hollywood movie. Haynes was limited to a minor role in another King Vidor film, the Civil War era romance *So Red the Rose* (1935), and minor roles in six other films—including three that were uncredited (Daniel L. Haynes; *So Red the Rose*).

Lincoln Perry, Paul Robeson, Ethel Waters, and Lena Horne are the most likely alternatives for a precursor to Black superstardom in Hollywood, and each attained more success than Nina Mae McKinney was able to attain. Lincoln Perry—more well-known as Stepin Fetchit—appeared with Clarence Muse in Fox's *Hearts in Dixie*, Hollywood's first all-Black cast movie. Similar to Bert Williams, audiences acknowledged his natural comedic talent. Yet, in much the same way that the NAACP later challenged *The Amos 'n Andy Show* for its stereotypical content, numerous viewers—including Black leaders—criticized the buffoonish and lazy coon persona who cowered before whites. Similar to Williams and McDaniel, Perry found himself torn between public opinion and finding steady work. Having appeared in 55 films between 1925 and 1976, Perry attained wealth and material success. Nevertheless, Hollywood studios never allowed him to become a leading man ("Stepin Fetchit"), and he certainly did not become an archetype for the Black leading man Hollywood would later accept.

Paul Robeson, similar to Josephine Baker and Nina Mae McKinney, had to travel to Europe to find appreciation for his talents. The former pro football player (long before pro football players were highly paid), former Columbia University law school student, singer, and actor was never allowed to become a Hollywood leading man. In 1925, Robeson appeared in *Body and Soul,* pioneering Black filmmaker Oscar Micheaux's controversial race film about a corrupt preacher, and Robeson gave a standout singing performance in the supporting role of Joe in Universal Studio's musical *Showboat* in 1936. Yet his career was more successful overseas. He appeared in several British films, including *Sanders of the River* (1935), which co-starred Nina Mae McKinney, and *Song of Freedom* (1936). Robeson also had many fans in Russia who "revered" him for his charisma and his powerful baritone vocals.

In the 1940s, numerous white people criticized Robeson for being a committed civil rights activist. Yet he was popular on Broadway, and he portrayed Othello in the longest-running version of the play in the United States ("Paul Robeson: Biography"' Rayme). Paul Robeson also developed a reputation as a Communist sympathizer. He had been well-received in Russia, and he perceived their socioeconomic model to be far less discriminatory than the version of democracy found in the United States. Other notable African Americans such as W. E. B. Du Bois had also referred to American democracy as a sham. Du Bois states, "Democracy alone is the method of storing the whole experience of the race for the benefit of the future, and if democracy tries to exclude women or Negroes or the poor or any class because of innate characteristics which do not interfere with intelligence then that democracy cripples itself and belies its name" (Du Bois, *The Wisdom of W. E. B. Du Bois* 37-8).

The U.S. government dealt a harsh blow to Robeson. It "revoked his passport and blacklisted him, severely affecting his income and reputation" (Rayme; "Scandalize My Name"). Targeted by the House Un-American Activities Committee as a reaction to his civil rights activism, like other blacklisted entertainers, Robeson's career was ruined (Rayme; "Scandalize My Name"). Unfortunately, his film career was limited to 13 credited roles in the United States and Britain between 1925 and 1942 ("Paul Robeson: Biography").

Ethel Waters made her Hollywood film debut in 1929 with a minor role in *On with the Show,* "the first 100% natural color, all-singing production" ("On with the Show"). This synchronous sound movie's official release came one month earlier than *Hallelujah's,* but Ethel Waters' breakout film role would not come until 1943, in *Cabin in the Sky,* when she reprised her role from the 1940 stage play of the same title. Unlike McKinney, Waters had already become well-known before entering the world of film. Waters thrived on stage before her film career, beginning in Black Vaudeville in 1917 and performing as a jazz and blues singer at the Cotton Club in the 1920s. According to "Ethel Waters: A Performance Biography" by Dwandalyn Reece King, Waters "broke into the mainstream" in 1933 when she appeared in Irving Berlin's Broadway musical revue *As Thousands Cheer* (1). As Hagar, the mother in *Mamba's Daughters* (1939), Waters became the first Black woman to star in a dramatic play on Broadway, defying the notion that Blacks were only suitable for dancing and singing (D. King 1). Similar to Nina Mae McKinney, Waters was conscious of Black role representations. In the 1920s, Waters had been hesitant about moving into what she and her friends called the "white time" in order to further her career. She stated: "I never exaggerated or overemphasized my characterizations. Most of the Negroes who were getting by on white time were like caricatures of human beings and portrayed buffoons who were lazy and shiftless beyond belief. And I ain't changing my style for nothing or nobody" (Waters 174).

Between 1929 and 1943, Waters appeared in several minor roles in feature films and shorts such as *Rufus Jones for President—* alongside a 7-year-old Sammy Davis Jr., in 1933 ("Rufus Jones for President"). In 1949, she starred as the grandmother of the passing-for-white protagonist in *Pinky*. Waters also played the titular role in the *Beulah* television series in 1951. She landed roles sporadically in television and film until 1972, five years before her death.

According to *Heat Wave: The Life and Career of Ethel Waters*, Waters was King Vidor's original choice for the role of Chick in *Hallelujah*, but Vidor's representative went to New York and was unable to find her (Bogle 173). Vidor never mentioned Waters or any actress other than Nina Mae McKinney when Nancy Dowd and David Shepard conducted interviews with him for the Directors Guild of America Oral History Series between 1970 and 1980 and asked questions about *Hallelujah* (Dowd 99). However, Vidor finally met Waters after the release of *Hallelujah* and told her that she had been his first choice. Donald Bogle states that Waters "never quite got over the loss of the *Hallelujah* role" (Bogle, *Heat Wave* 173). Some scholars believe that casting Ethel Waters, who was medium brown in complexion, in *Hallelujah* might have created a different archetype for Hollywood's Black actresses in leading roles. However, this is unlikely. Without makeup, Ethel Waters' complexion was not much darker than McKinney's. A Black woman who was neither dark-skinned nor able to pass for white proved the best of both worlds for the white male gaze. She was a woman who was not white, which upheld the dominant white standard of beauty, but she was still the exotic other. Both Waters and McKinney fit such a description. Even if King Vidor had cast Ethel Waters in *Hallelujah*, the studio likely would have lightened her skin tone with makeup if her complexion became an issue.

Moreover, MGM failed to even promote McKinney after *Hallelujah*. MGM squandered McKinney's five-year contract, and her career stalled after her supporting role in *Safe in Hell* in 1931, which was a terrible demotion from her leading role in *Hallelujah* in 1929. One must consider how crucial stars were to Hollywood studios. If MGM had signed Ethel Waters, she would have received the same mistreatment and neglect. Moreover, had Vidor found Waters instead of Honey Brown and kept McKinney on standby as he did when he began shooting with Brown, McKinney still would have likely received the role. Despite Vidor's alleged resistance to replacing Brown initially, Vidor and Irving Thalberg ultimately agreed that the role of Chick was made for Nina Mae McKinney. There is no reason to suggest that Ethel Waters, although wonderful in her later film roles, would have carried the role of Chick better than McKinney did.[15]

Lena Horne had no easy path as an actor, but by the 1940s, at least she did not have to be the one to endure the pain of paving the way for others as Nina Mae McKinney did. Horne became the first Black actor to enjoy a taste of stardom when she became the first openly promoted Black actor in Hollywood, but this did not occur until 1942, thirteen years after McKinney became Hollywood's first Black leading lady. This reveals a contradiction between the white Jewish studio heads' stance on race and other white Jews' growing support for the Black civil rights struggle. Discrimination against Blacks in Hollywood was more severe while the studios were establishing themselves in the 1920s and 1930s. By 1942, Lena Horne would receive the opportunity denied to Nina Mae McKinney in 1929. The timing also coincided with the struggle against discrimination in the United States military during the World War II era and the courtroom battles that preceded the grassroots movements of the modern civil rights era of the 1950s and 1960s.

Before becoming an actor, Horne began her entertainment career as a singer and a dancer. At age 16, she began dancing. Eventually, she began singing at the Cotton Club in Harlem, where white audiences enjoyed up-and-coming Black entertainers. In such a high-pressure atmosphere, especially for someone so young, Horne experienced highs and lows. Fortunately, legendary performers Cab Calloway and Duke Ellington chose to mentor her ("Lena Horne"). Horne's first film appearance was in 1935 as a dancer in Cab Calloway's musical short *Jitterbug Party*. In 1938, Horne appeared in *The Duke is Tops* opposite race film actor Ralph Cooper, the "Dark Gable," who was also a dancer, singer, former Apollo theater emcee, and one of the first Black actors, if not the first, to have a fan club (Gavin 64; "Ralph Cooper Fans in Cincinnati Organize"). Cooper, who had been unable to break into Hollywood acting, had recently become a partner in the race film company Million Dollar Productions. He had hoped to cast Nina Mae McKinney for the lead role as Ethel Andrews in *The Duke is Tops*, but she was unavailable at the time (Gavin 64). Cooper wasted little time in contacting Lena Horne, whom the *Pittsburgh Courier* hailed as the "Prettiest Girl in Show Business" (Gavin 64). The film was released in June 1938, and Horne shined in the role. In response to Horne's soaring popularity, the studio re-released the film as *The Bronze Venus* ("The Duke is Tops").

After signing with MGM in 1942, Horne appeared in her first MGM film. Horne was an uncredited singer in *Panama Hattie*, starring Red Skelton ("Lena Horne"; "Panama Hattie"). Her next film would be her breakthrough. Horne would land the role of temptress Georgia Brown in *Cabin in the Sky*, MGM's first all-Black cast musical since *Hallelujah* and the first from any other Hollywood studio since *The Green Pastures*, a 1936 Warner Bros. film that Black critics and audiences blasted for its stereotypical representation of Black people (Gavin 115). Featuring Ethel Waters, Eddie "Rochester" Anderson, Rex Ingram, and Louis Armstrong, *Cabin in the Sky* was released in 1943.

Immediately after Horne signed with MGM, family friend Walter White of the NAACP was concerned about her future and the representation of both Horne and her race because Black people were still relegated to stereotypical roles in comedies and musicals. Horne's newfound status showed some degree of progress, and it would have been a shame to see her reduced to degrading or subservient roles (Bogle, *Dorothy Dandridge: A Biography* 96). It was refreshing for Black audiences to see Horne on screen and in person. Her persona, always displaying her beautiful smile, was charming and elegant.

Born Lena Mary Calhoun Horne in 1917 in Brooklyn, New York, she was the daughter of Edwin 'Teddy' Horne Jr. and Edna Scottron Horne, the light-skinned and "green-eyed daughter of a Native American mother and a successful Portuguese Negro inventor" who dreamed of stardom as an actress (Gavin 12). Her grandfather, Edwin Horne Sr., was part English and part American Indian but was passing for Black because arguably "during Reconstruction, Native Americans had suffered worse discrimination than Blacks" (Gavin 10).

Lena's grandmother Cora Calhoun Horne had more white people in her immediate ancestry than Black. Cora deeply resented whites and instilled that in young Lena. Edwin Sr. and Cora had been quite active in the cause of civil rights. Cora would later sign up a 2-year-old Lena for the NAACP (Gavin 11-13). Both of Lena's parents came from families who, due to their light complexions, lived much more comfortably than most Black people. They were college-educated and lived comfortably, but Lena's father, Teddy, rejected his family's expectation that he would attend college. Instead, he relied on his charm and good looks, soon becoming a con artist, gambler, and "master hustler" (Gavin 10-12). When Lena was three years old, her father left her and her mother. He lied about being sick, "perhaps with tuberculosis," to have an excuse to leave. Although he later sent her gifts and an allowance, his absence left her with the pain of abandonment, and she grew up unhappy much of the time (Gavin 13).

Lena Horne would become the first Black actor openly billed and promoted as a Hollywood star, even though the major studios denied her the opportunity to land a major dramatic role like her white peers such as Ava Gardner, who received the role Horne desired as the "mulatto" Julie in MGM's *Show Boat* remake (97).

Despite having received a taste of stardom, Horne only had 14 credited movie roles. Ten occurred after *Cabin in the Sky* and *Stormy Weather*, both released in 1943 ("Lena Horne"). According to *Dorothy Dandridge: A Biography*, by the time MGM was ready to consider a Black woman for a dramatic lead, the studio felt that Lena Horne was too old. Convinced that selling youth was vital, the studio instead considered Dorothy Dandridge (Bogle 217).

Dorothy Dandridge was born in Cleveland, Ohio, on November 9, 1922, and she began performing in a singing duo with her sister, Vivian, after their mother, Ruby Dandridge, pushed them in that direction. Ruby Dandridge was an actress known for her minor roles late in the 1962 television series *Father of the Bride* and the films *Cabin in the Sky* in 1943, *Home in Oklahoma* in 1946, and *A Hole in the Head* in 1959 ("Dorothy Dandridge;" "Ruby Dandridge"). The Dandridge Sisters, first calling themselves "The Wonder Children," traveled and sang in Black Baptist churches, hoping to eventually get into show business (LoBianco). Occasionally, their mother joined them in their performances. Hoping to find employment during the Depression, they moved to Los Angeles.

Dorothy and her sister made minor appearances in films such as *The Big Broadcast of 1936*, starring the Nicholas Brothers (dancing duo), and *Easy to Take*, both in 1935 (Bogle, *Dorothy Dandridge: A Biography* 42; "Dorothy Dandridge"). In *The Big Broadcast of 1936*, the Dandridge Sisters—Dorothy Dandridge, Vivian Dandridge, and Etta Jones—and the Nicholas Brothers—Harold and Fayard—appeared in separate scenes (Bogle 41; "Dorothy Dandridge"). Dandridge first appeared on her own in minor roles in films such as *Teacher's Beau*, one of Hal Roach's *Our Gang* shorts, in 1935, and *A Day at the Races*, a Marx Brothers' feature, in 1937 ("Dorothy Dandridge"). She also appeared without her sister in *Sun Valley Serenade* in 1941, and this time, she performed in a scene with the Nicholas Brothers: a rendition of "Chattanooga Choo Choo" (LoBianco). Studios first began to take notice when she appeared in *Tarzan's*

Peril in 1951. She was willing to play the exotic African princess, but similar to Nina Mae McKinney early in McKinney's career, she refused maid roles.[16] Studios began to take her more seriously when she starred in *Bright Road* in 1953 with Harry Belafonte (LoBianco). Hollywood became willing to acknowledge Dandridge as a sex symbol, as long as she did not have kissing scenes with white men.

In 1954, Dorothy Dandridge received her breakout role in *Carmen Jones*, a film adaptation of the Bizet play *Carmen*. The film's male lead was Harry Belafonte, who went on to become one of the most famous Black actors of all time (with an active career spanning 1953 to 2018), was the first Black actor to win an Emmy ("Outstanding Performance in a Variety or Musical Program or Series" for "Revlon Review" on CBS's *Tonight with Harry Belafonte* in 1960), and was the first recording artist to have an album (*Calypso*, featuring "Day-O" in 1956) sell more than one million copies ("Harry Belafonte"; "Harry Belafonte: Emmy Awards, Nominations and Wins"; "Harry Belafonte: 2014 Governors Awards"). Dandridge and Belafonte delivered masterful performances in *Carmen Jones* and their chemistry was convincing. Meanwhile, Dandridge was also in demand as a nightclub singer (LoBianco).

Dorothy Dandridge went on to become the first African American to receive an Academy Award nomination for "Best Actress." She was nominated for her eponymous role in *Carmen Jones* (1954), but Grace Kelly would win for her role as Georgie Elgin in *The Country Girl* ("1954 Academy Award Winners and History"). Despite the milestone Oscar nomination, she had to wait three years for her next movie, *Island in the Sun*. Her opportunities, including the typical male "gaze" role, remained limited. Before her death, she appeared in only five more films, including *Tamango* (in which Dandridge's role violated the Hays Code's anti-miscegenation rule) in 1958 and *Porgy and Bess* in 1959 ("Dorothy Dandridge"). Dandridge, arguably "the first black *major* movie star" (emphasis mine, Mills 10), was on the brink of superstardom but was denied the chance to realize it. Professional and personal struggles took their toll on her. Unfortunately, her career was cut short by her tragic death from an "acute overdose of Tofranil," an anti-depressant, on September 8, 1965, in West Hollywood (LoBianco; "Dorothy Dandridge").[17]

Similar to Nina Mae McKinney, Dorothy Dandridge had a troubled personal life, including two failed marriages. Dandridge's were more widely publicized, of course, because she had been able to go much farther in Hollywood. Dandridge's first marriage was in September 1942 to Harold Nicholas of the Nicholas Brothers dancing duo, whom she met on the set of *The Big Broadcast* of 1936 (LoBianco). Dandridge's affair with her *Carmen Jones* director Otto Preminger is also well-known. It was perceived as scandalous because Preminger was white and an accomplished Hollywood director. It has been easy for people to accuse Dandridge of trying to use her relationship with Preminger to get ahead in her career, but it seemed that she genuinely wanted to marry him. She became pregnant with his child, but he left her alone, and she had an abortion ("Dorothy Dandridge"). The downward spiral in Dandridge's personal life worsened. In 1959, Dandridge made the mistake of marrying Jack Denison, a white man who had the reputation of being a "gold digger" (LoBianco). He left her after depleting all her funds through his "get rich quick" schemes (LoBianco). Dandridge and Harold Nicholas had a daughter who was born with brain damage, which impaired her mental development. In addition to the stress of her profession, the difficulties involved in caring for her daughter took a toll on Dandridge. She suffered tremendous stress and depression, and she developed an alcohol problem ("Dorothy Dandridge"). Around the same time as her relationship with Denison, she was also deeply concerned about her sister's health, especially when she was unable to contact her (Bogle, *Dorothy Dandridge: A Biography* 401).

Unlike Fredi Washington, Lena Horne did not have the complexion or hair texture to pass for white, but Lena's skin color was lighter than Nina Mae McKinney's. Thus, compared to Nina Mae's, Lena's appearance was even less threatening to whites' commonly held belief that white women were the standard of beauty and womanhood. Each of them possessed the talent and the "it" factor that warranted the spotlight. They knew how to project the persona of a star and sex symbol for any audience without reducing themselves to being Jezebel figures, but Dorothy Dandridge's complexion and hair texture were more similar to Nina Mae McKinney's than Lena Horne's.

Although there seems to be no record of Lena Horne or Dorothy Dandridge acknowledging Nina Mae McKinney as one of their influences, it is fitting to end this chapter with Horne and Dandridge since they were the Black actresses who pushed their way through the door that McKinney cracked open. An overview of the careers of Nina Mae McKinney's predecessors, contemporaries, and successors recognizes some of the most prominent Black figures in early twentieth-century entertainment. They gained acclaim, fame, and fandom. Yet none of McKinney's forerunners achieved Hollywood stardom, and neither did most of her peers. Indeed, Hollywood's first Black leading lady, Nina Mae McKinney, was the first Black star in Hollywood and the most logical precursor to Black superstardom in Hollywood.

Conclusion

McKinney's Rightful Place in History

As an on-screen actor, Nina Mae McKinney was the first Black star in Hollywood and the most logical precursor to Black superstardom in Hollywood. McKinney would have become the first *major* Black star or superstar in Hollywood if institutionalized racism and sexism had not prevented her from realizing her full potential. Delving more deeply into the matter than just a simple condemnation of racism and sexism, *Nina Mae McKinney: At the Dawn of Black Hollywood Stardom* seeks to present an overview of McKinney's Southern background and the mechanisms that were in place at the major film studios. It also illustrates the challenges of an early twentieth-century society in which institutionalized racism was deeply rooted and upheld at all costs. It explains that even though the studios were willing to exploit the dollars of the female audience and to appropriate the culture and creativity of Black people, the assimilated European Jews who ran the Hollywood studios were careful to avoid taking actions that the dominant group of white males in America might perceive as promoting gender or racial equality.

Through a comparative study of elite white actors Barbara Stanwyck, Carole Lombard, and Miriam Hopkins and non-white actors Anna May Wong and Lupe Vélez, this book has illustrated that Hollywood studios denied nonwhite actors—especially Black actors such as McKinney—opportunities to create their own public personas and enjoy non-stereotypical roles, the perquisites of stardom, and long-term career growth.

Even in light of Hollywood studios' discrimination against McKinney after her appearance in *Hallelujah*, she was not content to simply find work in race films. In her attempt at agency, she chose strong, non-stereotypical, or at least balanced, leading roles. She was also determined to find success on her own terms overseas.

McKinney's one major Hollywood role as Chick in *Hallelujah* is equally important to Black stardom as the entire careers of white actors such as Clara Bow and Greta Garbo are to female stardom and stardom, in general. McKinney's more well-known successors Lena Horne and Dorothy Dandridge did not have an easy path, either, but at least they are widely remembered today as important trailblazers. Nina Mae McKinney should be equally well-known outside of a small circle of scholars and film enthusiasts, and today's actors should come to recognize her as their predecessor.

While lavish, reckless lifestyles have always been a destructive force in Hollywood culture, perhaps treachery and malicious gossip are even more ingrained. Especially considering some critics' negative but unsubstantiated comments about McKinney's role in *Hallelujah* as well as the drug rumors and the seductress or Jezebel rumors, it is apparent that McKinney's legacy as an entertainer needs to be rescued and that her reputation needs to be restored. The history of American pop culture is filled with imperfect people and tragic heroes who have wrestled with various demons. For example, an unflinching look at Ray Charles in the film *Ray* (2005) served to elevate his status, not condemn him for his mistakes. Some critics have vilified Charles for secularizing gospel music and for abusing drugs. Yet we rightfully acknowledge him as a true pioneer and one of our most influential entertainers. He was also a musical genius who did not allow a racist society to strip away his dignity. Although Dorothy Dandridge's career was curtailed by her tragic death, she is rightfully remembered for her contributions and her influence on later actresses and singers. We must also recognize Nina Mae McKinney's humanity and her presence as a preeminent archetype in film.

Before her death, Nina Mae McKinney was denied a chance to tell her story. Unlike notable Black performers such as Ethel

Waters, publishers rejected McKinney's autobiography (Bourne 89). Regrettably, details about her life and her career have been lost as a result. For example, according to a short report in the February 13, 1958, issue of *Jet* magazine, McKinney explained that her Hollywood movie opportunities disappeared because she "refused to 'act right' with certain wolfish producers" ("Ex-Movie Actress Nina Mae McKinney"). McKinney refused to be a "service girl" who would "do anything" for a break, and she refused to be the Jezebel or vixen that some critics and scholars have unjustly mislabeled her as. Her autobiography might have provided stories and details about these and other topics from her life and career. Publishers might have welcomed candid reflections about McKinney's life choices, but her book likely went much further. It might have also included a thorough exposé of the terrible things that powerful white people, including racists and sexists, did or tried to do to her and the people close to her.

Similar to her character Chick, McKinney paid the price for setting such a high standard and boldly coming to the forefront. McKinney's career followed a pattern opposite that of talented white actresses who were allowed to grow after their breakout Hollywood performances. McKinney made her debut as an actress in a leading role in 1929, only to be reduced to supporting as well uncredited roles and eventually relegated to the very role she bitterly resisted early in her acting career—the maid—on screen in the 1940s and in real life by the 1960s.

Early in her career, McKinney had the talent, beauty, and stamina to become the first Black superstar in Hollywood. She was a convincing actor who possessed a pleasant voice, a curvaceous figure, and a pretty face according to her audiences. McKinney became the archetype for the Black leading lady Hollywood would later accept in terms of talent and physical characteristics. Ever since *Hallelujah*, later actresses, Black and non-Black, have borrowed or demonstrated McKinney's spunk, playfulness, quirky facial expressions, eye acting, mannerisms, rhythm, and stage presence, even if they are unaware of her being the original source. The spirit of an independent city girl and a womanly yet girlish presence distinguishes McKinney's performance in *Hallelujah*. Although flawed and human, Chick represents a modern woman and perhaps a heroine or antihero figure several decades ahead of her time—the likes of which did not become widely popularized in Hollywood until Pam Grier's female leads in the 1970s.

In *Hallelujah*, a certain "it factor" is apparent in Nina Mae McKinney's presence and in her acting. The industry and its fans usually honor actors for their body of work, even if certain scenes stand out in particular movies. Despite Hollywood constraints that limited her career growth, McKinney shines in noteworthy performances in films such as *Gang Smashers* and *Safe in Hell*. Yet it is McKinney's breakout role in *Hallelujah* that highlights the full range of talent she possessed.

In addition to revealing Nina Mae McKinney's indomitable independence, audacity, and desire for artistic integrity, *Nina Mae McKinney: At the Dawn of Black Hollywood Stardom* presents McKinney and Chick as modern women ahead of their time who sought to control their own destinies instead of adhering to the typical story arcs of a tragic mulatto or a vixen. This book should inspire research on other early-twentieth-century figures in entertainment who deserve more recognition than they have received, and it might lead to new revelations about Nina Mae McKinney. This book has sought to reveal McKinney's self-determination, restore her reputation, and promote a greater appreciation for her legacy. It is long overdue. Nina Mae McKinney must take her rightful place in history.

Nina Mae McKinney in *Hallelujah* (MGM, 1929) publicity photo.
Courtesy of the Margaret Herrick Library at the Academy of
Motion Picture Arts & Sciences.

Nina Mae McKinney in *Hallelujah* (MGM, 1929) publicity photo 2.
Courtesy of the Margaret Herrick Library at the Academy of
Motion Picture Arts & Sciences.

Nina Mae McKinney in *Hallelujah* (MGM, 1929) publicity photo 3. Courtesy of the Margaret Herrick Library at the Academy of Motion Picture Arts & Sciences.

Nina Mae McKinney in *Hallelujah* (MGM, 1929) publicity photo 4. Pictured (left to right): William Fountaine as Hot Shot, Nina Mae McKinney as Chick, and Daniel L. Haynes as Ezekiel. Courtesy of the Margaret Herrick Library at the Academy of Motion Picture Arts & Sciences.

Nina Mae McKinney in *Hallelujah* (MGM, 1929) – close-up.

Nina Mae McKinney in *Hallelujah* (MGM, 1929) – close-up 2.

Nina Mae McKinney in *Hallelujah* (MGM, 1929) – riverside sermon.

Nina Mae McKinney in *Pinky* (Twentieth Century Fox, 1949).
Publicity photo by Gilles Petard/Redferns.

Lancaster County Wall of Fame photo 1. Commissioned by the Lancaster County Council of the Arts. Paintings by Ralph Waldrop (1985). Photo by Dabian Witherspoon. Featured historical figures (left to right): President of the United States Andrew Jackson, "father of modern gynecology" J. Marion Sims, businessman/author/World War I pilot Col. Elliott White Springs, actor/singer/dancer Nina Mae McKinney, and astronaut Charles M. Duke Jr.

Lancaster County Wall of Fame photo 2: Nina Mae McKinney close-up. Commissioned by the Lancaster County Council of the Arts. Painting by Ralph Waldrop (1985). Photo by Dabian Witherspoon.

Works Cited

"Academy of Motion Picture Arts and Sciences." Oscars.org. Academy of Motion Picture Arts and Sciences, n.d.

"Adolph Zukor Biography." IMDb.com. Internet Movie Database. Amazon, n.d.

African American Legacy of the Woodlawn Cemetery. The Woodlawn Cemetery, n.d. www.thewoodlawncemetery.org/africanamerican. html.

Akbar, Na'im. "Racism: A Mental Disorder." Interview by Listervelt Middleton. *For the People*. South Carolina Educational Television. SC ETV, SC, 1987. TV.

Alberoni, Francesco. "The Powerless 'Elite': Theory and Sociological Research on the Phenomenon of the Stars." *Stardom and Celebrity: A Reader*. Ed. Sean Redmond and Su Holmes. Thousand Oaks, CA: Sage Publications, 2007: 65-77.

American Masters: Vaudeville. Writ. Greg Palmer. KTCS Seattle, 1997. DVD.

Anae, Nicole. "'They Will All Be My Color': Nina Mae McKinney and Black Internationalism in 1930s Australia." *To Turn the Whole World Over: Black Women and Internationalism*, Eds. Keisha N. Blain and Tiffany M. Gill. Black Internationalism series. Urbana: University of Illinois Press, 2019: 123-148.

Anderson, Lisa M. *Mammies No More: The Changing Image of Black Women on Stage and Screen*. New York: Rowman & Littlefield Publishers, Inc., 1997. Print.

"An Oral History with Leo C. Popkin." Interview by Douglas Bell. Oral History Program. Margaret Herrick Library. Academy of Motion Picture Arts and Sciences 2007: 90+.

Anna Christie. Dir. Clarence Brown. Perf. Greta Garbo and Charles Bickford. MGM, 1930. Warner Bros, 2005. DVD.

BaadAsssss Cinema: A Bold Look at 70's Blaxploitation Films. Dir. Isaac Julien. IFC, 2002. DVD.

"Bakay, Garbage, Armstrong, Hudgins, and 'Hallelujah' on Dazzling Regal Bill." *Chicago Defender* 1 Feb. 1930: 10. *Black Entertainers in African American Newspaper Articles. Vol. 1: An Annotated Bibliography of the Chicago Defender, the Afro-American (Baltimore), the Los Angeles Sentinel, and the New York Amsterdam News, 1910-1950.* Ed. Charlene Regester. Jefferson, NC: McFarland & Company, 2002: 37. Entry 589. Print.

Baker, Jean-Claude and Chris Chase. *Josephine: The Hungry Heart.* New York: Random House, 1993. Print.

Baldwin, Faith. "Do Hollywood Women Spoil Their Men?" *Photoplay* 53.5 (May 1939): 18. Print.

Baldwin, James. "The Devil Finds Work." *James Baldwin Collected Essays.* 1976. The Library of America. New York: Penguin, 1998: 477-572. Print.

Ball, Christine. "The Silencing of Clara Bow." GadflyOnline.com. Gadfly Productions. Mar./Apr. 2001. Web. n.d.

"Barbara Stanwyck." IMDb.com. Internet Movie Database. Amazon, n.d. Web. 8 Mar. 2014.

Barker, Chris. *Cultural Studies: Theory and Practice.* Thousand Oaks, CA: Sage Publications, 2011. Print.

Bartira, Donyale. "Nina Mae McKinney (1912-1697)." *Black Jazz Artists (19–20th Century),* 14 Mar. 2021, blackjazzartist. blogspot.com.

Bass, Jack, and Marilyn W. Thompson. *Strom: The Complicated Personal and Political Life of Strom Thurmond.* Cambridge, MA: Public Affairs/Perseus Books, 2005. Print.

BBC: The Voice of Britain. Dir. Stuart Legg. Prod. John Grierson. Perf. Nina Mae McKinney and H.G. Wells. GPO Film Unit. 1935.

"Being Too White is the Problem of Fredi Washington." *Afro-American* 19 Jan. 1935. Fredi Washington Papers, 1925-1979. Amistad Research Center, Inc. Tulane University, New Orleans, LA. Microfilm.

Benshoff, Harry M., and Sean Griffin. *America on Film: Representing Race, Class, Gender, and Sexuality at the Movies.* Malden, MA: Wiley-Blackwell, 2011. Print.

Berry, Venise T., and Carmen L. Manning-Miller, eds. *Mediated Messages and African American Culture: Contemporary Issues.* Thousand Oaks, CA: Sage Publications, 1996. Print.

"Bert Williams." IMDb.com. Internet Movie Database, n.d. Web. 26 Feb. 2014.

The Big Parade. Dir. King Vidor and George W. Hill. Perf. John Gilbert. MGM, 1925. Warner Bros, 2013. DVD.

Bird of Paradise. Dir. King Vidor. Perf. Delores del Rio and Joel McCrea. RKO Radio Pictures, 1932. IMDb.com. Internet Movie Database.

Birth of a Nation. Writ. Thomas F. Dixon Jr. Dir. D.W. Griffith. David W. Griffith Corp., 1915. IMDb.com. Internet Movie Database.

"The Birth of Hollywood (1907-1920)." *Moguls & Movie Stars: A History of Hollywood.* Turner Classic Movies, 2010. Vol. 2. DVD.

Black and Tan Fantasy. Dir. Dudley Murphy. Perf. Fredi Washington and Duke Ellington. RCA, 1929. Hollywood Rhythm Volume I: The Best of Jazz & Blues/The Paramount Musical Shorts. Kino Video, 2001. DVD.

Blackbirds. Dir. and Prod. Lew Leslie. Broadway. 1928. IBDb.com. Internet Broadway Database.

Blackbirds. Dir. and Prod. Lew Leslie. Broadway. 1939. IBDb.com. Internet Broadway Database.

The Black Film Center/Archive. College of Arts and Sciences. Indiana University Bloomington. <http://www.indiana.edu/~bfca.shtml.> Web. 11 Oct. 2011.

"'The 'Black Garbo': Nina McKinney.'" *African American Registry.* <http://www.aaregistry.org/historic_events/view/Black-garbo-nina-mckinney.> Web. 24 Oct. 2011.

The Black Network. Dir. Roy Mack. Perf. Nina Mae McKinney and the Nicholas Brothers. Vitaphone Corp./Warner Bros, 1936. *Hallelujah* DVD Release. Warner Bros, 2006.

"Blacks Attack Man: Race Riot Is Averted." *The Lancaster News* 9 Aug. 1929: 1. Microfilm.

Blight, David W. *Race and Reunion: The Civil War in American Memory.* Cambridge, MA: Belknap of Harvard UP, 2001. Print.

The Blood of Jesus. Dir. Spencer Williams. Amegro Films/ Sack Amusement Enterprises, 1941. IMDb.com. Internet Movie Database.

Bogle, Donald. *Bright Boulevards, Bold Dreams: The Story of Black Hollywood.* Fourth Edition. New York: One World/Ballantine Books, 2005. Print.

Bogle, Donald. *Dorothy Dandridge: A Biography.* New York: Amistad, 1997. Print.

Bogle, Donald. *Heat Wave: The Life and Career of Ethel Waters.* New York: Harper, 2011. Print.

Bogle, Donald. *Toms, Coons, Mulattoes, Mammies, and Bucks: An Interpretive History of Blacks in American Films.* Fourth Edition. New York: Continuum, 2001. Print.

Bordwell, David, Janet Staiger, and Kristin Thompson. *The Classical Hollywood Cinema: Film Style & Mode of Production to 1960.* New York: Columbia University Press, 1985. Print.

Bourne, Stephen. *Nina Mae McKinney: The Black Garbo.* BearManor Media, 2011.

Bret, David. *Greta Garbo: Divine Star.* London: The Robson Press, 2013. Print.

"Bride 13." IMDb.com. Internet Movie Database, n.d. Web. 26 Feb. 2014.

"The Broadway Melody." IMDb.com. Internet Movie Database, n.d. Web. 15 Mar. 2014.

Broadway: The American Musical. Dir. Michael Kantor. Nar. Julie Andrews. 6 Vols. PBS, 2004.

The Bronze Buckaroo. Dir. Richard C. Kahn. Perf. Herb Jeffries and Lucius Brooks. Hollywood Pictures Corporation, 1939. IMDb.com. Internet Movie Database.

"Brother, Can You Spare a Dream? (1929-1942)." *Moguls & Movie Stars: A History of Hollywood.* Turner Classic Movies, 2010. Vol. 4. DVD.

Brown, Beth. "Making Movies for Women." *Moving Picture World* 26 Mar. 1927: 34. Print.

Burr, Ty. *Gods Like Us: On Movie Stardom and Modern Fame.* New York: Anchor, 2013. Print.

Cabin in the Sky. Dir. Vicente Minelli. Perf. Ethel Waters, Lena Horne, and Eddie "Rochester" Anderson. MGM, 1943. IMDb.com. Internet Movie Database.

"'Cabin in the Sky,' a Musical Fantasy." *New York Times*, 28 May 1943.

"Carl Laemmle Biography." IMDb.com. Internet Movie Database. Amazon, n.d. Web. 5 Mar. 2014.

Carman, Emily Susan. "Independent Stardom: Female Stars and Freelance Labor in 1930s Hollywood." UMI/ProQuest. Ph.D. Dissertation. UCLA, 2008.

Carmen Jones. Dir. Otto Preminger. Perf. Dorothy Dandridge and Harry Belafonte. Otto Preminger Films/Carlyle Productions, 1954. Twentieth Century Fox, 2001. DVD.

"Carole Lombard." IMDb.com. Internet Movie Database. Amazon, n.d. Web. 8 Mar. 2014.

Caves, Richard E. *Creative Industries: Contracts Between Art and Commerce.* Cambridge: Harvard UP, 2000. Print.

Censorship Report. 15 Oct. 1929. *Hallelujah* Core Collection Clippings File. Margaret Herrick Library. Academy of Motion Picture Arts and Sciences.

"Charles Gilpin." IMDb.com. Internet Movie Database, n.d. Web. 26 Feb. 2014.

Chilton, John. *Who's Who of Jazz.* Fourth Edition. New York: De Capo Press, 1985. Print.

Chocolate and Cream. London. Leicester Square Theater. 13 Feb. 1933.

"Chorus Girl, Latest Model: No Boyish Figure Here." *The Lancaster News* 6 Sept. 1929, News About Town and County sec.: 4. Microfilm.

Chude-Sokei, Louis. *The Last "Darky": Bert Williams, Black-on-Black Minstrelsy, and the African Diaspora.* Durham, NC: Duke UP, 2006. Print.

Church of the Transfiguration (New York, New York). "Historic 'Little Church Around the Corner' Celebrates 175th Anniversary." *Episcopal News Service* 3 Oct. 2023. <https://www.episcopalnewsservice.org/pressreleases/historic-little-church-around-the-corner-celebrates-175th-anniversary/>.

"City Schools Open Thursday (September 5)." *The Lancaster News* 3 Sept. 1929, News About Town and County: 3. Microfilm.

"Clara Bow." IMDb.com. Internet Movie Database, n.d. Web. 20 Feb. 2024.

"Clara Bow Resents Compliment to Nina." *Lincoln Journal Star* 1 Nov. 1929: 5. www.newspapers.com/image/66430834.

"Col. Jason S. Joy." MPPDA.flinders.edu.au. MPPDA Digital Archive/Flinders Institute for Research in the Humanities, 2013. Web. 04 Dec. 2013. <http://mppda.flinders.edu.au/people/297>.

Col. Jason S. Joy Letter to George Kann at MGM. 6 Oct. 1928. *Hallelujah* Core Collection Clippings File. Margaret Herrick Library. Academy of Motion Picture Arts and Sciences.

Colonel Joy Memo. 4 Oct. 1928. *Hallelujah* Core Collection Clippings File. Margaret Herrick Library. Academy of Motion Picture Arts and Sciences.

Col. Joy's Letter to George Kann, 1929. 11 July 1929. *Hallelujah* Core Collection Clippings File. Margaret Herrick Library. Academy of Motion Picture Arts and Sciences.

Col. Joy Letter to Lamar Trotti. 29 Oct. 1928. *Hallelujah* Core Collection Clippings File. Margaret Herrick Library. Academy of Motion Picture Arts and Sciences.

"Col. Leroy Springs—Re: I Have an Old Bible." Query. Ancestry. com. Ancestry, 2 Sept. 2002.

"Col. Leroy Springs—Re: The True Story of the Springs Mills Industries/African American Descendants." Query. Ancestry. com. Ancestry, 22 Sept. 2002.

"Col. Leroy Springs, 12 Nov 1861–7 Apr 1931." Memorial Page. ID: 204303255. [database online]. Find a Grave, https://www. findagrave.com/memorial/204303255/leroy-springs. Accessed 25 Jan. 2024.

Colonel Joy's Resume. 22 Feb. 1929. *Hallelujah* Core Collection Clippings File. Margaret Herrick Library. Academy of Motion Picture Arts and Sciences.

"Color Question Stirs England: Labor Legislator to Push Matter When Parliament Reassembles." *The Lancaster News* 29 Oct. 1929: unknown. Microfilm

Copper Canyon. Dir. John Farrow. Perf. Ray Milland and Hedy Lamarr. ParamountPictures,1950. Paramount, 2003. DVD.

Corliss, Richard. "The 25 Most Important Films on Race." *Time.* Entertainment. Time, Inc., 2013. Web. 29 Nov. 2013.

Courtney, Susan. "Picturizing Race: Hollywood's Censorship of Miscegenation and Production of Racial Visibility through *Imitation of Life.*" *Genders* vol. 27. 1998. Genders Online Journal. Boulder, CO: University of Colorado. Web. https://

web.archive.org/web/20130530175734/http://www.genders. org/g27/g27_pr.html.

Cripps, Thomas. *Slow Fade to Black*. Oxford University Press, 1977. Print.

"Curtain Time: Negro Cast Presents Well-Acted Performance of 'Rain' at Bedford." *Brooklyn Daily Eagle* (Brooklyn, NY). 16 Aug. 1951:5. <www.newspapers.com/image/52856961>.

Dancer, Maurice. "Charley, Gloria and Race Screen Stars Mix at Vidor Party." *Pittsburgh Courier* 9 Feb. 1929: 1. *Black Entertainers in African American Newspaper Articles. Vol. 2: An Annotated Bibliography of the Pittsburgh Courier and the California Eagle, 1914-1950*. Ed. Charlene Regester. Jefferson, NC: McFarland & Company, 2009: 74. Entry 2293. Print.

Danger Street. Dir. Lew Landers. Perf. Jane Withers and Robert Lowery. Pine-Thomas Productions, 1947. Reel Enterprises, 2007. DVD.

"Daniel L. Haynes." IMDb.com. Internet Movie Database, n.d. Web. 20 Feb. 2024.

Dark Waters. Dir. André de Toth. Perf. Nina Mae McKinney, Merle Oberon, and Franchot Tone. Benedict Bogeaus Production, 1944. Dark Waters Productions/Image Entertainment, 1994. DVD.

"Darlings of Royalty: Beautiful U.S. Negro Women Win Hearts of Many Men of Noble Blood in Europe and Asia." *Ebony* (June 1953): 36-39.

"Darryl F. Zanuck Biography." IMDb.com. Internet Movie Database. Amazon, n.d. Web. 5 Mar. 2014.

"David O. Selznick Biography." IMDb.com. Internet Movie Database. Amazon, n.d. Web. 5 Mar. 2014.

"David Sarnoff." IMDb.com. Internet Movie Database. Amazon, n.d. Web. 5 Mar. 2014.

Davis, Angela Y. *Blues Legacies and Black Feminism: Gertrude "Ma" Rainey, Bessie Smith, and Billie Holiday*. New York: Vintage, 1999. Print.

De Leighbur, Don. "Nina Mae, First Glamour Gal of Pix, Makes Good in Comeback." *Los Angeles Sentinel* 15 June 1944.

Delgado, Richard, and Jean Stefancic. *Critical Race Theory: An Introduction.* New York: New York UP, 2001. Print.

De Santis, Christopher C., ed. *The Collected Works of Langston Hughes: Essays on Art, Race, Politics, and World Affairs.* Vol. 9. Columbia, MO: University of Missouri Press,2002. Print.

"Describes Robeson Film as Best British Hit." *Pittsburgh Courier* 27 Apr. 1934: 8. *Black Entertainers in African American Newspaper Articles. Vol. 2: An Annotated Bibliography of the Pittsburgh Courier and the California Eagle, 1914-1950.* Ed. Charlene Regester. Jefferson, NC: McFarland & Company, 2009: 207. Entry 5965. Print.

The Devil's Daughter. Dir. Arthur H. Leonard. Perf. Nina Mae McKinney, Ida James, and Jack Carter. Sack Amusement, 1939. IMDb.com. Internet Movie Database.

"The Devil's Daughter." IMDb.com. Internet Movie Database. Web. 2 Dec. 2013.

"'Didn't Raise My Daughter to Be an Actress,' Says Mama McKinney, But She's Glad Nina Mae Made Good." *Afro-American* 15 Feb. 1936.

Dirks, Tim. "Film History Before 1920."*Film History Before 1920.* AMC Networks, n.d. Web. 15 Sept. 2013.

"Dirt Craze Due to Women." *Variety* 103.1 (16 June 1931): 1.

"Dorothy Dandridge." IMDb.com. Internet Movie Database. Web. 2 Dec. 2013.

Douglass, Frederick. *Narrative of the Life of Frederick Douglass, An American Slave.* Reprinted Ed. New York: Penguin Books USA, Inc., 1982. Print.

Dowd, Nancy, David Shepard, and King Vidor. *King Vidor.* Metuchen, NJ: Directors Guild of America & The Scarecrow, 1988. Nancy Dowd and David Shepard interview director King Vidor. Print.

"The Dream Merchants (1920-1928)." *Moguls & Movie Stars: A History of Hollywood.* Turner Classic Movies, 2010. Vol.3. DVD.

Du Bois, W.E.B. *Souls of Black Folk.* 1903. New York: Penguin, 1996. Print.

Du Bois, W. E. B. *The Wisdom of W. E. B. Du Bois.* Aberjhani, ed. New York: Citadel Press, 2003. Print.

The Duke is Tops. Dir. William L. Nolte. Perf. Lena Horne. Million Dollar Productions, 1938. IMDb.com. Internet Movie Database.

"The Duke Is Tops." IMDb.com. Internet Movie Database, n.d. Web. 29 Nov. 2013.

Dyer, Richard, and Paul McDonald. *Stars.* British Film Institute, 2008. Print.

Egan, Bill. *Florence Mills: Harlem Jazz Queen.* Lanham, MD: Scarecrow, 2004. Print.

Elliot White Springs. State of South Carolina Certificate of Birth. South Carolina Department of Archives and History, Columbia, South Carolina. Web. South Carolina Delayed Births, 1766-1900 and City of Charleston, South Carolina Births, 1877-1901 [database online]. Ancestry.com, 2007. 14 Dec. 2013.

The Emperor Jones. Dir. Dudley Murphy. Perf. Paul Robeson and Fredi Washington. United Artists, 1933. East West Entertainment, 2008. DVD.

Eschner, Kat. "Remembering Paul Robeson, Actor, Sportsman and Leader." *Smithsonian Magazine* 23 Jan. 2017. < https://www.smithsonianmag.com/smart-news/remembering-paul-robeson-actor-sportsman-and-leader-180961834/.>

Ethnic Notions. Writ., dir., and prod. Marlon Riggs. California Newsreel, 1987. Signifyin' Works, 2004. DVD.

Everett, Anna. *Returning the Gaze: A Genealogy of Black Film Criticism 1909-1949.* Duke University Press, 2001. Print.

"Ex-Movie Actress Nina Mae McKinney." *Jet* 13 Feb. 1958: 64.

Fagan, Daniel. *America's Film Legacy: The Authoritative Guide to the Landmark Movies in the National Film Registry*. New York: Continuum, 2009.

"Famous Vaudeville Team Appears Tonight in Talkie at Empire." *Hawaii Tribune-Herald* 10 July 1931: 2.

"The Films of King Vidor." Program Notes. *Hallelujah*. 28 May 1971. Raw data. Los Angeles County Museum of Art, n.p. From May 7, 1971, through June 12, 1971, the Los Angeles County Museum of Art screened the films of King Vidor. Notes on *Hallelujah* are presented here.

"Flash! Flash! Flash!" *Pittsburgh Courier* 15 Oct. 1938: 20. <https://www.newspapers.com/image40092809>. A quote from the first line of the story is used here because the article's title is missing.

"Florence Mills Biography." Bio.com. A&E Networks Television, n.d. Web. 28 Nov. 2013.

"Florence Mills: The Little Blackbird." FlorenceMills.com. Bill Egan, n.d. Web. 26 Feb. 2014.

Forbes, Camille F. *Introducing Bert Williams: Burnt Cork, Broadway, and the Story of America's First Black Star*. New York: Basic Civitas Books, 2008. Print.

Fornäs, Johan. *Cultural Theory and Late Modernity*. London: Sage Publications, 1995. Print.

"Four Awaiting Death in Chair." *The Lancaster News* 10 Sept. 1929: 1. Microfilm.

Fredi Washington Papers, 1925-1979. Amistad Research Center, Inc. Tulane University, New Orleans, LA. Microfilm.

Friedman, Ryan. *Hollywood's African American Films: The Transition to Sound*. Rutgers University Press, 2011. Print.

Furia, Philip. *The Poets of Tin Pan Alley: A History of America's Great Lyricists*. New York: Oxford, 1990. Print.

Gang Smashers. Dir. Leo C. Popkin. Perf. Nina Mae McKinney, Laurence Criner, Mantan Moreland, and Monte Hawley. Ted

Toddy Picture Company/Million Dollar Productions, 1938. IMDb.com. Internet Movie Database.

"Gang Smashers." IMDb.com. Internet Movie Database. Amazon, n.d. Web. 28 Oct. 2013.

Garbo. Dir. Kevin Brownlow and Christopher Bird. Nar. Julie Christie. TCM Archives. Turner Entertainment Co./Warner Bros, 2005. DVD.

Gavin, James. *Stormy Weather*. New York: Atria/Simon & Shuster, 2010.

Gates, Jr., Henry Louis and Evelyn Brooks Higginbotham, Eds. *Harlem Renaissance Lives: From the African American National Biography*. Oxford: Oxford University Press, 2009. Print.

"Gentleman Jo Louis Will Win, Says Actress." *Daily News* [Perth], 25 August 1937: 1.

Glynn, Dean. "On the Spot." *The New York Age* 16 Apr. 1932: 6. www.newspapers.com/image/40889976.

God's Step Children. Dir. Oscar Micheaux. Perf. Ethel Moses and Jacqueline Lewis. Micheaux Pictures Corp., 1938. IMDb.com. Internet Movie Database.

Gone with the Wind. Dir. David O. Selznick. Perf. Clark Gable, Vivien Leigh, Hattie McDaniel, and Butterfly McQueen. Warner Bros., 1939. Warner Bros, 1999. DVD.

The Great Train Robbery. Dir. Edwin S. Porter. Perf. A.C. Abadie and Gilbert M. 'Bronco Billy' Anderson. Edison Manufacturing Co., 1903. IMDb.com. Internet Movie Database.

"The Green Pastures." IMDb.com. Internet Movie Database. Amazon, n.d. Web. 20 Feb. 2024.

Hall, Mordaunt. "*Hallelujah*! (1929)." *New York Times* 21 Aug. 1929. NewYorkTimes.com. The New York Times Company, 2013. Web. 5 Nov. 2013.

"Hall of Fame Inductees." Black Filmmakers Hall of Fame Awards. <http://www.Blackfilmmakersawards.com/Halloffamers.html.> Web. 25 Oct.2011.

Hall, Gladys. "Lombard---As She Sees Herself." *Motion Picture* Nov. 1938: 67-8. Print.

Hall, Stuart. "Cultural Identity and Cinematic Representation." *Film Theory: An Anthology*. Robert Stam and Toby Miller, eds. Malden, MA: Blackwell, 2000. 704-714. Print.

Hall, Stuart. "Culture, Media, and the 'Ideological Effect.'" *Mass Communication and Society*. James Curran, Michael Garevitch, and Janet Woollacott, eds. London: Edward Arnold, 1977. 315-348. Print.

Hall, Stuart. "Encoding, Decoding." *The Cultural Studies Reader*. Simon During, ed. London: Routledge, 2007. Print.

Hallelujah. Dir. King Vidor. Perf. Nina Mae McKinney, Daniel L. Haynes, and William Fountaine. MGM, 1929. Warner Bros, 2006. DVD.

"*Hallelujah*." IMDb.com. Internet Movie Database. Amazon, n.d. Web. 28 Oct. 2013.

Hallelujah Clippings File. Nina Mae McKinney. Margaret Herrick Library. Academy of Motion Picture Arts & Sciences, Los Angeles, CA.

"'Hallelujah' Shown to Whites Only in L.A." *Chicago Defender* 26 Apr. 1930: 9. *Black Entertainers in African American Newspaper Articles. Vol. 1: An Annotated Bibliography of the Chicago Defender, the Afro-American (Baltimore), the Los Angeles Sentinel, and the New York Amsterdam News, 1910-1950*. Ed. Charlene Regester. Jefferson, NC: McFarland & Company, 2002: 41. Entry 662. Print.

"Hallelujah" Silent Version Suggested Deletions. 13 Sept. 1929. *Hallelujah* Core Collection Clippings File. Margaret Herrick Library. Academy of Motion Picture Arts and Sciences.

"'Hallelujah' Star Overcome by Heavy Movie Tasks." *Pittsburgh Courier* 18 May 1929: 15. www.newspapers.com/image/40104931.

Halsey, Stuart, & Co. "The Motion Picture Industry." *The American Film Industry*. Tino Balio, ed. Madison: University of Wisconsin Press, 1976: 195-217. Print.

Handy, D. Antoinette. *Black Women in American Bands and Orchestras*. Second Edition. Scarecrow Press, 1998.

Hanson, Elizabeth. "'She Can Even Cook.' An Interview with Elizabeth Hanson," *Melbourne Table Talk*, 30 September 1937, 8.

"Harlemites Go 'First Nighter' for Sepia Film: 'Gang Smashers' Opened with Pomp of Hollywood's Best." *Pittsburgh Courier* 11 Feb. 1939: 21. *Black Entertainers in African American Newspaper Articles. Vol. 2: An Annotated Bibliography of the Pittsburgh Courier and the California Eagle, 1914-1950*. Ed. Charlene Regester. Jefferson, NC: McFarland & Company, 2009: 356. Entry 9773. Print.

Harrison, Daphne Duval. *Black Pearls: Blues Queens of the 1920s*. New Brunswick: Rutgers University Press, 1993. Print.

"Harry Belafonte: Emmy Awards, Nominations and Wins." Emmys. com. Television Academy, Academy of Television Arts & Sciences, n.d. Web. 13 Jan. 2024.

"Harry Belafonte." IMDb.com. Internet Movie Database, n.d. Web. 13 Jan. 2024.

"Harry Belafonte: 2014 Governors Awards." Oscars.org. Academy of Motion Picture Arts and Sciences, n.d. Web. 13 Jan. 2024.

"Harry Cohn." IMDb.com. Internet Movie Database. Amazon, n.d. Web. 8 Mar. 2014.

Harvey, David. *The Condition of Postmodernity: An Enquiry into the Origins of Cultural Change*. Malden, MA: Blackwell, 1995. Print.

"Hattie McDaniel Biography." IMDb.com. Internet Movie Database. Amazon, n.d. Web. 26 Feb. 2014.

"Heading for Paris." *Argus-Leader* (Sioux Falls, ND) 1 Apr. 1949: 15. <www.newspapers.com/image/229811550>.

"Hearts in Dixie." IMDb.com. Internet Movie Database. Amazon, n.d. Web. 28 Oct. 2013.

Hershfield, Joanne. "Dolores del Rio, Uncomfortably Real: The Economics of Race in Hollywood's Latin American Musicals." *Classic Hollywood, Classic Whiteness.* Daniel Bernardi, ed. Minneapolis: University of Minnesota, 2001. Print.

Hershfield, Joanne. *The Invention of Delores del Rio.* Minneapolis: University of Minnesota Press, 2000.

Hollywood Singing and Dancing: A Musical History–The 1920s—The Dawn of the Hollywood Musical. Dir. Philip Dye. Great Musical Treasures, 2008. DVD.

Howe, Herbert. "A Jungle Lorelei." *Photoplay* July 1929: 36+. Print.

Imitation of Life. Dir. John M. Stahl. Perf. Claudette Colbert, Louise Beavers, and Fredi Washington. Universal, 1934/1962. Universal, 1998. VHS.

"In Race for 'Miss Olympics.'" *New York Age* 19 Mar. 1932: 7. <www.newspapers.com/image/40889362.>

Index to Marriages. Nina Mickey. Marriage Certificate. City Municipal Archives. New York, New York. Borough: Manhattan. Vol. No. 14. U.S. Marriage License Indexes, 1907-2018 [database online]. Ancestry.com; 11 Jan. 2012.

Indiana, U.S., Marriages, 1810-2001 [database online]. Provo, UT, USA: Ancestry.com Operations, Inc., 2014. Original data: Indiana, Marriages, 1810-2001. Salt Lake City, Utah: FamilySearch, 2013.

"Indian Maharaja at Feet of Nina Mae." Afro-American. 16 Nov. 1929: 10.

"Information on Getting Married in New York State." Health.NY.gov. New York State Department of Health, Sept. 2011. Web. 26 Nov. 2013. <http://www.health.ny.gov/publications/4210/>.

"Irving Thalberg Biography." IMDb.com. Internet Movie Database. Amazon, n.d. Web. 5 Mar. 2014.

It. Dir. Clarence G. Badger and Josef Von Sternberg. Perf. Clara Bow and Antonio Moreno. Famous Players-Lasky Corp./Paramount Pictures, 1927. Kino Video, 2001. DVD.

"It May Be of Interest." *Gaffney Ledger.* 29 Apr. 1930: 3. <www.newspapers.com/ image/78037060>.

"It's a Premiere." *Clarion-Ledger* (Jackson, MS). 16 Aug. 1988: 33. <www.newspapers.com/image/184038175>.

Jackson, Carlton. *The Life of Hattie McDaniel.* Lanham, MD: Madison Books, 1990. Print.

Jacobs, Harriet. *Incidents in the Life of a Slave Girl.* 1861. Oxford: Oxford University Press, 2015.

J.B.M. Fisher Memo to Mr. McKenzie at MGM. 25 Oct. 1929. *Hallelujah* Core Collection Clippings File. Margaret Herrick Library. Academy of Motion Picture Arts and Sciences.

Jewell, Richard. *The Golden Age of Cinema: Hollywood, 1929–1945.* Malden, MA: Wiley-Blackwell, 2007. Print.

Jitterbug Party. Dir. Fred Waller. Perf. Cab Calloway and Lena Horne. Paramount Pictures, 1935. Hollywood Rhythm Volume I: The Best of Jazz & Blues/The Paramount Musical Shorts. Kino Video, 2001. DVD.

Jones-King, Morgan. "South Carolina Department of Archives and History." SC Birth Certificates at the Archives, SC Department of Archives and History. 3 Mar. 2020. <scdah.sc.gov/news/2020-03/sc-birth-certificates-archives>.

"Joseph Schenk Biography." IMDb.com. Internet Movie Database. Amazon, n.d. Web. 5 Mar. 2014.

"Josephine Baker Biography." Bio.com. A&E Networks Television, n.d. Web. 01 Dec. 2013. <http://www.biography.com/people/josephine-baker-9195959>.

The Josephine Baker Collection. Kino Video, 2005. DVD.

Judge Priest. Dir. John Ford. Perf. Will Rogers, Stepin Fetchit, and Hattie McDaniel. Fox Film Corp., 1934. IMDb.com. Internet Movie Database.

"Judge Priest." IMDb.com. Internet Movie Database. Web. 13 Jan. 2024.

Jules-Rosette, Bennetta. *Josephine Baker in Art and Life: The Icon and the Image.* Urbana: University of Illinois Press, 2007. Print.

Kato, M. T. *From Kung Fu to Hip Hop: Globalization, Revolution, and Popular Culture.* Albany: SUNY, 2007. Print.

Kentucky Minstrels. Dir. John Baxter. Real Art Productions/Universal Pictures (UK), 1934. IMDb.com. Internet Movie Database.

King, Dwandalyn Reece. "A Performance Biography of Ethel Waters (1896-1977)." Dissertation. Department of Performance Studies. New York University, 2000. UMI Microform 9956686. PDF.

King, Susan. "Film Pioneers." *Los Angeles Times* 31 Jan. 2011. Print.

King, Theresa. "Local Resident's Play Features Pioneer Star." *Clarion-Ledger* 21 July 1988: 69, 74. <www.newspapers.com/image/184081173>.

"King Vidor Exposed." *Pittsburgh Courier* 26 July 1930: 10. *Black Entertainers in African American Newspaper Articles. Vol. 2: An Annotated Bibliography of the Pittsburgh Courier and the California Eagle, 1914-1950.* Ed. Charlene Regester. Jefferson, NC: McFarland & Company, 2009: 94. Entry 2870. Print.

"King Vidor's Colored Folk Movie Shows at Embassy, Too; Rates 3 Stars." *Daily News* (New York, NY) 22 Aug. 1929: 239. www.newspapers.com/image/413062910.

Kisch, John, and Edward Mapp. *A Separate Cinema: Fifty Years of Black-Cast Posters.* New York: Farrar, Straus, and Giroux, 1992. Print.

Knight, Arthur. *Disintegrating the Musical: Black Performance and American Musical Film.* Durham, NC: Duke UP, 2002. Print.

La Caze, Marguerite. "If You Say So: Feminist Philosophy and Antiracism." *Racism in Mind.* Michael P. Levine and Tamas Pataki, eds. Ithaca: Cornell UP, 2004. Print.

"Lamar Trotti." MPPDA Digital Archive. MPPDA Digital Archive: Documents from the Motion Picture Producers and Distributors of America, Inc., 1922-1939/ Flinders Institute for Research in the Humanities, 2014. Web. 27 Apr. 2014.

"Lancastrian in Top Rated Movie." *The Lancaster News* Fri. 3 Feb. 1950, front page. Microfilm.

"Larry King Live with Shirley Temple Black." *Larry King Live*. CNN. 25 Oct. 1988. YouTube. 1 Apr. 2014. 12:27. <www.youtube.com/watch?v=Z_KacEMBJg0&list=WL&index=3>.

"Last Day Friday for Pinky." Midway Theater Ad. *The Lancaster News* Fri. 10 Feb.1950, Social and Personal: 7. Microfilm.

Leiman, Melvin M. *Political Economy of Racism*. London: Pluto, 1993. Print.

"Lena Horne." IMDb.com. Internet Movie Database, n.d. Web. 29 Nov. 2013.

Letter Re: MGM's New York Exchange. 18 Mar. 1930. *Hallelujah* Core Collection Clippings File. Margaret Herrick Library. Academy of Motion Picture Arts and Sciences.

Levine, Michael P., and Tamas Pataki, eds. *Racism in Mind*. Ithaca: Cornell UP, 2004. Print.

"Lewis Selznick Biography." IMDb.com. Internet Movie Database. Amazon, n.d. Web. 5 Mar. 2014.

LoBianco, Lorraine. "Dorothy Dandridge Profile." TCM.com. Turner Classic Movies, n.d. Web. 04 Dec. 2013.

Locke, Alain. *The New Negro*. 1925. New York, NY: Simon & Schuster, 1997. Print.

London's Famous Clubs and Cabarets. British Pathe. 1933.

The Lonely Trail. Dir. Joseph Kane. Republic Pictures, 1936.

Luck, Adam. "Eartha Kitt's Life Was Scarred by Failure to Learn the Identity of Her White Father, Says Daughter." *The Guardian*. Guardian News and Media Limited, 19 Oct. 2013. Web. 21 Oct. 2013.

"Madame Sul-Te-Wan Biography." IMDB.com. Internet Movie Database. Amazon, n.d. Web. 7 Nov. 2013.

Malcolm X. *February 1965: The Final Speeches.* Clark, Steve, ed. Malcolm X Speeches and Writings Series. 1992. Atlanta, GA: Pathfinder Press/Betty Shabazz, 2010.

"Manhattan Serenade." IMDb.com. Internet Movie Database. Amazon, n.d. Web. 11 Sept. 2013.

Manhattan Serenade. Dir. Sammy Lee. Perf. The Brox Sisters and Nina Mae McKinney. MGM, 1929. IMDb.com. Internet Movie Database.

Mantan Messes Up. Dir. Sam Newfield. Perf. Mantan Moreland, Monte Hawley, Lena Horne, and Nina Mae McKinney. Lucky Star Productions/Toddy Pictures Co., 1946. IMDb.com. Internet Movie Database.

Mapp, Edward. *African Americans and the Oscar: Seven Decades of Struggle and Achievement.* Lanham, MD: The Scarecrow Press, Inc., 2003. Print.

"Marcus Loew Biography." IMDb.com. Internet Movie Database. Amazon, n.d. Web. 5 Mar. 2014.

"Mary Pickford: Timeline." *American Experience.* PBS.org. PBS, 23 July 2004. Web. 13 Dec. 2013. <http://www.pbs.org/wgbh/amex/pickford/timeline/>.

Maslon, Laurence. *Broadway: The American Musical.* New York: Bulfinch Press, 2004. Print.

Mata Hari. Dir. George Fitzmaurice. Perf. Greta Garbo and Lionel Barrymore. MGM, 1931. *The Garbo Silents Collection.* TCM Archives. Turner Entertainment Co./Warner Bros, 2005, DVD.

Matthews, Ralph. "Mother of Harlem's Movie Queen Wanted Her to Be a School Teacher." *Afro-American* 15 Feb. 1936: 10. *Black Entertainers in African American Newspaper Articles. Vol. 1: An Annotated Bibliography of the Chicago Defender, the Afro-American (Baltimore), the Los Angeles Sentinel, and the New York*

Amsterdam News, 1910-1950. Ed. Charlene Regester. Jefferson, NC: McFarland & Company, 2002: 224. Entry 4056. Print.

Maynor, Georgie. Letter to Hedda Hopper. 5 July 1950. MS. Hedda Hopper Papers. Margaret Herrick Library. Academy of Motion Picture Arts & Sciences, Los Angeles, CA.

McMurray, Marjorie C. "Black Lancaster." *Tap Journal*. Spring 1977: 18-22. Print.

McMurray, Marjorie C. "Nina Mae McKinney Receives Award Posthumously." *The Lancaster News* Wed. 19 Apr. 1978. Here & There: 5B. Print.

McMurray, Marjorie C. "Nina Mae McKinney Was Lancaster's Only Cinema Star." *The Lancaster News* Wed. 5 Feb. 1986. Here & There: 1C. Print.

MGM Cinema Press Books. n.d. NY Public Library. Reel 5. *Hallelujah* Core Collection Clippings File. Margaret Herrick Library. Academy of Motion Picture Arts and Sciences. Microfilm.

Midnight Ramble. Dir. Bester Cram and Pamela Thomas. PBS. The American Experience. Synergy Entertainment, 2010. DVD.

Miller, D. Quentin. *Re-Viewing James Baldwin: Things Not Seen*. Philadelphia: Temple UP, 2000. Print.

"Million $ Pic Held Over Second Week." *California Eagle* 8 Dec. 1938: 2. *Black Entertainers in African American Newspaper Articles. Vol. 2: An Annotated Bibliography of the Pittsburgh Courier and the California Eagle, 1914-1950*. Ed. Charlene Regester. Jefferson, NC: McFarland & Company, 2009: 349. Entry 9616. Print.

"Million $ Pic Enters 3rd Big Week." *California Eagle* 15 Dec. 1938: 10. *Black Entertainers in African American Newspaper Articles. Vol. 2: An Annotated Bibliography of the Pittsburgh Courier and the California Eagle, 1914-1950*. Ed. Charlene Regester. Jefferson, NC: McFarland & Company, 2009: 349. Entry 9628. Print.

Mills, Earl. *Dorothy Dandridge*. Los Angeles: Holloway House, 1997.

"Minimum Contract for Artists." 14 Aug. 1931. Warner Bros. Pictures, Inc., Producer. Warner Bros. Archives. USC School of Cinematic Arts. This is an additional contract for Nina Mae McKinney's role of Leoni in the feature film *Safe in Hell* executed by S.E.M. (initials only). Print.

"Minimum Contract for Artists." 14 May 1931. Warner Bros. Pictures, Inc., Producer. Warner Bros. Archives. USC School of Cinematic Arts. This is Nina Mae McKinney's contract for the role of Leoni in the feature film *Safe in Hell* executed by Albert Warner. Print.

Mintz, S., and S. McNeil. "Chronology of Film History." Digital History. University of Houston, 2013. Web. 11 Sept. 2013. <http://www.digitalhistory.uh.edu/historyonline/film_chron.cfm>.

"Miriam Hopkins." IMDb.com. Internet Movie Database. Amazon, n.d. Web. 8 Mar. 2014.

Mitchell, Dawn. "Indiana Was a Scandalous Marriage Mill and Valentino Took Advantage." *IndyStar* 4 July 2019. <https://www.indystar.com/story/news/history/retroindy/2019/07/04/indiana-scandalous-marriage-mill-and-valentino-took-advantage-gretna-green-weddings/1621342001/>.

Moguls & Movie Stars: A History of Hollywood. Turner Classic Movies, 2010. 7 Vols. DVD.

Monceaux, Morgan. *Jazz: My Music, My People*. New York: Knopf, 1994. Print.

Morgan, Edmund S. *American Slavery, American Freedom: The Ordeal of Colonial Virginia*. New York: W.W. Norton & Co, Inc., 1975. Print.

Morin, Edgar. *The Stars*. Trans. Richard Howard. University of Minnesota Press, 2005.Print.

Morris, Earl J. "1938 Banner year for Negro Movie Industry." *Pittsburgh Courier* 21 Jan. 1939: 21. *Black Entertainers in*

African American Newspaper Articles. Vol. 2: An Annotated Bibliography of the Pittsburgh Courier and the California Eagle, 1914-1950. Ed. Charlene Regester. Jefferson, NC: McFarland & Company, 2009: 354. Entry 9729. Print.

MPPDA Deletions Report. 11 Aug. 1939. *Hallelujah* Core Collection Clippings File. Margaret Herrick Library. Academy of Motion Picture Arts and Sciences. Print.

MPPDA Letter to Col. Jason S. Joy. 5 Oct. 1928. *Hallelujah* Core Collection Clippings File. Margaret Herrick Library. Academy of Motion Picture Arts and Sciences. Print.

MPPDA Letter to Louis B. Mayer at MGM. 21 Apr. 1939. *Hallelujah* Core Collection Clippings File. Margaret Herrick Library. Academy of Motion Picture Arts and Sciences. Print.

MPPDA Report: *Hallelujah* Re-Issue Approved Without Limitations. 11 Aug. 1939. *Hallelujah* Core Collection Clippings File. Margaret Herrick Library. Academy of Motion Picture Arts and Sciences. Print.

Murphy, Reece. "Lancaster Actress Nina Mae McKinney Was Regarded as 'The Black Garbo' of Her Generation: Before Lena Horne and Dorothy Dandridge, There Was Nina Mae." *The Lancaster News* Sun. 10 Feb. 2013: 1. PDF.

Nanook of the North. Dir. Robert J. Flaherty. Les Frères Revillon, 1922. Reel Enterprises, 2006. DVD.

"NC Theater Takes Poll on '*Hallelujah.*'" *Afro-American* 31 May 1930: 8. *Black Entertainers in African American Newspaper Articles. Vol. 1: An Annotated Bibliography of the Chicago Defender, the Afro-American (Baltimore), the Los Angeles Sentinel, and the New York Amsterdam News, 1910-1950.* Ed. Charlene Regester. Jefferson, NC: McFarland & Company, 2002: 43. Entry 718. Print.

"Negro Film Star, Dancer Married at Crown Point." *Indianapolis Star* 24 Oct. 1930: 10.

"Negro Man Found Dead." *The Lancaster News* 3 Sept. 1929, News About Town and County sec.: 3. Microfilm.

"Negro Pastor Knifed After Church Meet." *The Lancaster News* 24 Sept. 1929: 1. Microfilm.

Nichols, Bill. *Ideology and the Image.* Bloomington: Indiana University Press, 1981. Print.

Night Train to Memphis. Dir. Lesley Selander. Perf. Roy Acuff, Allan Lane, and Nina Mae McKinney. Republic Pictures, 1946. IMDb.com. Internet Movie Database.

"Nina Mae Collapses on Irish Stage." *California Eagle* 5 Mar. 1937: 3. *Black Entertainers in African American Newspaper Articles. Vol. 2: An Annotated Bibliography of the Pittsburgh Courier and the California Eagle, 1914-1950.* Ed. Charlene Regester. Jefferson, NC: McFarland & Company, 2009: 280. Entry 7898. Print.

"Nina Mae Makes Four Parlophone Records." *Pittsburgh Courier* 27 Apr. 1935: 21. <www.newspapers.com/image/40231291>.

"Nina Mae McKinney." *California Eagle* 9 May. 1940: 7. *Black Entertainers in African American Newspaper Articles. Vol. 2: An Annotated Bibliography of the Pittsburgh Courier and the California Eagle, 1914-1950.* Ed. Charlene Regester. Jefferson, NC: McFarland & Company, 2009: 405. Entry 10915. Print.

"Nina Mae McKinney." IMDb.com. Internet Movie Database. Web. 30 Nov. 2013.

"Nina Mae McKinney Libeled in Nasty Magazine Article." *Afro-American* (Baltimore) 29 Mar. 1930: 22.

"Nina Mae McKinney of Harlem and London." *Vanity Fair* Dec. 1935: 41. Print.

Nina Mae McKinney. Obituary. *Amsterdam News* 13 May 1967.

Nina Mae McKinney. Obituary. *Daily News* (New York, NY) 8 May 1967.

Nina Mae McKinney. Obituary. *Pittsburgh Courier* 20 May 1967: 1.

"Nina Mae McKinney Reported Married." *Chicago Defender* 19 Dec. 1931: 1. *Black Entertainers in African American Newspaper*

Articles. Vol. 1: An Annotated Bibliography of the Chicago Defender, the Afro-American (Baltimore), the Los Angeles Sentinel, and the New York Amsterdam News, 1910-1950. Ed. Charlene Regester. Jefferson, NC: McFarland & Company, 2002: 88. Entry 1556. Print.

"Nina Mae McKinney, 12 Jun 1912–3 May 1967." Memorial Page. ID: 6863095. Cosmos, Section 196/197. Woodlawn Cemetery. Bronx, Bronx County, NY. Find a Grave, https://www. findagrave.com/memorial/6863095/nina-mae-mckinney. [database online]. Accessed 25 Jan. 2024.

"Nina Mae Seeks Annulment of Marriage." *Afro-American* (Baltimore) 29 Nov. 1930: 1. *Black Entertainers in African American Newspaper Articles. Vol. 1: An Annotated Bibliography of the Chicago Defender, the Afro-American (Baltimore), the Los Angeles Sentinel, and the New York Amsterdam News, 1910-1950.* Ed. Charlene Regester. Jefferson, NC: McFarland & Company, 2002: 57. Entry 985. Print.

"Nina Mae Monroe." U.S., Border Crossings from Canada to U.S., 1895-1960. Ancestry.com [database online]. Lehi, UT, USA: Ancestry.com Operations, Inc., 2010. The National Archives in Washington, DC; Washington, DC, USA; *Manifests of Passengers Arriving in the St. Albans, Vermont, District Through Canadian Pacific Ports, 1929-1949*; NAI: *4492491*; Record Group: *Records of the Immigration and Naturalization Service, 1787 - 2004*; Record Group Number: *85*; Series Number: *M1465*; Roll Number: *018*. Accessed 25 Jan. 2024.

"Nina Monroe." New York, U.S., Arriving Passenger and Crew Lists (including Castle Garden and Ellis Island), 1820-1957. Ancestry.com [database online]. Lehi, UT, USA: Ancestry.com Operations, Inc., 2010. The National Archives in Washington, DC; Washington, DC, USA; Passenger and Crew Lists of Vessels Arriving at New York, New York, 1897-1957; Microfilm Serial or NAID: T715; RG Title: Records of the Immigration and Naturalization Service, 1787-2004; RG: 85. Accessed 25 Jan. 2024.

"1918-1928: Triumph of American Film and the First of its Rebels." *The Story of Film: An Odyssey*. Writ. and dir. Mark Cousins. Vol. 2. Hopscotch Films, 2011.

"1929-30 Academy Awards Winners and History." Filmsite.org. American Movie Classics Company, Ltd., 2013. Web. 2 Nov. 2013.

"1954 Academy Awards Winners and History." Filmsite.org. AMC. American Movie Classics, n.d. Web. 04 Dec. 2013.

No Way Out. Dir. Joseph L. Mankiewicz. Perf. Sidney Poitier, Richard Widmark, and Linda Darnell. Twentieth Century Fox., 1950. IMDb.com. Internet Movie Database.

"Objects to Negress Named After Her." *The Lancaster News* Sun. 5 Nov. 1929: 2. Microfilm.

Ogidi, Ann. "Black British Film." *BFI Screenonline*. BFI. British Film Institute, n.d. Web. 02 Dec. 2013. <http://www.screenonline. org.uk/film/id/1144245/>.

On Velvet. Dir. Widgey R. Newman. Perf. Wally Patch and Nina Mae McKinney. Widgey R. Newman Productions/Columbia Pictures (UK), 1938. IMDb.com. Internet Movie Database.

"On with the Show." IMDb.com. Internet Movie Database. Web. 3 June 2024.

"One-Time Movie Star Nina Mae McKinney Is Seriously Ill in Harlem Hospital." *Longview News-Journal* (Longview, TX). 20 July 1960:4. <www.newspapers.com/image/1785/49827>.

"Panama Hattie." IMDb.com. Internet Movie Database. Web. 30 Nov. 2013.

Parker, Laurence, Donna Deyhle, and Sofia Villenas, eds. *Race Is . . . Race Isn't: Critical Race Theory and Qualitative Studies in Education*. Boulder, CO: Westview Press, 1999. Print.

Parsons, Louella O. "Actress to Wed Engineer." *L.A. Examiner* 18 Apr. 1948. Print.

"'Part in 'Imitation' is Not Real Me,' Says Fredi." *Chicago Defender* 11 Jan. 1935. Fredi Washington Papers, 1925-1979. Amistad Research Center, Inc. Tulane University, New Orleans, LA. Microfilm.

Passing the Buck. Dir. Roy Mack. Perf. Alexander Gray and Nina Mae McKinney. Warner Bros., 1932. IMDb.com. Internet Movie Database.

"Paul Robeson: Biography." IMDb.com. Internet Movie Database, n.d. Web. 22 Feb. 2013.

"Peepshow Pioneers (1889-1907)."*Moguls & Movie Stars: A History of Hollywood.* Turner Classic Movies, 2010. Vol. 1. DVD.

Pettus, Louise. "Nina McKinney." Nina McKinney. Ancestry.com, 1999. Web. 1 Oct. 2013. <http://www.rootsweb.ancestry.com/~sclancas/records/bios/ ninamckinney.htm>.

Pettus, Louise and Ron Chepesiuk. "Lancaster Brick Wall Pays Tribute to Notable Citizens of That Area." *The Herald* [Clover, SC] 17 Feb. 1988: n. pag. Louise Pettus Archives & Special Collections. Winthrop University. Print.

Pettus, Louise, and Ron Chepesiuk. "Nina Mae McKinney—Deserving of a Place in History." *Index-Journal* (Greenwood, SC) 21 Feb. 1988: 19. <www.newspapers.com/image/69972701>.

Pie, Pie Blackbird. Dir. Roy Mack. Perf. Nina Mae McKinney, Fayard Nicholas, Harold Nicholas, and Eubie Blake. Vitaphone Productions/Warner Bros. Pictures, 1932. *Hallelujah* DVD Release. Warner Bros, 2006. DVD.

Pinky. Dir. Elia Kazan. Perf. Ethel Waters, Jeanne Crain, and Ethel Barrymore. Twentieth Century Fox, 1949/1972. Twentieth Century Fox, 2005. DVD.

"Pinky." IMDb.com. Internet Movie Database. Web. 2 Dec. 2013.

The Power of the Whistler. Dir. Lew Landers. Perf. Richard Dix, Janis Carter, and Nina Mae McKinney. Darmour Inc./Columbia Pictures, 1945. IMDb.com. Internet Movie Database.

"Prattis Gives 1930 Review of Theater: Says Race Has Made Great Strides." *Chicago Defender* 27 Dec. 1930: 7. *Black Entertainers in African American Newspaper Articles. Vol. 1: An Annotated Bibliography of the Chicago Defender, the Afro-American (Baltimore), the Los Angeles Sentinel, and the New York Amsterdam News, 1910-1950.* Ed. Charlene Regester. Jefferson, NC: McFarland & Company,2002: 59. Entry 1029. Print.

Princess Tam Tam. Dir. Edmond T. Grèville. Perf. Josephine Baker. Productions Arys, 1935. Kino Video, 1989. *The Josephine Baker Collection.* Kino Video, 2005. DVD.

Rain. Writ. W. Somerset Maugham. Apollo Theater. 1951.

"Ralph Cooper Fans in Cincinnati Organize." *Pittsburgh Courier* 3 Dec. 1938: 21. *Black Entertainers in African American Newspaper Articles. Vol. 2: An Annotated Bibliography of the Pittsburgh Courier and the California Eagle, 1914-1950.* Ed. Charlene Regester. Jefferson, NC: McFarland & Company, 2009: 348. Entry 9610. Print.

Rayme, Mary. "Scandalize My Name: Stories from the Blacklist." *Zinn Education Project.* Web. 21 Feb 2024. <https://www.zinnedproject.org/materials/scandalize-my-name>.

Reckless. Dir. Victor Fleming. Perf. Jean Harlow and William Powell. MGM, 19 April 1935. McKinney had a cameo as a singer.

"Reckless." IMDb.com. Internet Movie Database. Web. 3 June 2024.

"Reel - Previews and Reviews - Two Pictures Now Being Cast to Net Race Group Thousands of Dollars." *California Eagle* 31 Aug. 1928: 8. *Black Entertainers in African American Newspaper Articles. Vol. 2: An Annotated Bibliography of the Pittsburgh Courier and the California Eagle, 1914-1950.* Ed. Charlene Regester. Jefferson, NC: McFarland & Company, 2009: 66. Entry 2040. Print.

Regester, Charlene, Ed. *African American Actresses: The Struggle for Visibility, 1900-1960.* Indiana University Press, 2010. Print.

Regester, Charlene, Ed. *Black Entertainers in African American Newspaper Articles. Vol. 1: An Annotated Bibliography of the Chicago Defender, the Afro-American (Baltimore), the Los Angeles Sentinel, and the New York Amsterdam News, 1910-1950.* Jefferson, NC: McFarland & Company, 2002. Print.

Regester, Charlene, Ed. *Black Entertainers in African American Newspaper Articles. Vol. 2: An Annotated Bibliography of the Pittsburgh Courier and the California Eagle, 1914-1950.* Jefferson, NC: McFarland & Company, 2009. Print.

"Reported Wed." *Chicago Defender* 31 Aug. 1929: 8. *Black Entertainers in African American Newspaper Articles. Vol. 1: An Annotated Bibliography of the Chicago Defender, the Afro-American (Baltimore), the Los Angeles Sentinel, and the New York Amsterdam News, 1910-1950.* Ed. Charlene Regester. Jefferson, NC: McFarland &Company, 2002: 30. Entry 447. Print.

"Revels in Rhythm." Prod. Charles B. Cochran. Perf. Nina Mae McKinney. London's Famous Clubs and Cabarets. The Trocadero Restaurant, London. 1933. British Pathé. <https://www.britishpathe.com/asset/65011/>.

"RKO Theater Chain to Present 'Gang Smashers': Picture Has Been Booked for Three Harlem Theaters." *California Eagle* 24 Dec. 1938: 20. *Black Entertainers in African American Newspaper Articles. Vol. 2: An Annotated Bibliography of the Pittsburgh Courier and the California Eagle, 1914-1950.* Ed. Charlene Regester. Jefferson, NC: McFarland & Company, 2009: 351. Entry 9659. Print.

"Robeson Film Wins High English Honor." *California Eagle* 17 Jan. 1936: 10. *Black Entertainers in African American Newspaper Articles. Vol. 2: An Annotated Bibliography of the Pittsburgh Courier and the California Eagle, 1914-1950.* Ed. Charlene Regester. Jefferson, NC: McFarland & Company, 2009: 238. Entry 6789. Print.

Robeson, Jr., Paul. *The Undiscovered Paul Robeson: An Artist's Journey, 1898-1930.* New York: John Wiley & Sons, Inc., 2001. Print.

"Robeson-McKinney Film Wins Coveted Annual English Award." *Pittsburgh Courier* 11 Jan. 1936: 7. *Black Entertainers in African American Newspaper Articles. Vol. 2: An Annotated Bibliography of the Pittsburgh Courier and the California Eagle, 1914-1950.* Ed. Charlene Regester. Jefferson, NC: McFarland & Company, 2009: 237. Entry 6780. Print.

Robinson, Cedric J. *Forgeries of Memory and Meaning: Blacks and the Regimes of Race in American Theater and Film Before World War II.* Chapel Hill: University of North Carolina Press, 2007.

Rogers, J.A. *Nature Knows No Color-Line.* 1952. St. Petersburg, FL: Helga M. Rogers/Cahill Law Firm, P.A., 1980. Print.

Rogin, Michael. *Blackface, White Noise: Jewish Immigrants in the Hollywood Melting Pot.* Berkeley: University of California Press, 1996. Print.

"Ruby Dandridge." IMDb.com. Internet Movie Database. Web. 2 Dec. 2013.

"Rufus Jones for President." IMDb.com. Internet Movie Database. Web. 22 June 2024.

Sadoul, Georges and Peter Morris. *Dictionary of Films.* Berkeley: University of California Press, 1972. Print.

Safe in Hell. Dir. William A. Wellman. Perf. Dorothy Mackaill, Donald Cook, Ralf Harolde, Nina Mae McKinney, and Clarence Muse. First National Pictures/Vitaphone, 1931. Warner Bros, 2011. DVD.

"Samuel Goldwyn Biography." IMDb.com. Internet Movie Database. Amazon, n.d. Web. 5 Mar. 2014.

Sanders of the River. Dir. Zoltan Korda. Prod. Alexander Korda. Perf. Paul Robeson and Leslie Banks. London Film Productions, 1935. Cozumel Films/UrbanWorks Entertainment, 2004. DVD.

"'Sanders of the River' Screens at 2 Theaters." *California Eagle* 8 Nov. 1934: 3. *Black Entertainers in African American Newspaper Articles. Vol. 2: An Annotated Bibliography of the Pittsburgh Courier and the California Eagle, 1914-1950.* Ed. Charlene

Regester. Jefferson, NC: McFarland & Company, 2009: 230. Entry 6599. Print.

"Scandalize My Name." IMDb.com. Internet Movie Database. Web. 21 Feb 2024.

Scar of Shame. Dir. Frank Peregini. Perf. Lucia Lynn Moses and Harry Henderson. Colored Players Film Corp., 1927. VHS.

Schatz, Thomas. *The Genius of the System: Hollywood Filmmaking in the Studio Era*. Pantheon Books, 1988. Print.

"Screen Actress Files Suit for Her Husband." *The Lancaster News* 27 Sept. 1929: 1. Microfilm.

Secretary's Report for Review Committee. 19 Nov. 1929. *Hallelujah* Core Collection Clippings File. Margaret Herrick Library. Academy of Motion Picture Arts and Sciences.

Secretary's Report for Review Committee. 6 Sept. 1929. *Hallelujah* Core Collection Clippings File. Margaret Herrick Library. Academy of Motion Picture Arts and Sciences.

Sherrer, Hans. "Film Star Clara Bow's Personal Secretary Was Wrongfully Convicted of Grand Theft." Justice Denied.org. *Justice Denied Magazine* 2.7. n.d. Web. 17 Feb. 2014.

Sherrod, Kerryn, and Jeff Stafford. "*Hallelujah!*" TCM.com. Turner Entertainment Networks, n.d. Web. 01 Nov. 2012. <http://www. tcm.com/this-month/article/ 17714|0/ *Hallelujah*-.html>.

Shohat, Ella, and Robert Stam. *Unthinking Eurocentrism: Multiculturalism and the Media*. New York: Routledge, 1994.

"Shuffle Along." 1921. IBDb.com. Internet Broadway Database, n.d. Web. 26 Feb. 2014.

"Sidney Poitier." IMDb.com. Internet Movie Database. Web. 20 Feb. 2024.

Singin' in the Rain. Dir. Stanley Donen and Gene Kelly. Perf. Gene Kelly and Debbie Reynolds. MGM, 1952. TCM.

Siren of the Tropics. Dir. Mario Nalpas and Henri Étiévant. Perf. Josephine Baker. La Centrale Cinématographique, 1927. *The Josephine Baker Collection*. Kino Video, 2005. DVD.

Smith, Frederick James. "Does Decency Help or Hinder?" *Photoplay* 26 (Nov. 1924): 36. Print.

Smith, Ian. "Drawing the Color Line: Lovely Negro Actress Gives Example." *Labor Daily*, 27 August 1937: 6.

Smith, Isadora. "Movie Star Weds 20-Year-Old Youth." *Pittsburgh Courier* 23 Sept. 1939: 21. <https://www.newspapers.com/image39548853>.

"Smith–Jones Go 'No Contest.'" *Pittsburgh Courier* 13 Sept. 1930: 14.

Smith, Theodora Shippy, and Mary Belk Mackey. *Lancaster County Black History: A Photographic and Literary Document, 1785-1991*. Lancaster County, South Carolina Black History Committee, 1993. Print.

"Solid Souths Hand Seen in Race Film End." *Chicago Defender* 3 Oct. 1931: 6. *Black Entertainers in African American Newspaper Articles. Vol. 1: An Annotated Bibliography of the Chicago Defender, the Afro-American (Baltimore), the Los Angeles Sentinel, and the New York Amsterdam News, 1910-1950*. Ed. Charlene Regester. Jefferson, NC: McFarland & Company, 2002: 82. Entry 1450. Print.

"So Red the Rose." Dir. King Vidor. IMDb.com. Internet Movie Database. Amazon, n.d. Web. 20 Feb. 2024.

"Sound Pictures Please Crowd: Sparkling Musical Show Makes a Big Hit at the Imperial Theater." *The Lancaster News* 5 Nov. 1929: 1. Microfilm.

South Carolina Death Records, 1821–1955. David McKinney. Certificate of Death. 30 Sept. 1918. Lancaster, Lancaster County, South Carolina. Certificate No. 017343. Vol. 37. South Carolina Department of Archives and History. [database online]. Ancestry.com; 17 Jan. 2024.

"South Carolina Department of Health and Environmental Control (SC DHEC)." Birth Certificates, Vital Records, scdhec.gov/vital-records/birth-certificates. Accessed 3 Aug. 2023.

Sperling, Cass Warner, Cork Millner, and Jack Warner Jr. *Hollywood Be Thy Name: The Warner Brothers Story*. Lexington, KY: University Press of Kentucky, 1998. Print.

Staiger, Janet. "The Hollywood Mode of Production: Its Conditions of Existence." *The Classical Hollywood Cinema: Film Style & Mode of Production to 1960*. Bordwell, David, Janet Staiger, and Kristin Thompson, eds. New York: Columbia University Press, 1985. 87-112. Print.

"Starring in Broadway 'Pic.'" *Pittsburgh Courier* 6 July 1934: 7. *Black Entertainers in African American Newspaper Articles. Vol. 2: An Annotated Bibliography of the Pittsburgh Courier and the California Eagle, 1914-1950*. Ed. Charlene Regester. Jefferson, NC: McFarland & Company, 2009: 218. Entry 6257. Print.

"Stars as Adam." *Chicago Defender* 28 Nov. 1931: 6. *Black Entertainers in African American Newspaper Articles. Vol. 1: An Annotated Bibliography of the Chicago Defender, the Afro-American (Baltimore), the Los Angeles Sentinel, and the New York Amsterdam News, 1910-1950*. Ed. Charlene Regester. Jefferson, NC: McFarland & Company, 2002: 87. Entry 1547. Print.

"Star Trek." 1966-1969. IMDb.com. Internet Movie Database, n.d. Web. 11 Jan. 2024.

Steen, Andee. "Destined to Be a Star: Local Woman Was First Black Actress in Hollywood." *The Lancaster News* Sun. 8 July 2001. Living. Print.

Stenn, David. *Clara Bow: Runnin' Wild*. First Cooper Square Press Ed. New York: Rowman & Littlefield, 2000. Print.

"Stepin Fetchit." IMDb.com. Internet Movie Database, n.d. Web. 26 Feb. 2014.

Stokes, Jane. *How to Do Media & Cultural Studies*. London: Sage, 2003. Print.

The Story of Film: An Odyssey. Writ. and Dir. Mark Cousins. 15 Vols. Hopscotch Films, 2011. TCM. Television.

Straight to Heaven. Dir. Arthur H. Leonard. Perf. Nina Mae McKinney, James Baskett, and Jack Carter. Million Dollar Productions, 1939. IMDb.com. Internet Movie Database.

"Straight to Heaven." IMDb.com. Internet Movie Database. Amazon, n.d. Web. 28 Oct. 2013.

"Sugar, Sugar." Writ. Jeff Barry and Andy Kim. Perf. The Archies (animated) and Ron Dante (voice of Archie). *The Archie Comedy Hour*. Writ. Dan DeCarlo and John L. Goldwater. The Archie Company/CBS/Filmation Associates, 1969. TV. IMDb.com. Internet Movie Database.

Swanee Showboat. Perf. Nina Mae McKinney, Mabel Lee, and Dewey "Pigmeat" Markham. Ajax Pictures Corporation, 1940. IMDb.com. Internet Movie Database.

Symphony in Black: A Rhapsody of Negro Life. Dir. Fred Waller. Perf. Billie Holiday and Duke Ellington. Paramount, 1935. *Hollywood Rhythm Volume I: The Best of Jazz & Blues/The Paramount Musical Shorts*. Kino Video, 2001. DVD.

"'The Talkies' Are Here!" *The Lancaster News* 5 Nov. 1929: 2. Microfilm.

Television Demonstration Film. Dir. and Prod. Dallas Bower. Perf. Nina Mae McKinney, Leslie Mitchell, and Elizabeth Cowell (commentary). BBC. 1937.

"Television's Influence on Cultures." *Communication Research Trends* 2:3 (1981): 1-8. PDF.

Television Show (title unknown). Prod. John Logie Baird. February 17, 1933 (airdate). London.

The Temptress. Dir. Fred Niblo and Mauritz Stiller. Perf. Greta Garbo and Antonio Moreno. MGM, 1926. *The Garbo Silents Collection*. TCM Archives. Turner Entertainment Co./Warner Bros, 2005, DVD.

That's Black Entertainment. Dir. William Greaves and G. William Jones. Skyline Entertainment Partners, 1990. DVD.

They Learned About Women. Dir. Jack Conway and Sam Wood. Perf. Gus Van and Bessie Love. MGM, 1930. Warner Bros, 2009. DVD.

"They Learned About Women." IMDb.com. Internet Movie Database. Amazon, n.d. Web. 11 Sept. 2013.

"Thompson Confident of Win Over Corbett." *Afro-American* 5 July 1930: 16. The Afro-American. AFRO Black History Archives. Web. 21 May 2013. <http://afro.com/afroBlackhistoryarchives/>.

Thompson, Marilyn W. "Marilyn Thompson on Essie Washington-Williams (1925-2013)." *Politico Magazine*. Politico, LLC, 22 Dec. 2013. Web. 04 Mar. 2014.

Together Again. Dir. Charles Vidor. Perf. Irene Dunne, Charles Boyer, and Nina Mae McKinney. Columbia Pictures, 1944. *Icons of Screwball Comedy* Vol. Two. Sony Pictures, 2009. DVD.

Trotti's Inter-Office Memo. 19 Oct. 1928. *Hallelujah* Core Collection Clippings File. Margaret Herrick Library. Academy of Motion Picture Arts and Sciences. Print.

Trotti's Inter-Office Memo—No Initials Copy. 19 Oct. 1928. *Hallelujah* Core Collection Clippings File. Margaret Herrick Library. Academy of Motion Picture Arts and Sciences. Print.

"The Truth About '*Hallelujah*.'" *Afro-American* 26 July 1930: 8. *Black Entertainers in African American Newspaper Articles. Vol. 1: An Annotated Bibliography of the Chicago Defender, the Afro-American (Baltimore), the Los Angeles Sentinel, and the New York Amsterdam News, 1910-1950*. Ed. Charlene Regester. Jefferson, NC: McFarland & Company, 2002: 49. Entry 817. Print.

"The Truth About '*Hallelujah*.'" *Afro-American* 2 Aug. 1930: 8. *Black Entertainers in African American Newspaper Articles. Vol. 1: An Annotated Bibliography of the Chicago Defender, the Afro-American (Baltimore), the Los Angeles Sentinel, and the New York Amsterdam News, 1910-1950*. Ed. Charlene Regester. Jefferson, NC: McFarland & Company, 2002: 49. Entry 824. Print.

Twentieth Century-Fox Memo from E.C. de Lavigne to Lew Schreiber dated 5 May 1937. UCLA Arts Special Collections. Print.

Uncle Tom's Cabin. Dir. Thomas Edison. Edison Manufacturing Co., 1903. IMDb.com. Internet Movie Database.

"The Unhappy Mr. Chevalier." *Photoplay* Dec. 1934: 69. Print.

"Uptown Fredi Washington Gives the Lowdown on Hollywood; No Great Hope for the Sepia Stars: Internationally Famous Actress-Dancer Finds Race Barrier Too Strong for Stardom—Claims New York Offers Most Liberal Outlet—Refuses to 'Pass.'" *Pittsburgh Courier* 14 April 1934. Fredi Washington Papers, 1925-1979. Amistad Research Center, Inc. Tulane University, New Orleans, LA. Microfilm.

U.S. Copyright Circular 15A. U.S. Copyright Office. Library of Congress. Web. 16 Dec. 2013. <http://www.copyright.gov/circs/circ15a.pdf>.

U.S. Federal Census, 1880. Napoleon McKenna [Napoleon McKinney]. Gills Creek, Lancaster, South Carolina. Roll 1232; Family History Film 1255232; Page 298B; Enumeration District 080. Web. TheNationalArchives.Gov. [database online]. AncestryLibrary.com; 11 Jan. 2012.

U.S. Federal Census, 1880. Nelson Crawford. Gills Creek, Lancaster, South Carolina. Roll 1232; Page 299D; Enumeration District 080. Web. TheNationalArchives.Gov. [database online]. AncestryLibrary.com; 11 Jan. 2024.

U.S. Federal Census, 1900. Dave McKenna [David McKinney]. Gills Creek, Lancaster, South Carolina. Roll T623_1533; Page 14A; Enumeration District 61. Web. TheNationalArchives.Gov. [database online]. AncestryLibrary.com; 11 Jan. 2012.

U.S. Federal Census, 1920. Leroy Springs. Gills Creek, Lancaster, South Carolina. Roll T625_1701; Page 16B; Enumeration District 91; Image 403. Web. TheNationalArchives.Gov. [database online]. AncestryLibrary.com; 11 Jan. 2012.

U.S. Federal Census, 1920. Nannie M. McKenna [Nannie M. McKinney]. Gills Creek, Lancaster, South Carolina. Roll T625_1701; Page 17B; Enumeration District 91; Image 405. Web. TheNationalArchives.Gov. [database online]. AncestryLibrary.com; 11 Jan. 2012.

U.S. Federal Census, 1930. Elliot W. Springs. Fort Mill, York, South Carolina. Roll 2216; Page 7A; Enumeration District 0032; Image 807.0. FHL microfilm 2341950. Web. TheNationalArchives. Gov. [database online]. AncestryLibrary.com; 11 Jan. 2012.

U.S. Federal Census, 1940. James Edwin Maynor. New York, New York. Roll M-T0627-02664; Page 11A; Enumeration District 31-1690. Web. 1940 United States Federal Census. [database online]. AncestryLibrary.com; 22 Jan. 2024.

U.S. Federal Census, 1950. Nina Mickey [Nina Mae McKinney]. New York, New York, New York. Roll 6149; Page 23; Enumeration District 31-2028. Web. TheNationalArchives.Gov. [database online]. AncestryLibrary.com; 11 Jan. 2012.

U.S., Find a Grave Index, 1600s–Current. James Edwin Maynor. Burial Details. 8 Mar. 1949. Queens, New York, New York. [database online]. Ancestry.com Operations, Inc., 2012; 22 Jan. 2024.

Vaudeville. Writ. Greg Palmer. American Masters. Thirteen/WNET, 1997. DVD.

Vidor, King. *A Tree is a Tree*. 1953. United Kingdom: S. French, 1989.

Virginia, U.S., Select Marriages, 1785-1940 [database online]. Provo, UT, USA: Ancestry.com Operations, Inc, 2014. Original data: Virginia, Marriages, 1785-1940. Salt Lake City, Utah: FamilySearch, 2013.

"Vixen." Def. 1. *Oxford English Dictionary*. Oxford: Oxford UP, 2013. OED.com. Web.1 Nov. 2013.

"Vixen." Def. 3. *Merriam-Webster Dictionary*. Springfield, MA: Merriam-Webster,2013. Merriam-Webster.com. Web. 1 Nov. 2013.

"Walter Albert Springs, 2 Mar 1894–24 May 1964." Memorial Page. ID: 263348330. [database online]. Find a Grave, https://www. findagrave.com/memorial/263348330/walter-albert-springs. Accessed 25 Jan. 2024.

"Wanted Coffee, Is Given Beating." *Pittsburgh Courier* 13 Jan. 1940: 1, 4. <www.newspapers.com/image/39549212>.

Warner Bros. Memo from Roy Obringer to Jack Warner dated 3 Oct. 1939. Miriam Hopkins Legal File. Warner Bros. Archives. USC School of Cinematic Arts.

"Watch for Pinky." Midway Theater Ad. *The Lancaster News* Fri. 13 Jan. 1950, Social and Personal: 7.

"Watch for Pinky." Midway Theater Ad. *The Lancaster News* Fri. 20 Jan. 1950, Social and Personal: 7.

Waters, Ethel, and Charles Samuels. *His Eye is On the Sparrow: An Autobiography*. 1950. Cambridge, MA: De Capo Press, 1992. Print.

Watkins, Mel. *Stepin Fetchit: The Life & Times of Lincoln Perry*. New York: Pantheon Books, 2005. Print.

Watts, Jill. *Hattie McDaniel: Black Ambition, White Hollywood*. New York: Amistad, 2005. Print.

Weisenfeld, Judith. *Hollywood Be Thy Name: African American Religion in American Film, 1929-2949*. Berkeley: University of California Press, 2007. Print.

White, Alvin E. "Nina Mae McKinney, Star of Early Theatre Buried." *Afro-American* (Baltimore) 20 May 1967: 11.

White, Alvin E. "Nina Mae McKinney, Star of Early Theatre Buried." *Washington Afro-American* 16 May 1967: 11.

"William Fox Biography." IMDb.com. Internet Movie Database. Amazon, n.d. Web. 5 Mar. 2014.

"William K.L. Dickson." IMDb.com. Internet Movie Database. Web. 16 Dec. 2013.

"William Springs, 1855–18 Sept 1939." Memorial Page. ID: 263343817. [database online]. Find a Grave, www.findagrave.

com/memorial/263343817/william-springs. Accessed 25 Jan. 2024.

Williams, Francis. "*Nina Mae McKinney: The Black Garbo.*" *Cinema* 35 (1976): 18-19. Williams, Iain Cameron. *Underneath a Harlem Moon: The Harlem to Paris Years of Adelaide Hall.* Bayou Jazz Lives Series. New York: Continuum, 2002.

Williams, John L. *America's Mistress: The Life and Times of Eartha Kitt.* London: Quercus Edition, Ltd., 2013. Print.

Williams, Lesley. "Paul Robeson: Artist and Man—An Interview with Nina Mae McKinney." *Inverell Times*, 26 November 1937: 8.

Williams, Tia. "Vintage Vamp: Nina Mae McKinney." *Essence* 6 Oct. 2010.<http://www.essence.com/2010/10/07/vintage-vamp-nina-mae-mckinney/>. Web. 3 Sept. 2011.

Wings. Dir. William A. Wellman and Harry d'Abbadie d'Arrast. Perf. Clara Bow and Charles "Buddy" Rogers. Paramount, 1927. Paramount, 2012. DVD.

Witherspoon, Mary Donnom. "Former Lancastrian Arouses Interest in Movie Showing Here: Nina Mae McKinney, Colored Native, Has Prominent Role in 'Pinky.'" *The Lancaster News* Fri. 10 Feb. 1950: 1. Microfilm.

Within Our Gates. Dir. Oscar Micheaux. Micheaux Book & Film Co., 1919. IMDb.com. Internet Movie Database.

Wollstein, Hans J. *Vixens, Floozies, and Molls: 28 Actresses of Late 1920s and Hollywood.* Jefferson, NC: McFarland & Co., 1999. Print.

Yates, Ted. "Nina Mae Tires of Playing 'Hell-Cat' Roles, Now She's a Lady in Revue." *Afro-American* 7 Sept. 1935: 9.

Zeitz, Joshua. *Flapper: A Madcap Story of Sex, Style, Celebrity, and the Women Who Made America Modern.* New York: Three Rivers Press, 2006. Print.

Zou Zou. Dir. Marc Allégret. Perf. Josephine Baker. Les Films H. Roussillon/ Productions Arys, 1934. Kino Video, 1989. *The Josephine Baker Collection.* Kino Video, 2005. DVD.

Appendix A

Firsts

- The first Black actor in a leading role in a Hollywood movie (as Chick in *Hallelujah*, 1929)
- The first Black star in Hollywood (1929)
- The first Black person to appear on television (appearing as herself in John Logie Baird's untitled early television show in London on February 17, 1933)
- The first African American movie actress to perform in Australia (*Hello Harlem* vaudeville tours, 1937)
- Possibly the first Black actor or actress to play a detective role in a feature film (as Laura Jackson in *Gang Smashers*, 1939)

Appendix B

Credited Film Roles

(documented performances in chronological order)

Hallelujah. Dir. King Vidor. Perf. Nina Mae McKinney, Daniel L. Haynes, and William Fountaine. MGM, 20 Aug. 1929. In this all-Black cast film produced by MGM, the drama unfolds when cabaret singer Chick (McKinney) cons a country newcomer, Zeke Johnson (Haynes), out of his money at a nightclub.

Manhattan Serenade. Dir. Sammy Lee. Perf. The Brox Sisters and Nina Mae McKinney. MGM, 21 Dec. 1929. McKinney sings in this musical short film.

Safe in Hell. Dir. William A. Wellman. Perf. Dorothy Mackaill, Donald Cook, Ralf Harolde, Nina Mae McKinney, and Clarence Muse. First National Pictures/Vitaphone, 12 Dec. 1931. Gilda (Dorothy Mackaill), a white woman who has resorted to prostitution to make a living, flees New Orleans after killing her rapist former boss. Gilda's boyfriend, Carl (Donald Cook), is a sailor who has been away for a year. He and Gilda go to an island in the Caribbean that has no extradition laws. He leaves her there, promising to return for her as soon as he can. McKinney plays Leonie, whom Gilda and Carl meet when they look for a hotel room. Leonie is not a vixen, but unrealistically, the white men at the hotel show no interest in her. She is pretty, and she looks too glamorous to be a barmaid. Leonie could be the hotel manager, an unusually high status for a Black character in a Hollywood film in 1931, but she might even be the hotel owner. The other character associated with the hotel is Newcastle (Clarence Muse), a Black porter. Leonie and Newcastle speak eloquently, and they are the only characters at the hotel who do not appear to have something to hide.

Pie, Pie Blackbird. Dir. Roy Mack. Perf. Nina Mae McKinney, Fayard Nicholas, Harold Nicholas, and Eubie Blake. Vitaphone Productions/ Warner Bros. Pictures, 4 June 1932. McKinney and the Nicholas Brothers, a famous tap-dancing duo, co-star in this musical short, which begins with her looking after the young brothers, ages 10 and 14. She is dressed as a nanny when she sets a pie on the kitchen table and tells them a story. Then, the film segues into a musical fantasy.

Passing the Buck. Dir. Roy Mack. Perf. Alexander Gray and Nina Mae McKinney. Warner Bros., 16 Dec. 1932. Musical short film.

"Revels in Rhythm." Prod. Charles B. Cochran. Perf. Nina Mae McKinney. London's Famous Clubs and Cabarets. The Trocadero Restaurant, London. 1933 (month and day uncertain). British Pathé. <https://www.britishpathe.com/asset/65011/>. McKinney appears at the 1:06 minute mark. The first intertitle reads, "London after dark and Mr. Cochran's Young Ladies are 'stepping out' in style to Annette Mills' melodies." The intertitle for McKinney's segment reads, "And with the 'Young Ladies'— Nina Mae McKinney, the famous West End Star." McKinney dances and sings "Bring Back the Charleston."

Reckless. Dir. Victor Fleming. Perf. Jean Harlow and William Powell. MGM, 19 April 1935. McKinney's singing cameo is in the film's trailer.

Sanders of the River. Dir. Zoltan Korda. Prod. Alexander Korda. Perf. Paul Robeson and Leslie Banks. London Film Productions, 26 June 1935. Bosambo (Robeson) is the loyal chieftain appointed by Sanders after African King Tofolaba and his soldiers come from the south and "threaten the peace." Nina Mae McKinney plays the role of Lilongo, the wife of Bosambo.

The Black Network. Dir. Roy Mack. Perf. Nina Mae McKinney and the Nicholas Brothers. Vitaphone Corp./Warner Bros., 4 Apr.

1936. Nina Mae McKinney and the Nicholas Brothers co-star in this Black-cast musical short, in which they compete in a talent show that is broadcast over the radio. McKinney's on-screen boyfriend (Babe Wallace) sings first. Then, the Washboard Serenaders perform. They are a band that sings and plays drums, guitars, and a kazoo (held inside of a drinking glass). Next, McKinney sings, "Only Half of Me Wants to Be Good." McKinney and Wallace dream of living on Sugar Hill but cannot afford to move there. After the talent show, he wins the lottery (a daily number), and their dream comes true.

Television Demonstration Film. Dir. and Prod. Dallas Bower. Perf. Nina Mae McKinney, Leslie Mitchell, and Elizabeth Cowell (commentary). BBC. 1937. McKinney sings a song, entitled "Papa Tree Top Tall."

Gang Smashers. Dir. Leo C. Popkin. Perf. Nina Mae McKinney, Laurence Criner, Mantan Moreland, and Monte Hawley. Ted Toddy Picture Company/Million Dollar Productions, 30 Dec. 1938. Rereleased as *Gun Moll* in the 1940s, this is a race film in which McKinney plays undercover detective Laura Jackson.

On Velvet. Dir. Widgey R. Newman. Perf. Wally Patch and Nina Mae McKinney. Widgey R. Newman Productions/Columbia Pictures (UK), 1938 (month and day uncertain). Musical and comedic short film.

The Devil's Daughter. Dir. Arthur H. Leonard. Perf. Nina Mae McKinney, Ida James, and Jack Carter. Sack Amusement, 7 Dec. 1939. In *The Devil's Daughter,* Nina Mae McKinney co-stars as Isabelle Walton, a woman who tries to scare off her sister Sylvia (Ida James) and take full control of the family business in Jamaica after their father's death. Isabelle pretends to practice Obeah, similar to Voodoo and also derived from West African religious roots. The film tries to balance the strengths of its performances against the story's stereotypical images, such as Isabelle's buffoonish servant Percy and his exaggerated dialect, irrationally superstitious Black people, and the fear and use of witchcraft. McKinney is quite convincing in her role. The quality of the cast and the theme of forgiveness are redeeming factors for this race film.

Straight to Heaven. Dir. Arthur H. Leonard. Perf. Nina Mae McKinney, James Baskett, and Jack Carter. Million Dollar Productions, 12 Dec. 1939. This is a race film in which McKinney plays Ida Williams, the mother of singing child prodigy Jimmy Williams and the wife of Joe Williams, a chemist who tries to expose a company that sells spoiled canned food and the racketeers who force local stores to sell it. After George Elliot causes Joe to lose his job, John "Lucky" Simon frames Joe for George's murder. Lucky, a local club owner, runs the racketeering ring. Joe is wrongfully arrested and convicted, and his lawyer friend Stanley Jackson tries to help Ida solve the case and clear Joe's name. Meanwhile, Jimmie is in danger with the racketeers after the club owner hears him singing outside with his friends and hires him to sing, of course, without consent from Ida.

Swanee Showboat. Perf. Nina Mae McKinney, Mabel Lee, and Dewey "Pigmeat" Markham. Ajax Pictures Corporation, 1940 (month and day uncertain). Musical and comedic short film. McKinney appears as herself.

Dark Waters. Dir. André de Toth. Perf. Nina Mae McKinney, Merle Oberon, and Franchot Tone. Benedict Bogeaus Production, 21 Nov. 1944. McKinney plays the role of the maid, Florella.

Mantan Messes Up. Dir. Sam Newfield. Perf. Mantan Moreland, Monte Hawley, Lena Horne, and Nina Mae McKinney. Lucky Star Productions/Toddy Pictures Co., 1946 (month and day uncertain). McKinney appears as herself in this comedy feature.

Night Train to Memphis. Dir. Lesley Selander. Perf. Roy Acuff, Allan Lane, and Nina Mae McKinney. Republic Pictures, 12 July 1946. McKinney portrays a maid.

Danger Street. Dir. Lew Landers. Perf. Jane Withers and Robert Lowery. Pine-Thomas Productions, 17 Apr. 1947. McKinney plays Veronica, a minor character.

Pinky. Dir. Elia Kazan. Perf. Ethel Waters, Jeanne Crain, Ethel Barrymore, and Nina Mae McKinney. Twentieth Century Fox, 11 Nov. 1949. Pinky (Crain) is a young Black woman who passes for white. When she returns home from nursing school, she is torn between her true identity and staying home (close to her roots) and her new identity, which involves being engaged to a white doctor. McKinney plays Rozelia, a maid. It is a stereotypical role of a Black woman who hides a switchblade in her stockings, but McKinney manages to play the role "her way." Rozelia has few lines but is well-spoken. She is the girlfriend of Jake, the man who had been cheating Pinky's grandmother out of her money. Still relatively young, at 37, McKinney's personal and career struggles seem to have aged her considerably. Although she only appears in a few scenes, some critics consider *Pinky* an important film for her. In this major Hollywood motion picture, McKinney shows that she is still a convincing actor.

Appendix C

Uncredited Film Roles

(documented performances in chronological order)

They Learned About Women. Dir. Jack Conway and Sam Wood. Perf. Gus Van and Bessie Love. MGM, 31 Jan. 1930. McKinney has a cameo as a singer. She sings "Harlem Madness."

Blood Money. Dir. Rowland Brown. 20th Century Pictures, Inc./ United Artists, 17 Nov. 1933. Nina Mae McKinney plays Rebecca, Ruby's maid. Lucille Ball also has an uncredited role in this film (as Drury's girlfriend in the racetrack scene).

Kentucky Minstrels. Dir. John Baxter. Real Art Productions/ Universal Pictures (UK), 1934 (month and day uncertain). McKinney sings in this film.

What Price Jazz. Dir. Sam Baerwitz. Perf. Ted Fio Rito Orchestra, George Irving, and Shirley Ross. MGM, 29 May 1934. McKinney is a dancer in this musical short.

The Lonely Trail. Dir. Joseph Kane. Republic Pictures, 25 May 1936. McKinney is an uncredited dancer in this John Wayne western.

Together Again. Dir. Charles Vidor. Perf. Irene Dunne, Charles Boyer, and Nina Mae McKinney. Columbia Pictures, 1944. Nina Mae McKinney steals the show in her one scene. Anne (Irene Dunne), the mayor, has a dinner meeting at a club. She enters the powder room after accidentally spilling a drink on her dress. An unnamed maid (McKinney) offers to iron the dress for her. Perceptively, the maid asks, "That man's really got you worried, ain't he?" She continues, "There's only three things that can make a woman start talking to herself—her bank account, her man, and her reputation. And they're all three the same things, ain't they?" Anne slowly responds, "My, my, it certainly is philosophical out tonight." When the maid finishes ironing, she and Anne hear whistles. The maid exclaims, "Uh-oh, here we go again!" She rushes over to peek out the door. Without hesitation, she turns around, tosses the dress to Anne, and goes out the powder room window. The police are raiding the club.

The Power of the Whistler. Dir. Lew Landers. Perf. Richard Dix, Janis Carter, and Nina Mae McKinney. Darmour Inc./Columbia Pictures, 19 Apr. 1945. IMDb.com. Internet Movie Database. McKinney plays the maid, Flotilda.

Copper Canyon. Dir. John Farrow. Perf. Ray Milland and Hedy Lamarr. Paramount Pictures, 2 Feb. 1950. Nina Mae McKinney plays the maid, Theresa.

Appendix D

Stage, Theatre, and Club Appearances

(documented performances in chronological order)

Blackbirds. Dir. and Prod. Lew Leslie. Broadway. 1928. IBDb.com. Internet Broadway Database. King Vidor discovered Nina Mae McKinney when she performed in the chorus line of one of these shows. Having had 518 shows between May 9, 1928, and June 15, 1929, it became one the longest-running shows on Broadway. The cast included several well-known Black entertainers such as Adelaide Hall, Bill Robinson, and Mantan Moreland.

Ballyhoo of 1932. Dir. Norman H. Anthony, Lewis E. Gensler, Bobby Connolly, and Russell Patterson. Prod. Ballyhoo Productions, Inc. Broadway. 1932. Internet Broadway Database. This busy show gave 95 performances between September 6, 1932, and November 26, 1932. Nina Mae McKinney sang "Love, Nuts, and Noodles."

Chocolate and Cream. London. Leicester Square Theater. 13 Feb. 1933. McKinney performed in this integrated revue.

"Revels in Rhythm." Prod. Charles B. Cochran. Perf. Nina Mae McKinney. London's Famous Clubs and Cabarets. The Trocadero Restaurant, London. 1933. British Pathé. <https://www. britishpathe.com/asset/65011/>. McKinney dances and sings "Bring Back the Charleston."

Hello Harlem. Australia. 1937. McKinney headlined a vaudeville revue that toured Australia.

Nina Mae McKinney's jazz band tours, 1939–1940. McKinney formed a jazz band (official name uncertain).

Blackbirds. Dir. and Prod. Lew Leslie. 1939–1940. IBDb.com. Internet Broadway Database. McKinney headlined the show with her jazz band.

Gay New Orleans. World's Fair. New York City. 1940. McKinney headlined the show with her jazz band.

Tan Manhattan. Perf. Flournoy Miller, Avon Long, and Nina Mae McKinney. Howard Theatre (Washington) and Apollo Theater (Harlem). 1941. In this all-Black musical comedy scored by Eubie Black and Andy Razaf, McKinney sings "Say Hello to the Folks Back Home" and "I'll Take a Nickel for a Dime."

Pancho Diggs and his Orchestra tours, 1942-1943. McKinney became the lead vocalist and the headliner, and the group became known as Nina Mae McKinney and her Orchestra.

Rain. Writ. W. Somerset Maugham. Apollo Theater. 1951. In a stage play based on Maugham's short story "Rain" (first produced in 1922), McKinney plays the role of jazz enthusiast and prostitute Sadie Thompson, who finds herself in conflict with a missionary over her soul.

Appendix E

British Radio and Television Performances

(documented performances in chronological order)

Television Show (title unknown). Prod. John Logie Baird. February 17, 1933 (airdate). London. The details are missing.

BBC: The Voice of Britain. Radio. Dir. Stuart Legg. Prod. John Grierson. Perf. Nina Mae McKinney and H.G. Wells. GPO Film Unit. 1935. McKinney sings a song, entitled "Dinah."

Ebony. Television. Prod. John Logie Baird. Perf. Nina Mae McKinney, Kirby Walker, and Rudy Smith. BBC. Saturday, February 27, 1937 (airdate). McKinney sings songs, entitled "Papa Tree Top Tall," "Harlem Moon," and "Why Am I So Blue?"

Dark Laughter. Television. Prod. Dallas Bower. Perf. Nina Mae McKinney, Leslie Thompson, Kirby Walker, and Yorke de Sousa. BBC. Saturday, June 5, 1937 (airdate). McKinney sings songs, entitled "Copper Coloured Gal of Mine" and "Big Boy Blue."

Acknowledgments

Hallelujah! I give God the highest praise and thanks for making all things possible. I give my most heartfelt thanks to Nina Mae McKinney for being such an enduring inspiration and to my family and friends for their prayers and support. Special thanks to every person and organization listed in my "Works Cited" section and everyone whose past work in film studies, Black Studies, or history has made future work possible. I would also like to recognize anyone who directly or indirectly provided assistance or encouragement during the process of publishing my book, including:

Monique L. Akassi

MK Asante

Jonathan Auxier

Colleen Aycock

BearManor Media

John Berry

Donald Bogle

Stephen Bourne

California African American Museum

Emily Susan Carman

Ron Chepesiuk

Mayme A. Clayton Library & Museum

Thomas Cripps

Marianna W. Davis

James Dawkins

Jovi Dominguez

Bill Egan, Scarecrow Press, Inc.

Joanne Ellis

Mary Felder

Eric Grace, Lancaster County Council of the Arts

Barbara Hall

Gary Harris

Lorene B. Harris

Dolan Hubbard

IMDb.com

Corey Jarell (Corey@Illkeepyouposted)

Sarah Joseph, PKJ Passion Global

Donald Juedes

Franklin Knight

Kristine Krueger

The Lancaster County Council of the Arts

The Lancaster County Library

The Lancaster News

The Lancaster Historical Society

Margaret Herrick Library, Academy of Motion Picture Arts & Sciences

Donald Matthews

Denise L. McIver

McKinney relatives and friends

Elaine McKinney

Marjorie Clinton McMurray

Keith Mehlinger

Joy Myree-Mainor

National Film Information Service, Academy of Motion Picture Arts & Sciences

James Nelson

Sara Nixon

Ben Ohmart

Alice Pendergrass

Lindsey Pettus

Louise Pettus

Louise Pettus Archives & Special Collections, Winthrop University

Dwandalyn Reece

Tonya Witherspoon Reed

Charlene B. Regester

Jimaki Witherspoon Roach

Bertha Maxwell Roddey

Susanne Schapowalow

The South Carolina Council for the Arts

The South Carolina Historical Society

South Caroliniana Library, University of South Carolina

Andee Steen

Charmaine Stradford

Greg Summers

The United States Bureau of the Census

The United States National Archives and Records Administration

Vital Records, South Carolina DHEC (Lancaster and Columbia)

Jimola Witherspoon Wade

Stone Wallace

Ronald Walters

J. A. White

Barbara Whitner

If I omitted any names, it was purely unintentional. Please accept my sincerest apologies and many thanks.

About the Author

Dabian T. Witherspoon is a native of Lancaster, South Carolina. He holds an M.A. in African American World Studies from the University of Iowa and a Ph.D. in English from Morgan State University, where one of his concentrations was "language and professional writing" (film studies and screenwriting). Dabian has conducted Black history presentations for schools, churches, and community organizations. He has taught history, film studies, composition, and literature at the high school and college levels. He has also taught drawing classes for children, tutored people of all ages, and worked as a screenplay analyst, copy editor, and project manager (book publishing). For booking and other information, please visit www.dabianwitherspoon.com.

Notes

1   The term "actor" is not gender specific. Some critics consider *actress* a sexist, lesser term. Similar to "singer," one may argue that the term *songstress* is unnecessary. This book uses *actor* for males and females, and it uses *actor* and *actress* interchangeably, out of convenience and with no sexist intentions.

2   Lewis Selznick went on to work at Paramount during the sound era. David O. Selznick left MGM to work at Paramount and then RKO before marrying Louis B. Mayer's daughter Irene and returning to MGM. In 1936, he started his own company Selznick International, which later produced *Gone with the Wind* ("David O. Selznick Biography").

3   People of any race can be Jews. It is a matter of religion and culture. Biblical Hebrews were Black people in Northeast Africa, of which the Middle East was considered a part before the term "Middle East" became commonly used in the mid-1900s. Racially, they were the same ancient people from what is now Sudan and its surrounding area, including Nubia and Kemet (ancient Egypt). They simply developed a different culture. They were dominant in the Old Testament world and lived in the region long before the people most associated with it since the seventh century CE. Many of the biblical Hebrews fled in all directions to escape being sold into slavery or slaughtered by the Romans. Immigrants and invaders later adopted/adapted the culture of the biblical Hebrews and migrated throughout Europe.

4   See Parker, Laurence, Donna Deyhle, and Sofia Villenas, eds. *Race Is . . . Race Isn't: Critical Race Theory and Qualitative Studies in Education.* Boulder, CO: Westview Press, 1999.

5   *The Broadway Melody* (1929) was MGM's first all-talking musical feature and both the first musical and the first sound film

to win an Academy Award for "Best Picture" ("The Broadway Melody").

6   See "Film Star Clara Bow's Personal Secretary Was Wrongfully Convicted of Grand Theft" by Hans Sherrer and "The Silencing of Clara Bow" by Christina Ball.

7   McKinney distinguished between reality and Hollywood treatment, stating that the story was exciting and "done with a lot of suspense," and she adds, " But it's about what happens to one girl. It doesn't take up any so-called problem as a whole and it doesn't say what the answer is for the kind of situations that girls like Pinky run into" (Wollstein 137).

8   See also Hershfield, Joanne. "Dolores del Rio, Uncomfortably Real: The Economics of Race in Hollywood's Latin American Musicals." *Classic Hollywood, Classic Whiteness.* Daniel Bernardi, ed. Minneapolis: University of Minnesota, 2001.

9   An actor credited as "Florence Mills" played a minor role as "Bride 9" in the 1920 silent film Bride 13. Her identity cannot be determined for certain as the credits and the source offer no details, footage, or photos. It is unlikely that she is the same Florence Mills whom Nina Mae McKinney named as her influence. McKinney's idol considered her big break to be her *Shuffle Along* stage performance in 1921. There were at least two other well-known performers named Florence Mills during that period. One was an actress and burlesque performer while the other was a cellist, and both women were white ("Bride 13"; "Florence Mills Trivia"). Moreover, in 1920, if the "groom" character in the film was white, there was no way that a Black actress could have played one of the brides.

10 Paul Robeson played the role in the film version released in 1933.

11 However, some Black viewers eventually took the stance that the "savage" portrayal of protagonist Brutus Jones was just as degrading (Forbes 307).

12 Company credits are unavailable for *Darktown Jubilee.*

13 Warner Bros. purchased Vitagraph in 1925 (Finler 284).

14 Eventually, the Black male would become dominant during the 1970s Blaxploitation era, including characters portrayed by actors such as Richard Roundtree. Unfortunately, after the genre that also featured powerful Black women portrayed by actors such as Pam Grier rescued Hollywood from its descent into the abyss, the genre's success was short-lived. Hollywood began to make cheap imitations, "reduced its value to simply borrowing some of its more 'non-threatening' elements, and ultimately, discarded it" (*BaadAsssss Cinema*). However, the industry has forced the Jezebel stereotype upon the Black female, even when she is far from it in reality or in her role on screen. The white female gaze upon the Black male has been all but forbidden while the white male gaze upon the Black female has not been, even when miscegenation was forbidden on screen. For decades, Hollywood resisted pairing a Black female with a white male, but with today's supposedly improved racial attitudes, it is still preferred over pairing a Black male with a white female or even pairing a Black male with a Black female—representing stable Black homes and families. Resistance to the latter suggests that it can only occur in a "Black movie," which too many whites still falsely claim cannot sell, especially in the international market.

15 Ethel Waters' biographies such as *Heat Wave: The Life and Career of Ethel Waters* by Donald Bogle make a few references to Nina Mae McKinney, and they vaguely mention key events such as the *Hallelujah* film casting. In *Heat Wave*, Bogle states that McKinney along with co-star Daniel Haynes simply "greeted" Waters at the Colored Artists Motion Picture Ball after Waters visited MGM studios in 1929 (Bogle 174). Unfortunately, cross-references to McKinney, such as interviews with King Vidor, neither make comparisons and contrasts between McKinney and Waters nor discuss any meaningful interaction between them.

16 *Dorothy Dandridge: A Biography* by Donald Bogle makes a few references to Nina Mae McKinney, generally about *Hallelujah* and the false hopes it brought Black actors. Bogle also mentions Joel Fluellen, a young Hollywood hopeful. Over time, one thing Nina Mae McKinney, Louise Beavers, Billie Holiday, Josephine Baker, Hattie McDaniel, and Sidney Poitier had in common was Fluellen. He was their platonic mutual friend (158-9). Unfortunately, cross-references to McKinney neither make comparisons and contrasts between McKinney and Dandridge nor discuss any meaningful interaction between them.

Index